Holy
Invitations

EXPLORING SPIRITUAL DIRECTION

Holy
Invitations

JEANNETTE A. BAKKE

BakerBooks

A Division of Baker Book House Co
Grand Rapids, Michigan 49516

© 2000 by Jeannette A. Bakke

Published by Baker Books
a division of Baker Publishing Group
P.O. Box 6287, Grand Rapids, MI 49516-6287
www.bakerbooks.com

Fourth printing, March 2006

Printed in the United States of America

Library of Congress Cataloging-in-Publication Data
Bakke, Jeannette A., 1939–
    Holy invitations : exploring spiritual direction / Jeannette-A. Bakke
      p.   cm.
    Includes bibliographical references.
    ISBN 10: 0-8010-6327-2 (pbk.)
    ISBN 978-0-8010-6327-5 (pbk.)
    1.-Spiritual direction. I.-Title.
BV5053.B345   -2000
253.5'3—dc21   00-027896

To the One who sends
Life's holy invitations,
Love's generous grace

Contents

Acknowledgments

This book has been growing for more than fifteen years and has been supported and cared for by many people. My first formal training in spiritual direction took place at Shalem Institute for Spiritual Formation, where I was encouraged to wait for God. In 1984, Dr. Tilden Edwards and Dr. Gerald May of Shalem identified that this was a book in the making. It has been a surprisingly long wait.

I am grateful to my directors and directees, Bethel Seminary students, and faculty colleagues who have influenced the writing in direct and indirect ways. President Carl Lundquist and Dean Gordon Johnson provided an environment in which spiritual formation could flourish and begin to shape this book.

Computer experts instructed and rescued me. Larry Hansen, Jim and Michele Anderson, Steve Brown, Preston Rash, and Gloria Metz answered endless computer questions and assisted in the preparation of the final draft.

Working with a collaborative, ecumenical team including Capt. Larry Horne, Chaplain, U.S. Navy; Dr. Charles Arn; Dr. Wilkie Au; Dr. Steve Harper; and Dr. Rueben Job to prepare and instruct Navy, Marine, and Coast Guard chaplains about spirituality and spiritual development enriched my understandings.

Bethel Seminary, Pat Pickering, and Father Joseph Campbell and Mary Lindholm at St. John's in the Wilderness offered quiet places to write. Sister Mary Bernadette and Visitation Convent provided a place of solitude.

God led me to people who have made countless contributions to this book. Friends generously prayed, read, and critiqued the manuscript. Early readers include Charette Barta, Rev. John Ackerman, Dr. Gary Klingsborn, Janet Hagberg, and Luci Shaw. More recent readers include Joann Nesser, who has shared the journey in spiritual direction from the beginning; Elsie Fuhrman, who prayed; Dr. Janet Ruffing, who prompted me to speak in my own voice; Dr. Nils Friberg, who encouraged me at Bethel and prayed, read, and critiqued every word; and Barbara Cohen, Sandy Little, Joan Simmons, and Nancy Pittner, the Michigan contingent who never told me anything—but prayed. I also want to acknowledge Sherrill Nelson and Mary Becker, whose insightful questions stirred me to think; Clodie Harrell, Marillyn Knuteson, and Peg Ruetten, who have been in this for the long haul, reading and praying; Rose Mary Dougherty, S.S.N.D., whose work in group spiritual direction is foundational; Dr. Carla Dahl, who helped me sort out contemporary language related to sexuality; Dr. Wilkie Au and Kay Vandervort, who contributed to my knowledge of Ignatian discernment, Scripture, and spiritual direction; and Lois Lindbloom, who asked helpful questions about group spiritual direction, and Scripture and spiritual direction. Madeleine L'Engle modeled and taught me the Christian discipline of paying attention to God's call to write.

Dr. Tom Schwanda looked over my shoulder on behalf of Baker Books with excellent observations, suggestions, and encouraging words. Bob Hosack, acquisitions editor at Baker Books, supported the work enthusiastically and saw God's invitations in it. Melinda Van Engen brought clarity and readability through her perceptive, careful editing.

Gerald May has been reading some form of this book off and on since 1984 and has continued to ask important questions, offer insights, pray, and encourage me to pray and struggle with developing ideas. My husband, Stan Bakke, watched this manuscript grow and change, read several versions, asked precise questions, and offered wise counsel, care, and opportunities to think about other things. Cody, our now geriatric springer spaniel, never let me or the book out of his sight.

The book includes many examples of spiritual direction conversations that are based on my experience and the experiences of others. Most often they are composite, fictionalized accounts. Where they are close to the experience of any individual or group, the details have been changed sufficiently to conceal the identities of all concerned.

Most of all, this book has been God's from the beginning—the One who continues to send holy invitations.

Introduction

This book was working in me long before I was working on it. In the 1980s and even for most of the 1990s, I felt I was somewhere that the rest of the Protestant world was not. It was a good place, and I was convinced that other Protestants participated in spiritual direction. They just didn't use the same language to describe their experience. Before 1983, I was unfamiliar with the term, though I had been giving spiritual direction for many years. I did not know there was a long history of Christian tradition that described and supported this ministry onto which I had stumbled. Now spiritual direction seems to be finding its way into Protestant conversations.

As I look back over the last twenty years, I see an enormous amount of change. I suppose that is true in any comparable length of time, but the pace of change from the early 1980s to the present seems to have been more exponential than linear. Perhaps the continuing expansion of computer technology and other media, or people's increasing dissatisfaction with the unmanageable pace of their lives, or the extending crassness of American society is awakening us to some important questions. Or perhaps it is a combination of those things plus myriad others. Could it be God? Whatever it is, at the beginning of a new century many seem willing and even eager to get a glimpse of their souls, to question God about the path and quality of their lives, and to pay attention to what they are shown.

This book describes a way of looking, a way of listening that has been helpful to many Christians who have felt drawn to search for a deepening faith relationship. Spiritual direction is the name given to a particular kind of helping relationship whose primary objective is to discern how God is inviting someone to be, to live, to appreciate, and to act in the midst of life.

This is a book about love. It is about our hunger to love and be loved as we are. But it is also about our desire to grow in love and to recognize and live out of the core of ourselves, which has been freed through relationship with Christ.

Some people wonder if they have ever experienced God's love for them or if they have truly loved anyone. Others are aware that they have much more love inside than what appears outside. We long to live out of our recognition of God's love for us and see it flow through us to others. We yearn to experience and express our lives as infused and intertwined with God's.

Our days are so full that these feelings may not come to our attention very frequently. Because of its great importance, however, our yearning does surface in quiet moments—like when we are working alone at a task in the kitchen or the basement or the yard or under the car. When our minds are engaged in routine tasks, there is often surprising roominess for other thoughts. Spiritual direction can help us identify these longings and provide us with companionship when we are ready to look at them more intentionally.

This book is for people who are not familiar with spiritual direction. It is for anyone who seeks to awaken to the presence of grace, the presence of the Holy Spirit. It is about being an ordinary human being with an extraordinary God and about wanting to hear and respond to God. Spiritual direction conversations include aspects of what some Christians have called "discovering God's will," and as you read, you will see how spiritual direction and discovering God's guidance are connected. We will address many aspects of discernment within the context of spiritual direction.

Overall, I hope to do two things in this book: (1) to encourage you to notice God's ever present love and invitations, and (2) to clearly describe the discipline of spiritual direction so that you are able to recognize whether the Spirit has been or is drawing you to participate in spiritual direction.

The book is divided into three sections: "An Introduction to Spiritual Direction," "Subjects Frequently Considered in Spiritual Direction," and "Possible Complications and Benefits of Spiritual Direction." Each of the sections has a distinctive place and tone. One may initially interest you more than the others. It is possible to read the sections in any order that looks inviting, but if you know very little about spiritual direction, it is a good idea to begin with section 1. The first section describes spiritual direction and compares it with pastoral counseling, mentoring, and discipling. It discusses Christian spirituality and addresses differences in language. It also describes who comes to direction and includes details to consider when beginning spiritual direction. Section 2 addresses some of the topics that are discussed in spiritual direction. Section 3 addresses both problems and benefits that may develop through spiritual direction.

Each chapter is followed by a reflection section that includes questions and tasks you may want to pray about or write about in a journal. Choose the ones that seem right for you. If you work with the questions, approach them with a prayerful openness, asking God to help you decide on the level of attention you give them in prayer, time, and energy. Otherwise, it is easy to become overly engaged in self-analysis rather than looking for God.

The reflection sections may be used individually, in pairs, or with small groups. Some of the activities are more suited to individual reflection because they require extended time for private consideration and response. Other questions provide for many different levels of response, and group members can choose what seems appropriate.

You will probably discover you already know more about spiritual direction than you realized. I hope you will see yourself in these pages and be encouraged and invited to explore the desires of your heart and God's.

JB

PART 1

An Introduction to Spiritual Direction

But yield who will to their separation,
My object in living is to unite
My avocation and my vocation
As my two eyes make one in sight.
Only where love and need are one,
And the work is play for mortal stakes,
Is the deed ever really done
For Heaven and the future's sakes.

Robert Frost,
"Two Tramps in Mud Time"[1]

What Is Spiritual Direction? | 1

Spiritual direction takes place when two people agree to give their full attention to what God is doing in one (or both) of their lives and seek to respond in faith. . . . Whether planned or unplanned, three convictions underpin these meetings: (1) God is always doing something: an active grace is shaping this life into a mature salvation; (2) responding to God is not sheer guesswork: the Christian community has acquired wisdom through the centuries that provides guidance; (3) each soul is unique: no wisdom can simply be applied without discerning the particulars of this life, this situation.

Eugene Peterson[1]

I have much more to say to you, more than you can now bear. But when he, the Spirit of truth, comes, he will guide you into all truth.

John 16:12

"How are you and God getting along?" Immediately a wall goes up to protect my inner privacy. Why does that question disturb me? Probably because the answer is not immediately clear. In fact, I'm not sure I know the answer. "How are God and I getting along?" I do a quick interior scan. "All right in some areas," "So-so," or "I haven't been giving this a lot of thought" cross my mind as possible answers I could give if pressed.

Life is full, complicated, and challenging. The days fly by quickly. Now and then we get a glimpse of just how quickly. Some days we feel as if we are being carried along by life's swift flow. We wonder what we might be missing. Our immediate circumstances influence whether questions such as the one my friend asked strike us as gentle inquiries or as questions that are essential for survival—questions we need to address.

When asked such a pointed question or others like it, we may wonder if God is nudging us to pay closer attention. Do we need encouragement to tend our desires for God, and, if so, where do we find it? We wonder where we might find support as we explore how we are connecting, communicating, and cooperating with God, and where we are struggling in our relationship. When these kinds of interests and questions come to the surface, spiritual direction may be what we are looking for.

What Is Spiritual Direction?

Spiritual direction is a spiritual discipline that has played a part in the lives of numerous Christians, and, like other Christian disciplines, it helps us hear, see, and respond to God. It is most often practiced in the context of a relationship between two people. However, spiritual direction conversations can also take place in groups.

The term *spiritual direction* has appeared only recently in Protestant vocabulary and still sounds unfamiliar to many as a Christian discipline. But our understanding and appreciation of its content—openness to God's presence, comfort, and guidance—has always been important to Christians and is something we desire. I have chosen to use the term *spiritual direction* because a vast body of literature can be explored most easily by using this term rather than any other. The bibliography at the back of this book includes books and web sites that provide a good place to begin further exploration.

No matter what our denominational affiliation or tradition, or the exact words we use to describe God's participation with us, we are aware of God's nearness and leading individually and collectively. We know that the Holy Spirit is the one who invites us initially and draws us onward in faith. We have been nurtured and prompted to listen to and follow God by the Spirit through many means including Scripture, worship, prayer, teaching, preaching, study, music, friends and family members, acts of kindness, communities of believers, life circumstances, inspirational writing, Christian classics, poetry, biographies, fiction, works of art, and the beauties of creation. Sometimes the Spirit speaks to us from the outside and sometimes from the inside through words, impressions, dreams, or pictures in our minds.

Spiritual direction is a kind of discernment about discernment. We explore what has seemed more and less important to us and how we are making choices and acting on our observations. We pay attention to how we interpret our experiences, thoughts, and feelings associated with our relationship with God and how that relationship influences our human relationships.

Whether we have heard the term before or not, *spiritual direction* is somewhat of a misnomer because spiritual direction is neither exclusively spiritual nor particularly directive. However, the words do fit in other ways. They clearly identify the primary guide we seek, the Holy Spirit. They acknowledge the connection between our human spirit and God's Spirit and our desire to nurture our dependency on God so that it permeates and takes precedence in our thoughts, attitudes, values, choices, and behaviors.

Present-day directors do not give answers or tell directees what to do in their relationship with God or when making life choices. Instead, they listen with directees for how the Spirit of God is present and active. Directors support and encourage directees as they listen and respond to God.[2]

Spiritual direction is a process that often affects our point of view—the way we look at things. At times directors will ask questions that encourage exploration of a particular Scripture passage, concept, or way of praying or journaling. These suggestions are intended to help directees clarify and examine their own questions and considerations.

The mixture of "spiritual" and "direction" are reflected in the following spiritual direction dialogue.

Directee: I've been thinking lately about how my spiritual life seems to be affecting the people I live with, especially my spouse, and how his lack of interest in God affects me.

Director: What's that like?

Directee: In a word, hard. I feel like I'm trying to function in two competing worlds . . . trying to please both of them, and I'm not satisfied in either area. It feels like I'm always taking shortcuts or doing things differently than what seems right for me.

Director: How is that influencing you?

Directee: I hate to say it, but I think I blame both of them.

Director: Oh.

Directee: Both God and my husband.

Director: What does that look like?

Directee: I'm trying to love God and listen to God and cooperate with what I hear. I'm trying to love my husband and listen to him and cooperate with what I hear. That sums it up pretty clearly.

Director: It seems like something is missing here.

Directee: What's that?

Director: You. You sound very intentional about wanting to listen to and please both your husband and God. I don't hear you saying anything about how you pay attention to your own heart, about what might be right for you. I wonder what might happen if you'd step back from your involvement with God and with your husband and ask yourself what is important for you.

Directee: It's important for me to be loved and have a sense of being loved by both God and my husband.

Director: What makes you feel loved?

Directee: When I think God and my husband would like what I'm doing.

Director: So you're saying that it's what you do or don't do that's important?

Directee: It does sound that way.

Director: What have your prayers been like?

Directee: Not wonderful. I find myself reporting in to God about what I've been doing, and waiting for a pat on the head that doesn't seem to come.

It would have been easy for the director to encourage the directee to analyze what might be going on in her relationships. But the director opened it to God in prayer, waiting to see what the Spirit of God invited.

Director: The Scripture that comes to me as I listen to you is Psalm 139. You could try spending time with that each day and notice if it seems helpful. Read slowly and pray whatever arises. You don't need to read the entire psalm. Read it as if you are talking to God. You might want to do some journaling.

One of the purposes of inviting directees to Scripture is to draw them away from their self-centered focus, to allow the Spirit to move them to a different place of perspective—hopefully to a place where they are able to hear again who God really is and how God thinks and feels about them. It is easy to lose sight of God's love for us.

Directee: It sounds like I need to get myself back to square one. Reading Scripture seems like a good idea. I've been going around in circles about this stuff and sure could use help to slow down enough so I might see where I am and what I might like to do. I've been mostly arguing with myself about it.

Director: Is there any particular place you're feeling the crunch?

Directee: I don't know that there is. I've just been feeling anxious about the whole thing. Sometimes my husband acts as if he's jealous of my spiritual life, which makes no sense to me. It's not like I'm giving my attention to another human being. Well, maybe it is a little, because it is an intimate relationship, though in different ways than our marriage.

Director: Do you notice any difference in your feelings toward your husband since you've been more intentionally making space for God?

Directee: In some ways I don't need him in quite the way I did. I suppose he feels that and is aware that even though I want to please him I'm not as obsessed with our relationship as I was. When I talk about it this way I realize it's healthier now. Some of my unrealistic expectations have softened. He should be glad about that.

Director: Are you saying there have been changes?

Directee: Oh yes. Now that I'm talking about this more I'm beginning to see why I've been feeling the pull between my relationship with God and my relationship with my husband. There is movement there, and I'm not entirely comfortable with the changes myself. As much as I disliked being so attached, it was familiar, and now I'm feeling unbalanced, like I don't know myself and my responses.

Director: It sounds like *you* are getting into the conversation now.

Directee: It was unrealistic to think I could figure it out the other way. I think I'm on the right track. My husband sure didn't get what he thought he was getting when he married me, but the changes in my life have been rather dramatic since I started spending more time with God. No wonder the poor guy is wondering what hit him. I suppose it will take some time to see where all this goes.

The faithfulness of God is at the core of spiritual direction. When we seek spiritual direction, we are utterly dependent on God and God's love reaching for us. Willingness to place our hope in God is also a necessary element. We long to experience God's presence in this shattered, exquisite world and need help to believe in our own ability to recognize God's voice. We need encouragement to trust God to be God, to trust the Holy Spirit in another person, and to trust God for a particular spiritual direction relationship. It is helpful to remember that all the initiative is not ours. In fact, any movement on our part toward God is an indicator that God has been seeking us.

When we seek God, we discover that God is trustworthy in ways that are far beyond anything we have imagined. Scripture assures us that God does respond, that God hears, cares, and answers.

> So do not fear, for I am with you;
>   do not be dismayed, for I am your God.

Isaiah 41:10

> Come near to God and he will come near to you.

James 4:8

> All that the Father gives me will come to me, and whoever comes to me I will never drive away.

John 6:37

> So I say to you: Ask and it will be given to you; seek and you will find; knock and the door will be opened to you. For everyone who asks receives; everyone who seeks finds; and to everyone who knocks, the door will be opened.

Luke 11:9–10 NIV ILE

> For where two or three come together in my name, there am I with them.

Matthew 18:20

Spiritual direction is a way to pursue God with all our heart and a way to respond to God, who is pursuing us. In direction we gather many threads together. We bring diverse prayers, impressions, and experiences into direction conversations to invite the Spirit of God to reveal themes and patterns, movements and countermovements that affect our spirit and life.

Spiritual direction is a way to give caring attention to our relationship with God—attention that is focused on life's foundations underneath ordinary busyness. We offer ourselves and our hopes and fears to God in an openness that affirms our intention to listen.

It is helpful to be wholly present and to assume an attitude of waiting rather than an activist stance when we want to be attuned to the Holy Spirit. This requires that we release ourselves and our lives gently into God's care. When we try to overmanage or control our relationship with God, we often pull back from desiring God and are easily diverted from really listening. We desire to be open to God in a receptive way—available and waiting.

Until very recently contemplative presence and practice were not adequately explained or taught within a Christian framework to most Protestants or Roman Catholics. In fact, many Christians viewed contemplation with a suspicious eye, due in part to popular Western culture, which places contemplation and action at two opposite ends of a continuum. Many considered contemplation to be a kind of passivity, perhaps even a kind of laziness. They assumed that people were waiting for God to do something rather than engaging in the challenges of life. But this is not how it has been lived out. It used to be common knowledge that people of prayer become people of action flowing out of their relationship with God. What we do and how we do it are influenced by listening to God. When both prayer and action are valued, we may pursue activities out of clarified motivations and attitudes.

God desires both contemplation and action. In Luke 10, Jesus strongly endorses both godly activity and contemplation. Luke 10:25–37 tells the story of active compassion on the part of the Good Samaritan. Jesus affirms Mary's choice to sit at his feet and listen in the story of Mary and Martha told in Luke 10:38–42.

We are pulled and motivated, drawn and repelled by a constant flow of ideas and experiences. Listening to God helps us sort the wheat from the chaff. We want to decide which avenues to pursue, which actions to take, and how much time and energy we should expend on particular pursuits from *within* the context of our relationship with God. When we take time to listen intentionally to the Holy Spirit, our actions have the potential of becoming truer expressions of who God has created and called us to be. In this way, contemplation and action become a unified whole, as shown in the following example.

I am part of a four-person spiritual direction group that has met for a morning or afternoon every four to six weeks for fifteen years. One of the things that has changed gradually is our awareness that the quality of our presence together (openness to the Spirit and each other) is enhanced by shared silence, even though we make time for prayer when we are alone. All four of us tend to let our lives become overcrowded, and we fit easily into the hurried pace of our culture. We need structure that acclimates us to a more contemplative mode when we are together. It is not something that just happens.

We greet each other and put a meal on the table. Then we cease social conversation and offer ourselves and the time to God. We ask for grace to be fully present to the Spirit of God and each other. Then we move into an hour of silence in which we eat and prepare for group spiritual direction. Sometimes there is music without words in the background and sometimes not.

We have discovered that the shared silence gives us the opportunity to notice what has been occupying our energy and attention. We may write in our journals, pray, go for a walk, or just relax in the quietness. We may consider what to talk about during our time together or explore whether the Spirit seems to be inviting or nudging us in any particular way.

This time of preparation fosters a more contemplative, waiting presence with God and each other when we come together for spiritual direction. Focused listening is work even in a contemplative place. We are learning little by little to be still and know God (Ps. 46:10). *The Message* describes it this way: "Step out of the traffic! Take a long, loving look at me, your High God."

Through intentionally providing for contemplative time together we nurture the possibility of being attentive to God in the midst of daily life. We hope that our shared practice will spill over so that we notice God's presence more consistently and then respond in ways that reflect this presence. This is part of what Paul means when he encourages us to pray always, to live with a moment-by-moment prayerful awareness of God (1 Thess. 5:16–18).

Who Is Involved in Spiritual Direction?

Spiritual direction takes place within the framework of a distinctive kind of friendship in which one person functions as the director, the other as the directee. The words *director* and *directee* may or may not be a part of your vocabulary. Other possible names are listed below.

director	directee
spiritual father/mother	spiritual son/daughter
shepherd	follower
pastor	parishioner
guide	seeker
midwife	child
soul friend	soul friend
prayer companion	prayer companion
spiritual friend	spiritual friend

The words used to describe the roles of two persons involved in spiritual direction capture some of the characteristics of what direction is, but none of them depicts all that is intended or actually occurs in direction meetings. The labels that emphasize the role of God's call and the maturity of the director could suggest some kind of exaggerated spiritual hierarchy. Others that imply mutuality may adequately reflect our shared, flawed humanity but do not seem to take into consideration the specific graces that draw us to a particular person for direction. Some Protestants who are only slightly acquainted with spiritual direction may be concerned about whether a director could come between them and God.

You might find it interesting to review the list of possible names for directors and directees and notice which of those names invite you and seem to fit into your experiences of faith, growth, and helpful relationships. The expressions and practices that most adequately communicate the heart of spiritual direction take into account the call of some persons as spiritual guides. They also maintain, protect, and provide for the freedom and responsibility of directees to nurture their dependency on God and come to their own conclusions based on prayer, Scripture, and discernment.

Directors and directees are dedicated to listening for God's ways, desires, and invitations. They meet together to listen to the Holy Spirit and to each other, for the benefit of the directee. Ultimately, though, the conversations are for God, because as directees become more attuned to God, their life and actions will reflect more of God's desires. Opening our ideas and feelings with another person and intentionally inviting God to be present is like opening the windows of a closed house to spring air. We harbor a mixture of true, partially true, and untrue perceptions, ideas, and impressions and are strongly influenced by the limitations of being only one person of a particular gender, age, culture, family, and personality with distinct preferences and dislikes. It is often easier to recognize what is essential when we speak out loud about our interior life.

The things we are most reluctant to discuss in spiritual direction are often the things that need care and attention. But sometimes resistance is good protection. There are patterns inherent in spiritual growth that support readiness for certain opportunities or challenges at specific times. It is important neither to rush nor delay. Only God knows when we are ready to address particular topics at a meaningful level.

Resistance is neutral in itself, but it usually points toward possibilities for prayer. There are some things we would rather not talk about to anyone, and some things we talk about with friends but not so easily with a spiritual director. The question we bring to our prayer is, "What is the Spirit of God inviting?" Maybe something has come to mind because God knows we are ready for expansion inward or outward, healing, deepening in love with God, or a call to carry God's love into the world. We long to hear the Spirit's timing rather than just our own.

Even when directors feel strongly that specific areas need addressing, they pray silently asking for God's perspective. They may test readiness with nonintrusive questions that invite directees to notice and consider possibilities. But they still leave choice and responsibility regarding exploring any subject to God and the directees.

Let's listen in on a spiritual direction conversation.

Directee: Today I'd like to think about hiddenness.

Director: What do you mean?

Directee: Well, I figure there is a huge amount of stuff in me that I am not aware of and I think that whatever is hidden has power simply because it is outside of my view. I suspect that I function rather automatically out of some of it.

Director: What interests you about that?

Directee: God sees it all.

Director: Yes.

Directee: It's not that I need or want to see everything that God sees, but I wonder whether there are things in that hidden place that God is interested in my knowing more about.

Director: Has anything in particular sparked your curiosity?

Directee: Yes, as a matter of fact it has. I've been praying about living in a more intentional way, with more of myself available to God. I think that most of the time I just go along not being particularly tuned in to God or to the Holy Spirit's presence with me. I'm wondering about what I might be missing.

Director: Interesting. It sounds like you are thinking about this from two different viewpoints—what you don't know about yourself and what you don't know about God. Are those related in your mind?

Directee: Maybe so, although I hadn't looked at it that way. It's like I'm looking for more of me to give to God, which isn't particularly rational but still feels right. What I mean by "not rational" is that when I dedicated my life to God I perceived that to be my whole self with nothing left outside.

Director: What do you think about that now?

Directee: That still seems right, but at times it's as if God asks me, "This too?" As if God recognizes that I may not have realized all I was offering God initially. I am seeing a lot more options and opportunities, even temptations. I'm amazed how my temptations have changed.

Director: Oh.

Directee: I used to think a lot about how I was perceived in my workplace. Which isn't necessarily a bad thing. But I've become aware that I was a whole lot more concerned about what other people thought than what God might be thinking. Now that I've recognized that, it doesn't seem to have so much power to determine my course of action. I am not saying I don't care or notice. But it has become just one of the factors I pay attention to. It is less dominating.

Director: So that was a specific example of something that was hidden from you and isn't any longer?

Directee: Yes. Maybe that's part of why I wonder what else might be hidden. I've enjoyed feeling so much freer at work, and it is making a difference. Funny, it has even improved other people's opinions of me. Now that's a paradox, isn't it?

Director: How does hiddenness show up in your prayer?

Directee: I think I've done more analyzing than praying, but I'm getting some ideas about how I'd like to try praying. I want to express my gratitude. This change has been good, and I'm aware that I did not do it. God did. So I'm grateful. Then I'd like to ask if there are other hidden things the Spirit would like to reveal that need healing. After this experience I have more courage in that regard. That feels a little scary and reckless, but I am getting the idea that whatever God brings up is likely to be something I'm ready for.

Director: That sounds good.

Directee: Now I get it. No wonder I have been wanting to figure out how to be more awake and available to God and to God's presence. I do not want to miss the good stuff. Not a particularly altruistic or spiritual motivation, but at least it's honest. Looks like I just found another topic for prayer.

No matter where we begin the conversation or what we choose to talk about, God is faithful to guide us toward what we need to consider and to nourish our lives and relationships with God and others.

Spiritual Direction and Its Relatives

Spiritual direction is a part of many elements of faith life including preaching, teaching, intercessory prayer, prayer for healing, and pastoral counseling, but spiritual direction is also a separate ministry. When a person feels called to listen to God, spiritual direction can offer a place of prayerful support and encouragement.

It is not always easy to differentiate between spiritual direction and its closest relatives: pastoral counseling, mentoring, and discipling. These helping relationships, while possessing some distinctive characteristics, also share some in common. One way to clarify the similarities and differences is by listening to how a counselor, mentor, discipler, and spiritual director describe what they offer. As you read, notice that these roles are different especially in regard to qualities of presence and focus of attention. When helpers have a preset agenda, it greatly influences the kind of listening they do. If they have an agenda, they may initiate the topics of conversation or attempt to insert material. If their agenda is to listen to God, they are prayerful and much more laid-back—permitting, inviting, noticing what arises and responding. There is a difference between a conversation in which you know the other person is eager to speak and one in which you know you can talk for as long as you like and the other person is praying and content to listen to your every word.

In *pastoral counseling,* or other pastoral enterprises, the helper might say, "*In the name of God I am here for you.* I give my attention to you and to our being together as a representative of God's love and care for you. I am a broken human expression of that love, but you have my attention and care while we are together and my prayers while we are apart."[3]

Mentoring shares many qualities with the other helping relationships but is more likely to imply a context such as a workplace, academic setting, or other institution. A mentor might say, "I walk alongside you for the purpose of your growth and development. I will listen to your perceptions, observations, and responses and try to help you understand the (workplace, academic setting, institutional) system. I will listen, advise, coach, challenge, and encourage. I hope to help you clarify, deepen, and extend your vision, wisdom, skills, and competencies. I desire to support you personally. I will share my experiences. *I give myself to you. Together we will seek your growth for God's sake, for your sake, and for the good of the system.*"

In *discipling,* a discipler might say, "I will teach you about God the Creator, Jesus the Messiah, and the Holy Spirit and encourage you to ask God to forgive your sins and participate in your life. I will introduce you to the Bible and show you where to begin and how to read, study, and interpret Scripture. I will teach you how to pray alone and with others and help you become involved in meaningful Christian worship, service, and outreach. Out of what I have learned by being a Christian and studying, I will teach you. I will pray with you and for you. *I give myself to you for God's sake.*"

In *spiritual direction,* the director might say, "My prayers are for God's will to be done in you and for your constant deepening in God. During this time we are together, I give myself, my awareness and attention, my hopes and heart *to God for you. I surrender myself to God for your sake.* I will listen with one ear to the Holy Spirit and with the other to your description of your prayer and relationship with God. I will support you in prayer as you describe and discern your experiences with God and respond to you out of my ongoing prayer and reflection."

The diagram below provides another way to look at some of the characteristics of each relationship:

Varieties of Spiritual Companionship

	Agenda	Process	Role of Helper	Goal of the Learner
Pastoral Counseling	set by counselee	problem solving crisis management healing of past wounds	facilitator	"healthy"
Mentoring	chosen by mentor and mentee and influenced by an "external" such as a workplace or educational institution	development	coach	improvement "like the external"
Discipling	set by the discipler	instruction	transmitter	learning incorporation "like the teacher"
Spiritual Direction	revealed by the Holy Spirit	noticing paying attention praying	pray-er listener	Imago Dei "like God" "like Christ"

From the conversations and the chart we see that counseling, mentoring, discipling, and spiritual direction overlap in their emphases on God's participation and the intention of one person to help another in some way. They differ, however, in their primary goals and processes. The four helping relationships also create different levels of interdependence that are shaped in part by the frequency of meetings. Pastoral counseling may take place once, on an ongoing basis, or when needed. Mentoring and discipling can be onetime occurrences but more often involve ongoing relationships with frequent meetings and social as well as spiritual aspects. Spiritual direction meetings usually take place once a month for an hour. Limited contact helps directees maintain responsibility for their own lives and refrain from becoming overly dependent on the director.

Pastoral Counseling Compared to Spiritual Direction

Pastoral counseling often focuses on problems we wish to resolve. Many people seek counseling when they are in a crisis situation. They are in the midst of personal distress, grief, or trauma and hope someone can help them make sense of their experience. Developmental issues such as the desire to function effectively in intimate relationships also draw people to pastoral counseling as do needs for healing from past wounds. Each of these reasons for seeking counseling may have spiritual dimensions as well.

We often pursue counseling when we are ready to accept help to clarify our understanding and modify perceptions, attitudes, and behaviors that hinder satisfying participation in daily life. Counseling usually lasts until a person has moved through a crisis or resolved questions that brought that person to counseling. When we seek counseling we may be asking, "How can I get through this crisis?" or "How can I live and function in more rewarding ways?"

People who choose spiritual direction do so because they want to pay closer attention to their relationship with God. Spiritual direction is for essentially healthy people and may continue indefinitely. Typical spiritual direction questions are "Where is God in this?" or "Where has God gone and why don't I sense any divine presence at all?" or "How am I being called to be Christlike?"

The education and practices of pastoral counselors vary greatly. Some counselors tend to use primarily psychological categories and tools to address the issues raised by their counselees. Others are acquainted with many frameworks for listening. Some pastoral counseling is close to, or may actually include, spiritual direction if the orientation of the counselor is toward spiritual material and if the counselor senses God's calling and gifting in this area.

People who are called to be spiritual directors, on the other hand, are aware that God is teaching them—that the Holy Spirit is their primary instructor. The "education" of spiritual directors begins and hopefully continues with God. Any kind of leading of the Holy Spirit toward formal education usually appears somewhere in the midst of rather than at the beginning of a person's intentional journey with God. People who become spiritual directors did not seek or intend to become directors. They have responded to the Spirit by setting aside time for prayer, Scripture reading, worship, solitude, and silence to nurture their responsiveness with God. They have allowed the Spirit to love and shape them.

Spiritual direction gifts are developed through the cooperative creativity of the Holy Spirit and a human soul within the context of ongoing prayer and a lifestyle that is deliberately attentive toward God. The awareness that one is developing as a spiritual director may be long and slow or appear rather suddenly. Whenever it becomes clear, however, it is obvious that the idea was God's rather than the person's own choosing. Often, the calling is confirmed by other people of faith who sense that something special is taking place in the life of a particular person and seek out this person to listen and pray.

If spiritual directors feel more intentional study could be helpful, they should pursue study that respects how God has been shaping them and offers helpful clarification rather than takes over what the Spirit has begun. It is important not to weigh down the work of inner development by study that feeds ego-serving desires to acquire status or knowledge. At the same time, study and prayerful reflection that are invited by God can enhance a director's freedom to hear and respond to the Spirit and to directees.[4] Appropriate educational experiences can expand knowledge, refine competencies, and nurture a director's awareness of God's calling and gifting. But even if directors receive extensive education, the Holy Spirit should always remain the primary resource for directors and directees. Spiritual direction arises out of inviting and listening to God.

Mentoring Compared to Spiritual Direction

People seek mentoring when they desire to develop particular competencies. They are looking for a coach, supporter, encourager who will honestly explain what is valued within an institution or system. They seek someone who has sufficient experience to recognize others' gifts and levels of development and who cares about encouraging and assisting growth. People who look for a mentor usually know in what areas they need help. They may wish to become more involved in decision making or to take more of an initiative in identifying and pursuing goals for themselves and for their institution. They may seek education or training. They may have goals such as learning to speak effectively in a group, teach a seminar, or guide a meeting. They may wish assistance in understanding the formal and informal rules and practices of the institution of which they are a part.

People who seek mentoring are asking questions such as, "What are my strong and weak qualities? Which ones are most important to me personally and professionally, and where should I focus my efforts? What is important in this particular setting, and how congruent is that with my priorities? How can I become a stronger, more skilled team member?"

Discipling Compared to Spiritual Direction

Disciplers often have definite plans that they follow step by step with those they disciple. Scripture talks about guarding and passing on what has been entrusted to us. (See 1 Tim. 6:20; 2 Tim. 1:12–14; and Jude 3.) One of the intentions of discipleship, therefore, is to teach—to pass on information about God, Scripture, Divine/human relationships, and to explore meaningful living that is based on a relationship with God. Discipleship includes a generally agreed upon body of knowledge. Disciplers help disciples become familiar with the information, struggle with it, understand it, and then assimilate and integrate what they have learned. Discipling includes significant intellectual endeavor that shapes the disciples' interpretations of experience—with other people and with God. Passing on knowledge that creates new options and possibilities is the purpose of discipleship. The outcomes are dependent on what the disciples decide to do in response to new information.

Spiritual directors, however, hold their agendas lightly or come to spiritual direction meetings without agendas. They invite the Holy Spirit to choose the topics, guide the discussion, and teach. Specific topics arise as the director and directee talk, and this material becomes the focus for prayer and reflection, rather than any set program. Instruction, when it does occur, is most likely concentrated around directees' prayer and choices related to what they believe God intends.

Both discipling and spiritual direction focus on God and a person's relationship with God but in a different way. The discipler frequently functions as a teacher and may talk more than the disciple. For all practical purposes, the relationship flows from God, to the discipler, to the disciple. This is particularly apparent if the discipler is identified as a strong, mature, skilled adult and the disciple is younger, undeveloped, immature, or new to faith. The primary relationship in spiritual direction, however, is between God and the directee. The director is a helpful, prayerful listener and is last in importance—God, directee, director.

Even though we drew lines of distinction among various ways of spiritual companioning, there is considerable overlap. It may seem unnecessary or unimportant, therefore, to try to distinguish so precisely among these closely related relationships—pastoral counseling, mentoring, discipling, and spiritual direction—except for the fact that the way we function is significantly influenced by our perception of what a relationship is "for." Both subtle and not so subtle differences emerge when we decide that a relationship is primarily for problem solving, coaching, instruction, or listening for the Holy Spirit. Of course, some instruction and problem solving are often intertwined with what brings us to spiritual direction, but grace plays a clearer role than in the other relationships.

Through counseling, mentoring, and discipling, many people explore managing life more effectively and may think of themselves as taking charge or accepting responsibility in clearer, stronger, and more intentional ways. In contrast with this approach, even though perceptions, values, and choices are influenced by willingly listening to and cooperating with the Holy Spirit, transformations that occur in spiritual direction are more dependent on grace than an outcome of our trying to resolve problems or change ourselves. Those seeking spiritual direction need to pray about and discern what they want to address with a spiritual director and what could be better cared for with other kinds of helping persons.[5]

Practicing Spiritual Direction

Spiritual direction involves information, but it also invites us to another kind of knowledge. The knowing desired in spiritual direction is more like the knowing of love that has a sense of wholeness. Seeking spiritual direction can raise our awareness and sharpen our realization of interior knowing that is not dependent solely on external facts. This knowing proceeds from the joining of our spirit with God's Spirit. Scripture says that through the Holy Spirit we "have the mind of Christ." Through spiritual direction we seek to recognize God's voice and God's mind (1 Cor. 2:10–16).

The following example from a direction session gives a glimpse of how this might look. The directee begins the conversation.

Directee:	I know that I know that I know that I know.
Director:	That sounds like you are pretty sure.
Directee:	I guess that would sound rather arrogant if I didn't say more. But this is all new to me and I'm quite taken by it. Grateful. I don't know if you can understand when I say, "It's not 'my' knowing."
Director:	Could you say more about that?
Directee:	I can try. It is *knowing,* which feels like pure gift. I did not struggle for it. I was not asking any question of which I was aware. I was just "hanging out with God," being grateful, but mostly quiet, just offering myself to God and inviting God to be with me. Deep inside something began welling up—a kind of assuring presence and then a kind of clarity that felt alive. It was unencumbered by my usual scattered-

ness. The best description I can manage is to say it was a *knowing* that was "given." It felt like it was filled with grace.

Director: Was the *knowing* "about" anything?

Directee: Not really. More than anything I think it showed me, God showed me, that I have the capacity to know in this way.

Director: What did that mean to you?

Directee: Good question. Maybe it set a kind of standard. If this appears again, I'd probably think it's the Holy Spirit and try to pay attention. I suppose there are counterfeits. Maybe I could rationalize or manufacture a similar experience. Putting any knowing next to what happened here seems like it would be helpful. It was way beyond intellect. No, it wasn't against intellect. It just wasn't about intellect—at least not human intellect and the way I see it functioning in myself and others. It was a kind of *total knowing*. I guess that means it includes intellect but is not limited by the human mind.

Spiritual direction gives people an opportunity to reflect on what they perceive as experiences with God. It is good to have a place to talk about such experiences and ask pointed questions. "Why did you think it was God? Is this the God you read about in Scripture?"

Director: Let's ask the "So what?" question. Does there seem to be anything coming out of this experience? with God? with others?

Directee: It sure was humbling—not in a groveling way, but in a way that made me take notice. What I mean is it makes me feel like the Creator of the universe, the One who made me and knows me totally, has just told me we are friends, intimate companions. It feels like a quality of relationship that's different from everything else. There is no temptation to think I'm Jesus Christ. After this it's clear that we're quite different, Jesus and I. I am not a particularly self-sacrificing person, but I am loved just as I am. I can't tell you the difference this is making everywhere I go. It's like I had a big drink of light and it's radiating through me. People ask me what's going on with me because I seem different. I guess I am different or becoming different . . . or willing to be.

Director: This sounds like a vulnerable place.

Directee: I'll say so. I'm surprised how much I've talked about it now. When others ask I sort of sidestep their questions. For right now I'm mostly savoring God and not inclined to blabber. It feels like talking about it just anywhere could take something away from the experience.

Director: It sounds like you are being very deliberate about this.

Directee: Yes. I had decided before I came today that it was okay to tell you. But I thought and prayed about doing so. I know I can't hold on to this feeling forever, but neither do I want to push it away. I'm asking God a lot of questions and feel like I'm being taught. I guess that's all I'd like to say about it for now.

Intentionality, discipline, and change are part of spiritual direction. Most models of counseling, mentoring, and discipling include components of intentional change that are dependent on instruction and a decision to behave differently. Although intentionality and self-discipline are crucial in implementing hoped-for changes, some practices seem to suggest that education and rational choice are sufficient after initial surrender to Christ.

In spiritual direction, however, the Holy Spirit continues to function and be perceived as both the teacher and the source of grace and power. We remain dependent on grace, seek to cooperate with the Spirit, and resist any illusions about our ability to be our true selves without God's help. Intentionally giving our attention to God is both the beginning and the end goal of spiritual direction. We are not seeking change per se. We are seeking God, seeking fuller communion with the Holy Spirit, and seeking to trust God for and in whatever unfolds. We want to be aware of God's presence with us, dwell more closely with God, and explore what it means to abide. We are learning to be more like Mary of Bethany, who sat at Jesus' feet (Luke 10:38–42). No set of doctrines alone can do this for us.

The essence of spiritual direction, then, is this deepening love and communion with God. Great and small transformations do flow out of this Divine/human connection, but they are not the main event. Our desire to be and become God's friend, follower, love, and faithful one is foremost.

After praying, learning about spiritual direction, and identifying our reasons for considering spiritual direction, it is time to let go of our pondering, trust the generosity of God, and move ahead. We hope to be freely natural and offer our best effort. Yet we know we remain dependent on more than ourselves for the outcome. In spiritual direction, we must rely on God.

Reflections

When we are considering a new kind of relationship, it is helpful to consider the relationships we have had and what they have meant to us.

1. Draw a lifeline that begins with the date of your birth and extends across the top of the page. Divide the line into five- or ten-year segments. Put the initials of friends who have been important to you where they belong on your lifeline. What do you notice about your friendships? Where do they appear in your life? What was going on when you discovered special friendships? Are your friends older than you, younger, or about the same age? Or is there a mixture of ages? How many are of your gender? The opposite gender? Which friendships had or have spiritual dimensions? What other things do you notice that seem significant to you?

2. Four kinds of helping relationships were described in this chapter: mentoring, pastoral counseling, discipling, and spiritual direction. What experiences have you had with each of these kinds of relationships? Add to your lifeline the initials of people who have shared these kinds of relationships with you. Label each name to indicate which kind of relationship it is or was (sf=social friendship, m=mentoring, pc=pastoral counseling, d=discipling, sd=spiritual direction). Some names may have more than one description. What role did you play in each relationship? What have been some of the benefits and hindrances of these relationships?

3. There are many ways to describe spiritual companionships. Some of them seem familiar and inviting to us; others are outside our experience. As you read the following material, you may discover new ideas about some of the possibilities of spiritual companionships. Notice which ones you have experienced and which ones you have not. Which ones seem inviting and interesting to you? Which ones might you like to learn more about or experiment with at this time in your life?

Informal Spiritual Direction

These relationships lack structure and role definition, and meetings are often irregular and spontaneous. There is nearly always an atmosphere of mutuality.

Wisdom sharing—like the wise older family member to whom everyone goes.

Spiritual friendship—the people you naturally talk to about your life with God.

Soul mates—lifelong relationships of support and care with deep inter-connectedness.

Occasional encounters—chance meetings (often onetime events) in which spiritual guidance occurs for one or more people.

Formal Spiritual Direction

These relationships are explicitly defined as spiritual direction and incorporate all that such a relationship entails.

Expert spiritual direction—people who are called by God and professionally trained. This is their work.

Gifted, charismatic spiritual direction—directors who are more called and gifted than trained. They rely on the Holy Spirit from beginning to end.

Master-disciple relationship—the director acts as a window to the divine.

Institutional direction—spiritual direction in the context of a seminary or other Christian institution. Someone assumes an official role and may have institutional authority over the directee.

Mentoring, discipling, and eldering relationships—usually focus more on moral and educational guidance.[6]

4. Answering the following questions can assist in determining if a relationship is one of pastoral counseling, mentoring, discipling, spiritual direction, or something else.

Who initiates the relationship?

How does the relationship pay attention to the person?

How does the relationship pay attention to God?

What is the agreed upon content?

What is the agreed upon climate (instructive, contemplative, etc.)?

What are the hoped for outcomes?

What controls the duration of the relationship? Is there a usual range?

What is the pattern of the meetings (frequency, setting, duration)?

How is responsibility divided and shared?

What is expected between sessions?

How is periodic evaluation provided for?

2 | The Heart of Spiritual Direction

> We define Christian spiritual direction, then, as help given by one Christian to another which enables the person to pay attention to God's personal communication to him or her, to respond to this personally communicating God, to grow in intimacy with this God and to live out the consequences of the relationship. The focus of this type of spiritual direction is on experience, not on ideas, and specifically religious experience, i.e., any experience of the mysterious Other whom we call God. Moreover, this experience is viewed, not as an isolated event, but as an ongoing expression of the ongoing personal relationship God has established with each one of us.
>
> William Barry and William Connolly[1]

> I no longer call you servants, because servants do not know their master's business. Instead, I have called you friends, for everything that I learned from my Father I have made known to you.
>
> John 15:15 NIV ILE

Conversation about our life with God can be awkward at best. No matter what words we choose or how we struggle to articulate the nuances of experience, we can never quite capture the reality that has touched us or say all we desire. It is impossible to completely describe or comprehend God. Yet, it is important to try to speak about our experience.

Added to the dilemma of trying to put words where words will never suffice is our recognition that each person's spiritual autobiography is unique. Our taste for and responses to conversation about God are strongly affected by our history.

Some faith-related words and phrases seem neutral while others awaken pleasurable memories of encounters with God. But not all expressions of Christian spirituality strike us in these ways. Some words and phrases related to faith make us anxious because they evoke memories of our being spiritually abused, taken advantage of, or manipulated, particularly when we were young. I am referring to practices such as inappropriate use of Scripture to control people, dominating shepherding relationships, overly restrictive lifestyle control, making people afraid to use their own God-given thinking abilities, and punishment in the name of God. Some ways of talking about spir-

ituality are so different from the way we have understood Christian faith
that they seem threatening. We may even question whether persons who
use language in certain ways are truly Christians. Their words and
phrases sound foreign to us.

When we have strong positive or negative reactions to faith-connected
words, it is helpful to listen carefully to our bodies and feelings and ask
what our reactions mean. Paying attention to rather than either pushing away or embracing our strong responses gives opportunity for healing and growth when we bring them into prayer and spiritual direction
conversations.

Spiritual Direction and Prayer

Spiritual direction is dependent on prayer during and outside of direction meetings. Prayer takes place when the human heart discloses itself
to God and is open to listen and respond. Spiritual direction takes place
within the context of prayer. In spiritual direction we ask another person to listen with us to the Spirit of God from *within* our relationship
with God. We desire to be together in the place where we commune most
intentionally and freely with God.

The director and directee choose to settle into a prayerful receptivity
and observe what follows. They are in an experience and watching it
simultaneously, or switching back and forth. Sometimes spiritual direction is a little like bird-watching—waiting quietly and noticing what
appears. We desire a prayerful place and quality in our time together.
We try to pay attention to how the Holy Spirit is with us now—in the
present. Whatever happens in a spiritual direction conversation points
toward how we are getting along with God. This kind of possibility does
not come about by accident. It is not something we can hope for and
presume it will appear. It is supported by the prayers of director and
directee when they are together and apart.

Effective spiritual direction meetings depend on both people intending to listen attentively for the Holy Spirit, which leans more toward
patient waiting than active striving to hear God. Prayer becomes a mixture of activity and passivity: an active intentionality to be available to
the Spirit and a passive, open willingness that invites God to set agendas for spiritual direction conversations. Directees do not need to have
what they describe as an outstanding or successful prayer life. But they
do need to be willing to pray regularly and explore the Spirit's invitations. The willingness of directors and directees to continue to pray and
seek God even when prayer is not satisfying or comfortable is essential
for spiritual direction to take place.

Descriptions and definitions of prayer abound. It is revealing and helpful to notice which aspects are important to us as we try to describe authentic prayer.

adoration	grace
asking	love
authenticity	receptivity
change	response
communion	surrender
confession	transformation
connectedness	truthfulness
courage	vulnerability

These are just some of the words that come to mind when we consider components of prayer. Is there a scriptural picture of relationship that captures the essence of prayer for you? In your prayer do you think of God as an unconditionally loving parent, like the father of the prodigal son (Luke 15)? Or does the Song of Solomon better characterize the depth of Divine/human desire for togetherness? Do you think about Jesus going away to be alone with his Abba? What other scriptural pictures of prayer attract you? How do you envision the participants in prayer, Divine and human? Which of the words in the above list are essential to your description of prayer, and what words would you add to the list?

Speaking about our prayer brings some of what we think to light. Let's listen in on a direction conversation.

Sitting by the table in the winter sun, they talked. God had been inviting changes, and Sue was trying to pay attention. She began by describing what her prayer times had been like—often hurried, sometimes cut short, occasionally missed. And then she said, "I'm beginning to wonder if there's some reason I'm avoiding time with God. My life seems busy enough right now, and maybe I'm afraid God is going to ask me to add something to my schedule."

Director: That's interesting. Is there anything in particular you think God is nudging you about?

Directee: Well, nothing comes to mind right away, and that's what makes me nervous. The things I usually consider as possibilities just don't seem to be it. When I sort through those in my mind, nothing clicks.

Director: Why does that make you uneasy?

Directee: As a matter of fact, whether or not I'm feeling overly busy, I do not want to miss anything God might be inviting. Sometimes I've been surprised what comes up when I really pay attention. Even when I have lots of questions, it seems that if I follow the questions—keep letting my honest concerns surface and bring them into prayer—some pretty interesting stuff happens.

Director: Like what?

Directee: Last year in a similar circumstance I felt prompted to call my aunt. You remember this is someone I talk to once a year. She said to me, "Oh, Sue, I'm so glad you called. You know it's funny, I was just wishing for an opportunity to talk to you. Those health concerns I mentioned earlier look like they really were pointing to some things I need to pay attention to and I'm not sure where to start." I was grateful I'd responded to that nudge. When I saw all that followed I became convinced that the Holy Spirit had been prompting me.

Director: Maybe there is some relationship, maybe not. Could you talk a little about what your prayer is like?

Directee: It seems like my concerns about the possibility of God asking me to do something is making it difficult for me to settle down when I finally do make space for prayer. I run off before I give myself or God a real chance to communicate.

Director: Now that you've said this, what do you think could be helpful to you?

Directee: I guess I might as well face this and get it over. No matter what it is, I don't like going along in this way, because it feels like I'm hiding and not available for the kind of relationship I need and want with God. I long for a sense of God's presence and guidance in this busy time.

Director: How does it seem right to provide for this?

Directee: It's been a while since I've taken a retreat day. If I get myself out of my own environment for a few hours, maybe that would help me relax, pay attention, and take time to write down some ideas I've been thinking about. Writing in my journal usually helps me realize how engrossed I've become in the details of life and helps me to back away and get a different perspective. As I continue writing I move through the surface clamor that occupies so much of my time. That seems to increase the likelihood of my being able to hear God. When I try to do this at home, my job jar seems to scream at me. Every cupboard I walk past shouts, "Clean me."

Director: I can identify with that. [They both laugh.]

Directee: Now that we've got that settled, there are a few other things I'd like to talk about. Every now and then a few words of Scripture come to mind, and I mull them over and pray about whatever they bring to my attention. So on that front I've been feeling like God has been taking care of me on the run even though I haven't been able to get it together around my prayer time.

Spiritual direction conversations focus a great deal on day-to-day prayer experience. These conversations about prayer take place *in the midst of prayer,* which is not the same as casually discussing our prayer with a friend.

In spiritual direction conversations, directors intentionally turn their attention and heart, their hopes and thoughts toward God and invite God to be present and to serve as the director. Their first ear is open toward God—a way of listening prayer. They listen to directees out of this place of prayerfulness. Directees also open themselves to God and invite the Spirit. Directees speak about what their relationship with God is like.

Directors and directees do not just begin talking about their experience with God. They try first to settle into their own experience and life with God. It is similar to when someone is deeply in love and this colors that person's other human relationships. Direction happens in the context of a loving Divine/human relationship. It is being in the relationship and trying to speak about it at the same time. Directors listen to the Holy Spirit and to directees and try to help directees attend to what they cannot hear by themselves.

When I invite another person to join me in the heart of my prayer, my love for God, my sense of life with God, and allow that person to see me and my ways of listening and speaking to God, I often receive the clarity necessary to recognize answers to questions such as, "How are God and I getting along? Where is grace distinctly active in my life? Where am I? At an impasse, hard-pressed, resisting God? Where are my blind spots? Where does God seem distant, and where do I feel God's love for me and my love for God?" When answers do appear, I often discover a new set of questions.

In order for a person to be open with another person about the true condition of the heart and its vagaries, that person has to believe such honesty can make a difference in the quality and closeness of his or her relationship with God.

Telling Our Stories

The prayerful context of spiritual direction becomes the environment for speaking, listening, doubting, questioning, challenging, teaching, counseling, clarifying, discerning, affirming, restoring, comforting, healing, and encouraging.[2] It provides an open space for us to talk, pray, and pay attention with someone who listens to us speak about our hopes, dreams, and fears and respects the way we perceive the realities of God with us.

Spiritual direction conversations contain cognitive and affective information and responses. We talk about what we think and what we feel. We describe concepts, understandings, and emotions and notice our responses even as we speak. There are moments of silence and times when we are aware of newness and of the Spirit's presence. We are often touched by deep gladness.

All of this takes place as we tell our stories. Stories of spiritual direction are stories of God embodied in the particularity of individual lives. Every person is uniquely addressed by grace. God initiates and invites in surprising ways. Perhaps someone is exploring old and new God-questions that were stirred up due to a family tragedy. Perhaps someone is falling in love with God and is not sure whether this is good news, bad news, or just news.

Even though people are drawn to spiritual direction for different reasons, which influence what they choose to discuss and where they decide to begin, it is important for them to hold their intended agendas lightly. Both director and directee hope to remain open to whatever comes to light during a direction conversation. Excessive prior planning or speculation can hinder the unfolding of a natural process of spiritual direction and narrow the exploration.

For people who are used to more structured interactions with planned agendas (which includes most of us), it can be unsettling not to plan. There is some sense of security or comfort in having a plan, even if things turn out differently than we expected. But it can help to remind ourselves that we are not entering a capricious process. Spiritual direction entails a different kind of preparation that encourages our receptivity to God and each other. We open ourselves to the Holy Spirit and invite God to speak with us as God desires. An open agenda leaves room for unexpected turnings. When spiritual direction unfolds as it is intended, we discover that God has graced the conversation with what was needed.

Nothing is wasted. No matter where we choose to begin describing what our life with God has been like since our last direction appointment, it seems a sufficient opening for the Spirit of God to bring the focus toward the core of our relationships—Divine and human. Perhaps this is because our speaking is a sign of our willingness and intention to listen to God during spiritual direction.

Sometimes we start off with an account of our life in recent days, describing the rhythm of ups and downs and our sense of God or lack of our sense of God and what that might mean. Or maybe we have been captured night and day by some event or issue that feels so huge it seems to fill the entire screen of our life.

People who have strong concerns may need to talk about them early in the conversation. If they try to hold them back for later in the session, trying to speak about more routine, less threatening matters first, sometimes nothing of real consequence happens. It is as if their true self is gathered in a kind of vigilance around the matter of deep significance and whatever they are discussing is not meaningful enough to keep them truly engaged, let alone sufficient to connect with their director.

The opportunity to tell our story unhindered, uninterrupted is rare. Most of the time people are so involved in their own concerns they do not listen with complete attention. It can be quite startling, therefore, to feel another person fully attending to you, present with you and for you, setting their own struggles aside in order to be available to God and you. Sometimes this is wonderfully freeing and at other times it is paralyzing. We find ourselves listening to ourselves, weighing our words, and considering if we speak authentically or frivolously.

Sometimes it is exhausting to open areas we have not spoken about before. We may wonder at our own courage or choices and ask more than once, "Who really is in charge here?" We didn't expect to bare our souls so abruptly. At other times we ask ourselves why we choose to remain hidden. We may know very well what we need to talk about but have great difficulty trusting another human being with our thoughts. Perhaps we fear that we are losing faith or becoming a heretic. Perhaps we fear we are going overboard for God, becoming someone who is likely to do anything the Spirit invites. Whatever our reluctance, it is real and we are stuck, which, of course, is one of the reasons we came to spiritual direction in the first place. We wanted a clearer view. Now we are not sure we need or want to know as much as we are beginning to understand about our ways of evading and following God. What we do not talk about is as significant as what we do.

But telling our story to a spiritual director is often a pure gift. As we speak we begin to see connections that were hidden. Insights arise or our perspective about circumstances or ourselves may shift. There are Divine and human affirmations and confirmations. Sometimes the words we needed to hear come from our own lips. Sometimes our director's response arising out of that person's open listening to God and us carries helpful information. Our director says what we needed to hear and could not have asked for, maybe because it was below our conscious awareness or we did not have the words to describe it.

Interior developments arise out of silence that are beyond our clear view. We just know that something has moved or changed and that God is active. We may have a sense that the Spirit is inviting us to rest or recognize more completely that we are not alone in our quest or our questions. It may feel as if God is watching out for us, preparing or protecting us, healing old wounds, or inviting us to something new, or we may only be able to recognize that God is near and appreciate this awareness.

The opportunity to tell our story opens us to hear God's story more deeply—God's presence and participation in our lives and in the life of the world. In God all human stories connect. And when we participate in spiritual direction, we seem to notice more of the connections. Perhaps it is because we are more awake and available. We are seeking to pay attention, and God is expanding our capacity for awareness, appreciation, and understanding. Maybe our openness to God's presence attunes us more often to God's involvement with other people. We see that God is alive and active in the world.

Reflections

1. What more would you like to know about spiritual direction?
2. You have told some of the stories of your life many times and others not at all. Some of these are God stories. You knew you were being nudged by God or you were thinking about significant spiritual issues. Perhaps you were feeling unusually blessed or delighted or maybe you were angry about God's apparent absence. Write down possible titles for some of your stories that you would like to talk about with a spiritual director. Choose one and write about it in your journal.

   How was God present?

   What was significant for you?

   What words would you use to describe the qualities of this encounter?

   As far as you know, what do you think has been the fruit of this story?
3. Choose a story that you have not spoken about with anyone. Write about it using the same questions.

   Why have you remained silent about this?

   Do you think God invites you to speak about this now or still remain quiet?

3 | **Who Comes to Spiritual Direction?**

Anyone on an identified spiritual path experiences a variety of pullings and pushings, inclinations and disinclinations, attractions and repulsions that affect the direction he or she will follow. For example, as I have been working on this book I have felt a pull to spend less of my time in formal prayer and more on writing. Should I follow that inclination, or remain firmly disciplined in the time I set aside for prayer? Is this feeling a legitimate calling of God, a self-generated excuse to avoid prayer, or the sly work of some "other" force? This is a matter for discernment. . . . In the spiritual life, we must make such discernments constantly, choosing our directions with care, consideration and prayer. But because of our inherent personal blind spots and self-deceptions, and because of our vulnerability to outside forces, it is necessary to have help. Thus the spiritual director aids us in finding our proper direction.

Gerald G. May[1]

"For I know the plans I have for you," declares the Lord, "plans to prosper you and not to harm you, plans to give you hope and a future."

Jeremiah 29:11

Spiritual direction involves the truest love any human being can experience—the love of God. We are invited to discover our true heart and desires, our authentic selves, from within the context of sacred love. The living core of Divine/human connectedness is present in Christ and in our willingness to let go of self and self-interest as the ultimate center of our attention. Satisfying Divine/human relationships are grounded in God's love for us and our responsive intention to be God's. When we surrender ourselves to God, the way opens for us to recognize and become all God intends.

Once we are on the journey of faith, we discover that receiving and responding to God's love and receiving and giving love in human relationships is a long-lasting invitation and opportunity. From time to time we yearn for God and search for a deeper, fuller, more complete relationship. Something, Someone seems to beckon us to explore new possibilities. We have probably noticed that our desires appear in spurts, in stops and starts, and that we are quite erratic in our appetite for God. We see that without support and encouragement or intentional attentiveness we easily miss the subtlety of God's initiatives toward us. Spiritual direction helps us hear, recognize, and pay attention to the voice of our faithful love who is God.

Our deepest hope is that we will hear the Holy Spirit, who awakens us to God's presence and draws, enlivens, and frees us to respond to God out of an awareness that is rooted in reality as only God knows it. When we discern accurately what the Spirit is saying and are willing to believe and follow, new prospects open for healing, love, growth, and service. The Holy Spirit enables us to love God, our neighbors, and ourselves.

Who Comes to Spiritual Direction?

Who comes to spiritual direction? Anyone who is feeling drawn in the ways described above. But there is much more to be said. People who seek spiritual direction are looking for God, but what motivates them to think that spiritual direction could be helpful at a particular moment in time arises out of the story of their lives.

People may choose spiritual direction as one way of trying to pay closer attention to God at any stage of life's journey—beginning, middle, or end. We change. Life circumstances change. The world changes. A continuous flow of new opportunities invites discernment of the Holy Spirit's intentions and invitations toward us. We meet our own varying willingness and learn to recognize our particular ways of resisting and following God.

Broad themes appear when we consider who comes to direction. There are certain times in human journeys when people are more likely to seek spiritual companionship, but there is no one-to-one correspondence or defining categorization. The following overarching themes are lived out in the midst of unique circumstances that point toward the mysteries of life and of God's activity with and within us.

People Experiencing a Faith Transition

Many people come to spiritual direction because they are no longer at home in their own world. They are exploring or reexploring their ideas about God and faith. Their pictures of God are changing, or their practices. But most of all, they notice their own struggling. They no longer feel comfortable where they used to sense they belonged. They ask who or what has shifted, God or them. The place they worshiped for years may have changed or their ideas or feelings are developing in different directions. They may not be able to say immediately what has changed, but whatever it is, they feel they are adrift and are finding it disquieting. They are asking what God might be saying or showing them. It may take a while to gather courage to give words to the discomfort.

The following conversation shows how insights may arise in spiritual direction.

Director: What have you noticed about your heart?

Directee: Funny you should ask. I've been thinking about myself as the Ice Queen.

Director: Why is that?

Directee: No feelings.

Director: Is that some kind of a change for you?

Directee: Oh yes. I used to have this love affair with God. It was so incredible. Like God was right there. That sense of God's love began in the midst of a difficult season, and it continued for several years.

Director: When did you notice something was different?

Directee: About five years ago.

Director: What was that like?

Directee: It felt very strange . . . like God had gone away, or at least my sense of Jesus had disappeared. That was unnerving. I come from a background where Jesus is all-important. I began to feel like some kind of a heretic.

Director: So what did you do?

Directee: I tried different kinds of prayer. I'd write letters to Jesus, to God in my journal, and ask where he'd gone. I looked at my life under a microscope trying to figure out if I'd committed some particularly terrible sin and didn't know it. I couldn't think of anything, but then I can be pretty blind, so I prayed that the Spirit would show me if there was something between us, something hindering our love. But nothing showed up.

Director: How has that affected your prayer and other things you do to nurture your life with God?

Directee: It seems like I pretty much do what I've done for several years. I try to take an hour at the beginning of the day. That doesn't always happen, but it's pretty regular. During that time I write in my journal, read Scripture, pray. Sometimes it goes fast, and sometimes it really drags.

Director: What's your prayer like?

Directee: It seems to be getting quieter and quieter. Sometimes it is, "Come, Holy Spirit," or maybe I'll begin with a phrase or two. "Holy God, you who love me, here I am." At times I notice something stirring within, but I can't say that there are feelings as such. It seems like there is some kind of activity going on, and it is God, but that's about all I am sure of.

Director: Does this seem related to your ordinary, outward life in some way?

Directee: I am under the impression that the answer is yes because even though I don't feel anything in the way I used to, I feel like the Holy Spirit is guiding me very directly.

Director: What do you mean by that?

Directee: I seem to know what I am to do, which job assignments to take, where to go, which people to make contact with.

Director: Why do you think that's God?

Directee: That's a good question. When I follow these impressions— I guess that's as good a word as any for them—the Spirit leads me to experiences that confirm that this was what God desired. It's like I am able to do what my part is and then God does something. It's fun to watch, but at times I feel like I'm the last to know what's going on.

Director: What do you think God's view might be of all this?

Directee: That's a new perspective. I wonder if God has been inviting me to a different kind of trust, more trust in the God I cannot see or feel, but showing me divine faithfulness and care all along the way. That would be a good way to describe what's happening.

Director: And the Ice Queen?

Directee: Maybe she doesn't have the hard heart that I feared she did. That feels like good news.

This may sound like an answer, but it is really only a beginning. The directee has begun to hope God is in this new place, but that does not mean she is clear about where the Spirit is leading her. The conversation has just opened. It could be a long time before it goes much further, but now someone else knows and is willing to pray with her and for her. She does not feel like quite the heretic she wondered whether she was becoming, but neither does she have answers in the usual sense. This kind of transition in the life of faith is what brings many people to spiritual direction.

When people are growing and this growth is causing them to see things differently, it is helpful to have a relationship with someone who knows this new way, who is acquainted with this stage of the faith journey. When people are questioning the adequacy or fullness of their ways of being a Christian, spiritual direction provides an opportunity to explore where God is in this transition. In a sense, these people are experiencing a loss, the loss of a faith life they were accustomed to or considered normal.

People Experiencing Loss

Losses of other varieties—our own or those of people we care about—also bring people to spiritual direction. We know we are dealing with a sense of loss when we notice we are experiencing the normal progression of emotions associated with grief: denial, anger, bargaining, depression, and acceptance. These stages do not proceed in any neat order; we usually move back and forth among these stages until we reach resolution and closure, which sets the stage for whatever comes next.

Physical losses, such as those that arise from normal aging or from traumatic events including accidents and disease cause people to ask, "Why me?" and "Where is God in this?"

The loss of material possessions also stimulates questioning. We lose things through forgetfulness, natural disasters, stock market changes, other people's actions, or through decisions we make ourselves, such as selling a home. We may experience a reduction of income that arises out of a choice to pursue an invitation of the Spirit, such as setting out on a vocational path that requires additional schooling and a loss of income. Perhaps the Spirit is challenging us to serve through a short- or long-term mission project. Maybe we are being drawn to a lower-paying, more service-oriented career. Our values are shifting, and the loss we experience is not entirely comfortable, even when we believe it is God's idea.

The loss of a significant relationship can stir old and new wounds and questions. It may be a permanent loss through death or divorce, or it may be a change within a relationship, such as the changes that take place as children grow up and eventually leave home and establish adult identities and independence.

People experiencing such losses may seek spiritual direction hoping to discover meaning in the midst of difficulties. They wonder how God is present and participating.

People Experiencing Changes in Self-Perception

Early in our marriage, I can remember loving my husband but feeling isolated and alone because our new life together did not provide everything a large network of relationships had offered before marriage. Before marriage, I lived near my family and extended family, was a busy college student, and had an active, happy circle of friends as well as this new love in my life. Now, suddenly, I was living in a different area of the country, knew no one except my husband, and discovered that I absolutely hated the job I was prepared to do. This points to another area of loss: a loss of self-esteem. This kind of awareness can stimulate our searching for God and God's guidance.

Feeling guilty about not living up to our own expectations or the demands we perceive from others, or even from God, affects our sense of self. Self-perception is more fluid than we often realize. It is easily influenced by physical patterns of sleep, nutrition, and our level of health and wellness. We feel different about ourselves when we are rested, well fed, and healthy than when we are exhausted, hungry, or sick. The ways we get along with people who are important to us and our present life circumstances also strongly influence our perceptions and opinions of ourselves. Messages we perceive from others have a loud voice. Anything that makes us sad, angry, disappointed, depressed, argumentative, or pushes us into denial may point to concerns that make spiritual direction look attractive.

It is difficult to find a place where we can speak openly and honestly about our self-perception because we fear looking self-centered, unworthy, or inadequate. Trusted friends may try to "fix" us or comfort us when really we need to address our thoughts by speaking out loud about them and by taking them into our prayer. Looking clearly at things in the presence of God brings clarity, healing, and growth. Spiritual direction conversations provide a setting in which to do this.

People Experiencing the Flow of Life

All of life, with its challenges, changes, and delights, has the possibility of bringing us to consider spiritual direction.

People often seek spiritual direction when they feel restless. They ask, "Is this all there is to human life?" Perhaps they were hoping for more—more from God, more from human relationships, more satisfaction in their work, play, or prayer. Or maybe we have experienced the opposite. The "more" arrived suddenly, and we are anxious because God is addressing us in new ways—through Divine presence, or unexplainable inner peace, or love that washes over us without a reason we can account for, or a sense of healing. Something significant has changed in us, and we know it was not our doing. God is being God outside of what we have come to expect. Sometimes this pleases us and sometimes it scares us; perhaps we are both delighted and scared at the same time. We are not sure which feeling to believe or how to pay attention to the mixture or to God.

Some people come to spiritual direction in response to new information. They have recently learned about the ministry of spiritual direction and recognize that it is what they have been seeking. They are not looking for a person to tell them what to think or feel about God. They want to talk to someone who will respect them and their experience and assist them in paying prayerful attention to what they are already thinking and feeling.

People Experiencing a Yearning for God

People seek spiritual direction when they are dealing with transitions, grief, wounds, and questions about discernment. No matter how directees describe their reasons for seeking direction, however, if we listen closely we can hear authentic yearnings for God woven into their stories. They are asking, "How is God in this?" Rather than looking merely for answers to life situations, they are looking for the presence of God, and they are wondering how to be awake and available to this ever present God. They long for Divine/human companionship. They may even say they are convinced that living life to its fullest potential is dependent on hearing God more clearly.

Sarah, a woman in her mid-fifties, entered spiritual direction through a slow process that stretched over three years. She was involved in a job, a church, and many satisfying friendships. She was coping with the pain of feeling caught in a bruising work environment resulting from changes in personnel, goals, procedures, and expectations. At times her opportunities were directly affected, but her central concern was whether the world itself was changing, becoming less hospitable. She wondered what that might mean about God's power and effectiveness. In addition to the disquiet of her workplace, she was concerned because many people at church were loudly expressing diverse opinions about significant congregational issues. She had strong opinions and wanted to voice them too, but the idea of losing church as a safe place troubled her.

Sarah frequently discussed her thoughts and questions with friends and prayed consistently, but these usual ways of dealing with her life no longer seemed sufficient. Then she noticed her prayer changing in disturbing ways. It seemed flat. In fact, she was avoiding prayer. She wanted to know where God was in all this. She wondered if there was anything she could do to have a more peaceful, trusting heart in the midst of uncomfortable circumstances and longed to move through them as quickly as possible. She did not want to stay in this place any longer than absolutely necessary.

She first heard about spiritual direction three years ago. Now and then the possibility of looking for a director crossed her mind. She read a little about direction and talked to friends. When she realized she was going around in circles with her concerns, she decided to give direction a try.

So far, after meeting once a month for six months with a spiritual director, Sarah says the meetings have offered her a place to talk about her relationship with God in ways she has not talked about it to anyone before, not even her friends. She is surprised how freeing it is. Sarah thought her personal prayers, Scripture reading, and church involvement should provide sufficient support for her continuing growth. She says she is getting a different perspective. Her director is helping her recognize the Holy Spirit's presence.

Some of the issues that were so important to Sarah are softening a bit, and her realization of what is most important to her is affecting her ability to trust God in the moment-by-moment flow of her life. She is noticing great and small graces more often and that gives her confidence that God is and will be there in whatever way she truly needs. Speaking to her director about her faith has helped Sarah notice where the Spirit is alive and active and also helped her identify some of her favorite ways of shutting out God and depending on herself.

She calls herself a happier person. Perhaps some of her satisfaction arises from her pleasure about "really doing something"—becoming more intentional about paying attention to her relationship with God and listening for the Spirit's invitations. From within that context she looks at her prayer, discernment, and chosen responses. She laughs when she says, "I am amazed how often when my director asks, 'How is that in your prayer?' I realize that whatever the item is, it has not appeared in my prayer in exactly the way I'm talking to him about it. It is amazing how much difference having another pair of prayerful eyes/ears makes."

Sam speaks differently about his journey. He is thirty-eight and married to Joan. They have three children. He would have called himself a Christian, desiring to be God's man, but he had drifted away from the church. Some of it was due to busyness, but there were other factors that he was not sure how to address even if he wanted to. He read Scripture now and then and prayed spontaneously. He was working on issues that were important to him, and he really cared about what God might want of and from him. When he attempted to discuss these ideas with others, however, they gave him answers he described as unreflective and insufficient.

When he read about spiritual direction in a newspaper article, he became interested. He called the newspaper, spoke to the reporter, and asked how he could make contact with the directors mentioned in the article. After discussing his questions with one of them, he entered spiritual direction. That was two years ago. When he looks back, he marks his decision as a major one. He says he continues to be surprised by how much more he sees than he used to. He wonders now how he could have been so unintentional, just rolling along, for so many years. But the most exciting part for him is his clearer recognition of God's moment-by-moment presence and love and his awareness that he and his wife and children are being guided into a deepening love for God and a desire to be God's people in the world.

Each Person Is Unique

People consider spiritual direction when they are

- feeling restless or challenged
- in transition
- dealing with losses
- looking for someone to share their journey who knows the new way they are feeling drawn
- feeling guilty about not living up to someone's expectations—their own, a person's they care about, or even God's
- wondering if this is all there is in a satisfactory life
- having spiritual experiences that are different from what they have known before
- opening to God's love, to receive and respond more fully
- exploring general or particular questions about discernment
- responding to information about spiritual direction
- yearning for God[2]

Yet, you are unique. I am unique. Every person in the long flow of history is one of a kind and so are the relationships with God that unfold through the details of individual lives. Further, our stories cannot be separated into spiritual and material components or inner and outer realities. We discover that all facets of life are inseparably related and the site of God's grace and activity. The specific qualities of each life and relationship with God provide the milieu, material, and reasons for choosing spiritual direction.

It is important to take personal individuality into account so we do not categorize people. An almost unconscious stereotyping can easily shape how we speak, listen, and respond, which, in turn, limits our openness to the Spirit. We can miss meaning and grace by not paying close enough attention to nuances that give distinctive shape and color to ourselves and others in direction relationships.

The circumstances of each life, including conception, birth, and place of birth, are the first pieces in the picture of who we are. There are no generic persons. Each human being is born out of the union of a particular man and woman. This joining of two genetic legacies carries with it everything for a new life, including gender, race, and physical and mental capacities and traits. Social influences, including cultural, generational, and ethnic characteristics, religious opportunities, and economic resources, also shape people.

At times we are grateful for our heritage. At other times, however, we may feel we have been cheated, perhaps by God. We may feel deprived. We may think that opportunities have been limited in ways that seem unfair or unusual or that our circumstances have been too difficult. Perhaps we feel wounded or think we are not whole, normal, or like others.

All people pay some attention to the events and qualities of their particular life. Many are drawn sooner or later to think about how God is connected with their being exactly who they are. We may inquire about meanings and purposes related to our conception, birth, family, schooling, timing, relationships, or work opportunities. We may interpret life events through a theological lens and thank or curse God on that basis. These interpretations of ourselves and our lives become part of how we perceive and present ourselves when we come to spiritual direction.

Along with our life situation, the human life cycle itself becomes the context of an ongoing relationship with God. We are strongly influenced by our stage in life, whether an infant, child, adolescent, young adult, middle-aged adult, or elderly person. What we recognize of God and how we interpret and respond is colored by many age-related physical, mental, and social characteristics. Each season of life carries distinctive opportunities and challenges that may invite us to enter spiritual direction.

Sometimes we can better prepare for these life changes by studying what developmental theorists have observed and learned about human behavior. Such study can help us understand important aspects of growth and reflect on our own. This information may help us recognize and participate in the kind of spiritual friendship called for at a particular time and place in life. We may deal more easily with some of our fears, gain a greater understanding of our changing self-concept, and react in a more positive way when faced with questions and struggles. Our study can also alert and encourage us to be more intentional about asking God to protect and guide us through seasons and transitions when we are likely to be unusually vulnerable.[3]

Human beings seem to depend radically upon familiarity; the changes that unfold as part of the normal life cycle can be unsettling. We often try to create predictable, comfortable relationships and environments to ease our anxiety about changes we sense in ourselves and the world.

But we cannot shield ourselves completely from recognizing that we do not know what comes next; we cannot see the future, and this can make us uneasy. Many of our questions and dilemmas are connected to this uneasiness and become the basis of spiritual direction conversations.

Our sense of God and God's intentions toward us within the context of a particular life become significant when we consider spiritual direction. Our personal characteristics as people who choose to love and follow God grow out of the specifics of our heritage, nurture, environments, and developmental opportunities and challenges. Our perceptions and interpretations of our own life and the Holy Spirit's interactions with us provide ongoing reasons to consider spiritual direction as well as material for spiritual direction conversations.

Why I Came to Spiritual Direction

I suppose I should not be surprised that this book arises out of my story with God or that it has been developing for many years. Telling my story in the one-to-one conversations of spiritual direction often stretches me; including some of my story in these pages stretches me farther. I am not eager to bare my soul to the world. But perhaps my attempts to describe portions of my journey and why I came to spiritual direction will make it easier for you to consider sharing your story with a spiritual director.

Once when I was asked to do a self introduction, I decided to write it in rhyme, which helped me communicate what seemed essential in a way that was quick and direct.

> To America my grandparents came in a boat,
> In the cattle hold stuffed with Swedes and a goat.
>
> Immigrant families flourished and grew.
> My parents were born—and finally me, too.
>
> I am a small town child from a family of five.
> On the edge of Chicago we grew and thrived.
>
> In the summer we walked the Lake Michigan Shore,
> At Bethany's beach, where we loved the wave's roar.
>
> Schools in rapid succession filled my young head
> With things from books and what teachers said.
>
> Wheaton, Cornell, and Minnesota—
> Twenty-two years seemed like more than my quota.
>
> God walked my path—I now know,
> And painful lessons began to show.

Family troubles grew and abounded.
Life became hurried, harried, and hounded.

I would wryly laugh as the list stretched and lengthened
And thought that we'd die; who'd guess we'd be strengthened?

Questions flourished in the dark of the night
And came out in bursts that were no delight.

I spit them at God and my friends and my foes,
Asking, "Why pretend?" and "What do you know?"

My figuring mind had not counted or planned
On God's reaching in and taking my hand.

Faced with Love I could not explain
God came alongside in the midst of my pain.

Hard questions still stand and evil is strong,
But God is enough to teach me life's song.

I live with one husband, one dog, and one cat
At the edge of a lake that is wavy and flat.

We ski in the winter and summer as well,
Read books by the fire and find stories to tell.

We listen to leaves blown in the wind,
Watch herons and gulls alight and ascend,

See cattails and clouds and float in a boat
Oops—it sounds like the beginning without Swedes or the goat.

People who come to spiritual direction usually want to tell their story with God as straightforwardly as possible. They hope to describe what the core of their life communicates about God's grace and love and the person God has created and called them to be. They may also wish to talk about how they have gotten sidetracked. What we select to tell our spiritual director and how we present our story is a way both to reveal and conceal our deepest selves. We may see our story in new ways due to the variations and nuances we select to tell as well as our heightened sense of intentionality.

You may have noticed I tried to tell a little of the core but then moved to less threatening, more peripheral information. We tell our stories as we are able and drawn to God, sometimes revealing, sometimes concealing, moving back and forth. Telling our story is a way of communicating, letting another glimpse who we are, and being willing to see ourselves more clearly. Some of our telling arises out of the normal, expected routines of life, some of it comes out of traumas, crises, and fractures of relationships, bodies, and minds, and some flows from joy.

A longer, more detailed version of what led me to spiritual direction looks like this. I was raised in a family that went to church and Sunday school weekly and sometimes attended a midweek service, read the Bible at home, and talked about God. When I was a little girl, I pictured myself racing through the door of heaven, leaping into Jesus' arms laughing, and announcing, "I'm home."

As a teenager I remembered that scene but felt embarrassed by my childhood enthusiasm and open love. In college I sang for God with great joy, worked in a parachurch group, and grew up (the first of many turns from adolescence toward maturity that I am now convinced is a lifelong process). I married after college and was sure we would have a Christian home, but I don't think I ever planned to get radically involved with God by risking very much. These kinds of thoughts were under the surface, and I did not have the courage or inclination to explore them.

But young adulthood brought painful intrusions into my life, including the birth of a nephew with visual limitations and a suicide in the family. These and other unwelcome realities inaugurated a long, difficult season. Yet we remained committed to God and involved in the church. It was years before I was ready, willing, and able to speak to God out of the truths of my own discoveries, anger, confusion, and newly shaping questions. But pain has a way of blowing our cover, revealing whatever is hidden. I figured that either God did or did not care about what we were experiencing, and I wanted to know which. If God did not care or did not exist, then it was time to stop pretending and really grow up, which meant making it on our own and learning to cope. I thought that if it became clear that God did exist and was loving, I would seek God's help. My primary goal was personal survival.

I went many places and asked whatever I liked, sometimes without much concern about how my questions might affect others. I went to healing meetings, prayer meetings, conferences, seminars, and retreats. I sought professional counseling for the depression I was battling and waited almost a year for an appointment with someone I had decided I might be able to trust. I thought I'd found someone who could tolerate hearing what I really thought and felt. In my search, I was drawn to many others. Some helped and some did not. I, in turn, by my behavior and questions, wounded some and assisted others.

What seemed most surprising were God's loving initiatives. God taught me through large healing gatherings; small groups of people who shared their stories, worshiped, prayed, and ate together; reading and praying with Scripture; writing in a journal; and prayers of empty agony when I was alone stretched out on my face on the floor. One afternoon when

I was with a small group of women including my mother, the Holy Spirit's love rinsed me, and I knew it unmistakably. The reservoir of pain was simply gone. I was free to recognize and respond to God in new ways. I believe that God answered the prayers others prayed for me when I was thoroughly enmeshed in self-preoccupation and dislike.

Many people were willing to listen to God with me in those early days of my search. I do not think any of them had ever heard the term *spiritual direction*, but they were doing it. They did not just give their best advice; they listened, prayed, waited, and watched what the Spirit brought forth. It was a long way down the road before I was to know what spiritual direction was and to seek it. But as I sought God, the Holy Spirit guided me to the resources I needed, whether I knew what they were or how to ask.

Somewhere in the midst of my healing, people began to come to me for prayer and conversation. Most of the time I knew I did not have the answers, although at times I would get sidetracked trying to fix someone. Learning to depend on God is a lifelong challenge. Yet as I grew in this area, my deepening prayer and growing dependency began to create a welcoming space for others. I was participating in spiritual direction as both a directee and a director but still had never heard the term. At times I was troubled by how deeply I was involved in others' lives and considered taking counseling courses, but something always stopped me. It was clear that the insights and transformations that occurred in these meetings happened through the prayers in and around the conversation. I was not doing the real work, God was.

I knew I wanted to learn more about personal spiritual development, so I entered a formal spiritual direction relationship as a directee and I applied to a study program. I was accepted because someone dropped out at the last minute. My involvement began to seem like God's providential grace when I began reading about spiritual direction. It was as if a door opened. The Holy Spirit had been teaching me about spiritual direction through my experiences as a directee and as a director. Now I was being introduced to the experiences, thoughts, and ministries of a long line of spiritual directors. It became rapidly apparent that others knew about what I had been experiencing, had words for it, and knew how to pay attention to it and to God in it.

Now, many years later, I am still involved as both directee and director. I have not arrived. I still yearn for whole and holy resolution to painful realities and questions. But the long-ago image of a homecoming with God has been renewed, and at times I see myself racing through the door of heaven into God's glad arms. For me, spiritual direction often contains a taste of that kind of resolution and homecoming because it has become a place where I remember God loves me, shares my fractured, ordinary life, and is present in grace no matter what may arise.

Everyone has a story about how God brings him or her to consider spiritual direction as a directee, a director, or both. You may want to discuss with family members, a pastor, or friends your decision to participate in spiritual direction, but when you do so, you are not seeking permission or approval. Although potential participants need to listen respectfully to others, the opinions of others should not be the determining factor in their decision whether to take part in direction. Ultimately, a decision regarding spiritual direction is based on God's leading and a person's desire to follow God wholeheartedly.

Who comes to spiritual direction? Anyone who would like to hear God and see God's part in their story in the context of a prayer-centered relationship.

Reflections

1. What are the positive and negative legacies that contribute to your being you? Set aside some quiet time to reflect on and write about the legacies that are shaping you.

   from your mother
   from your father
   circumstances of your birth
   physical, mental, emotional capacities and traits
   educational and economic conditions and opportunities
   religious and spiritual heritage
   extended family and family systems
   particular crises
   others

   If you could write a chapter about each legacy, what chapter title would you give each one?

2. Look at the list on page 54 that describes when people consider spiritual direction. In a time of quiet, prayerful reflection invite God to show you which of these might be drawing you to consider spiritual direction. Choose two or three of the possibilities on the list to pray about and write about in your journal.

Spiritual Direction and Trust | 4

But for a Christian, there are, strictly speaking, no chances. A secret Master of the Ceremonies has been at work. Christ, who said to the disciples, "Ye have not chosen me, but I have chosen you," can truly say to every group of Christian friends, "You have not chosen one another, but I have chosen you for one another." The friendship is not a reward for our discrimination and good taste in finding one another out. It is the instrument by which God reveals to each the beauties of all the others. . . . At this feast it is He who has spread the board and it is He who has chosen the guests. It is He, we may dare to hope, who sometimes does, and always should preside. Let us not reckon without our Host.

C. S. Lewis[1]

Trust in the LORD with all your heart
and lean not on your own understanding.

Proverbs 3:5

"Trust me." Can I? Should I? Will I? What would that mean? Where could it lead? Words that are intended to assure us often put us on guard and raise suspicions about whether we should believe the one who speaks. Hearing the words "Trust me" may make us more hesitant than if nothing had been said. At times, trusting is straightforward, uncomplicated, and easy. At other times, however, trusting feels life threatening or at least potentially hazardous to something we hold dear.

I am involved in relationships that require trust. So are you. So is everyone. Sometimes we decide to proceed slowly and carefully, to consider the possible outcomes of our trust. On other occasions, even if we are usually inclined to act cautiously, we may feel drawn or compelled to take risks.

Human experience offers frequent opportunities to trust or not. Should we believe the results of medical tests and follow the recommended course of treatment? Should we purchase a used car, an old house, a piece of fine jewelry? Can we believe the reasons our child gave for breaking curfew? Is the information in this course, book, or web site accurate? Will our friend keep what we told him in confidence? Can we depend on our ability to hear God accurately?

Every aspect of life reinforces our awareness that we dwell in an inter-dependent network of trust. Human survival, continuance, and fulfill-ment depend on cooperation. Even when we were very young, we had some awareness of whether we could rely on the persons around us. Every human environment is a mixture of what can and should be trusted and what cannot and should not be trusted. We may become unsettled when we realize that the people with whom we live or work are not com-pletely reliable, but we may become even more troubled when we sus-pect that we ourselves are not fully trustworthy.

The web of trust is complicated and far-reaching and functions both within and beyond our conscious attention. We may never recognize all the factors that influence our trust, nor is it necessary to do so. How-ever, it is helpful to recognize that each of us has a history of trusting that affects all present relationships, including those involved in spiri-tual direction. Our own history, and whether our caregivers, significant others, mentors, colleagues, and acquaintances have been worthy of trust, influences our ability and willingness to trust other human beings, ourselves, and God.

Trusting God

Trusting God is not only about trusting Divine intentions through life's challenges and circumstances, it also includes trusting God to teach us about God. As we grow, God shows us more about Divine love, care, and perspectives. The following direction discussion is about God teach-ing someone about God.

Directee: When I returned to my retreat room after supper I was sur-prised to see I had left a candle burning. It was safe because it was in a glass container, but I had intended to put it out. The flickering candlelight drew me to be quiet. I got com-fortable sitting on the bed, resting against the pillows along the wall, and just sat for a while, thanking God for the soli-tude, the beauties of winter with sunshine on snow and long, blue shadows early and late in the day. I settled more and more deeply into the quiet prayer that drew me. There was a springlike artificial flower arrangement on the win-dowsill, next to the candle. It looked fresh: white daisies, deep blues, soft pinks, a shower of green. The beauty of the candlelight and flowers drew me, and then I noticed in my prayer I was addressing God as "Beauty of the Trinity."

Director: What was that like?

Directee: Really gentle. And, as a matter of fact, it was a great relief.

Director: What do you mean?

Directee: You may remember I told you how uneasy I was because I felt like I had lost Jesus. Suddenly, it was like I connected with him again, and he was inviting me to pay attention to being in relationship with the Trinity. Scripture came to mind, the place in John 17 where Jesus prays to the Father for everyone who will believe in him and asks the Father that they (the believers) will be "in us" and be "one as we are one." I looked up the passage to read it again. It says that those who follow Jesus will be drawn into a relationship with the Trinity that is similar to the way the members of the Trinity are related to each other and that Jesus wants his followers to have the same kind of interdependent relationship with God and each other. This sounds pretty heady, but it really wasn't at the time. It was more like enjoying God's company in a new way, something about the largeness of God's love and presence.

Director: What have you noticed since then?

Directee: I'm not so nervous about losing Jesus like I was, and I have a sense that this is the beginning of something new, maybe a new chapter with God.

Director: Any idea what the title of the new chapter might be?

Directee: It's too early to guess.

Director: Are you doing anything different or differently in your prayer time since this experience?

Directee: Just addressing God as "Beauty of the Trinity" sometimes and praying in whatever way seems invited. And, of course, asking God a million questions about what this all means and what I am supposed to be praying about or doing related to my new awareness.

Director: That seems like a good place to begin.

"Trust in the LORD with all your heart, and do not rely on your own insight," is a clear command of Scripture (Prov. 3:5 NRSV). But it is quite likely that sometime we will discover we are primarily or even exclusively trusting God to be God in the ways we have become accustomed to thinking about God. Trusting God beyond the God we have understood or known up until now can feel very uncomfortable. Then we are called to depend more on God than we do on ourselves—a very unlikely possibility unless we are aided by grace. We feel more secure relying on what we are able to perceive through our direct senses and what we have already learned about living in relationship with God. We like to observe, analyze, and chart our course.

When we are preoccupied with managing ourselves, it is easy to feel responsible, competent, and independent, at least for a while. It is important to know ourselves and to be good stewards of the life God has given us, but independence from God is not God's intention for us. We were created to be God's companions. Psalm 139 states that God was present in our creation, has known us always, and has great interest in us.

> For You did form my inward parts, You did knit me together in my mother's womb. I will confess and praise You, for You are fearfully wonderful, and for the awful wonder of my birth! Wonderful are Your works, and that my inner self knows right well. My frame was not hidden from You, when I was being formed in secret and intricately and curiously wrought (as if embroidered with various colors) in the depths of the earth [a region of darkness and mystery]. Your eyes saw my unformed substance, and in Your book all the days of my life were written, before ever they took shape, when as yet there was none of them.
>
> verses 13–16 AMP

We cannot comprehend all that this means or implies, but at the very least, it suggests that God desires the best for us. Some of us find this difficult to believe and others seem to have always known and remain convinced of God's love for them even in the midst of challenging circumstances.

We may or may not have grown up or live in an environment that encourages us to believe in and trust God, and all of us question God's trustworthiness at times. Ordinary human life is fraught with difficulties. But when we are drawn to spiritual direction, we discover that we have enough trust to desire a closer relationship with God, to see more clearly who God is, and to hear more clearly what God says. We have come at least to a tentative conclusion that perhaps God is trustworthy, possibly more trustworthy than we are, and that it could be to our great benefit to hear and follow God.

We are more than merely curious about God and God's ideas. We are exploring how to align ourselves more intentionally with God's loving presence, desires, instruction, and care. In some measure, we enter spiritual direction because we want to trust and follow God more easily and more completely. We hope for a quality of openness in our hearts and willingness and courage to hear and act on what God invites.

Some people who choose spiritual direction have had a wide range of experiences of trusting God over a span of many years. They have come to a deep appreciation of the numerous ways they have recognized God's presence and care. In fact, they are more likely to trust God than themselves.

Although we may not consciously acknowledge that this is what we are doing, we quite often describe the edges of our trust of God. Susan says she trusts God "for forever." She adds, "If I die suddenly, I know I'll go to be with God because of Jesus, but sometimes I'm not sure about God for now." Bill describes his trust in God with a smile. "I have a sense of being loved, loved, loved by Divine Love. It's so strong that it helps me act out of a love for others that I know is more than, different from my human love. The love has a fuller, freer quality than I'd be likely to attribute to myself—I know myself better than that." Ann says, "God and I are really in a trust war. It is not going well at work; in fact, I'm afraid I will be part of the next staff reduction. I feel myself clamoring after God with endless questions. Maybe that's good. I'm still running *to* God even though I feel fractured. My behavior shows me I am at least wanting to trust God in spite of the fact that I am not feeling particularly peaceful or hopeful about whatever the outcomes might be." These are contemporary examples of struggling with Divine/human trust considerations.

The likelihood of our trusting God at all is deeply colored by our perception of who God is and what God is like. (Chapter 10, "Experiencing God," includes some of these considerations.) Oftentimes our perceptions of God are based on what we know of God from Scripture. Opportunities to trust God have been presented to humankind over and over in different forms. The Bible includes stories about many people who trusted God before the incarnation of Christ, such as Abraham and Sarah, Moses, Noah, Deborah, and David and Abigail. The focus in the New Testament is on Jesus' life, healing, teaching, death, and resurrection, which adds essential information and insight and is beneficial to our willingness and ability to trust God.

Jesus knew that his obedience to God the Father would result in his death. He also knew that his death and resurrection would bring about our rescue from domination by sin and its consequences. Christ's self-offering is the basis of God's invitation to us to trust in the extent, quality, and completeness of Divine love. Jesus is the perfect example of divine trustworthiness. Romans 5:8 describes it this way: "But God proves his love for us in that while we still were sinners Christ died for us" (NRSV).

During Christ's earthly life, his disciples learned to trust him gradually by watching, listening, asking questions, and making mistakes. Through their day-to-day relationship with Christ, they experienced continuing opportunities to recognize and rely on God. We tend to think that the disciples had a distinct advantage over us because of their shared life with Jesus. But even they did not understand many things of significance. Some of those things became clear later. Some did not. Like the disciples, our trust in God begins and grows in the midst of ordinary living and develops and deepens according to a pattern of repeating encounters with God.

Through believing that Jesus is our way to God, we choose to trust God in surrender, commitment, and relationship. We release ourselves into God's care, and God transforms and enlarges us both slowly and suddenly. By grace, we grow or are grown in our willingness to trust God more and rely less on our own ideas or our culture's values.

We respond to our awakening to God in various ways. At times, we sense the Spirit asking us to release our whole selves into God's care, and we are conflicted. Our answer is, "Yes and no." Even though we think we would like to be God's without reservation, we also like having a sense of control over our destiny. Releasing our life to another, even to God, is not easy. We become aware that the Spirit of God invites us to wholeheartedly choose to offer ourselves again and again to God.

As life progresses and new possibilities emerge, we almost seem to hear the Spirit asking, "Do you still want to trust me? Now that you have seen this, what will you choose to believe? God or no God? A God you can trust or not? Whose wisdom will you choose, yours or mine?" The calls to participate in self-surrender usually come in areas in which we are strongly attached to our perceptions, choices, or privileges.

I was not happy with God or myself when I caught a glimpse of behavior that seemed to indicate I was treating the academic year as if it were God's but summer as mine. In some measure, the weekends and evenings were mine as well. I was surprised to see these aspects of myself. It was not so much that I was consciously going my way rather than God's but that I was oblivious to how I was thinking about and using large blocks of time. I saw that sometimes I felt imposed upon and resentful even when it was clear that a particular request was initiated by God, as when I was invited to teach a singles' retreat over a Labor Day weekend. "Not me!" I worried whether I would get sufficient preparation time, family holiday enjoyment, Sabbath, or play.

I get tense even now while I am writing this thinking about my blindness. It makes me uneasy to see how blind I was about time and suspect that I could be just as undiscerning now about other things. This awareness draws me to pray that the Spirit will help me trust in God's goodness related to everything I do not know or see. Facing observations such as these by writing in my journal, praying about them, and talking about them with my spiritual director is often uncomfortable, later helpful, and finally freeing.

I have discovered that when I seek to discern God's desires in regard to my work, I am better able to identify and avoid the canyons of under- and overcommitment and have a clearer view of my mixed motivations and what God is saying to me. I have learned that when I bring my questions, fears, and hopes into the open, the way clears to new possibilities. God often brings me to more adventurous, interesting options, places, work, and circumstances than I could have planned or foreseen. God also surprises me with unexpected respites and even vacations.

When I am willing to order my schedule in a prayerful consciousness, inviting God into all considerations, my tendencies to control lessen. But even when I am more intentional about asking God to help me see whatever is influencing me, I often still struggle with both seeing and doing—with identifying what the Holy Spirit is inviting and being willing to follow God's desires.

I am grateful for opportunities to talk about these things with my spiritual director. I am often surprised by what God does with them and me when I bring them intentionally into my prayer. One day when I was praying it seemed as if God was saying the following to me, and I wrote it in my journal:

> You cannot see what I want you to see unless you stand in a particular place. Remember how it has been before. When you discern the place I want you to be, then I can show you things that it would be impossible to show anywhere else in exactly the way I mean it to be. Particularity is everything. The nuances of specific interrelationships are unique to each moment, setting, configuration. I like to be the one who sets the stage and sometimes I share that delight with you. Trust me that when I am taking you away from this wonderful, fragrant summer place I take you to something better—Myself. I know you'd rather stay home, but in the end you'll say, "I wouldn't have missed it." Trust me. I will never waste the time you give to me or anything else. Whatever you truly let go of and place fully in my keeping becomes a seed planted for the kingdom. I am the only One who really knows what that means. But I will teach you when you are willing to learn this glorious way.

When I look at these words or remember them and the events that followed when we traveled to communist-dominated Eastern Europe in the mid-1980s, it helps me to trust in God's love and guidance. We discovered that we were in exactly the right place at the right time. We took about fifty photographs of our friend J's family, including some warm, smiling pictures of her father. Two weeks after we delivered the pictures to J, her father died unexpectedly. We had been able to take in needed food and clothing, but even more importantly, J's dad had heard that his daughter and her family were doing well, and J's dad and mom had received her written messages of love and encouragement.

We experienced God's faithful presence and care directly and also in people we met. The daughter of an Orthodox priest not only told us what to do but made arrangements for a taxi to meet us at night and take us where we wanted to go. She also went along with us to assure our safety and translate for us. Because of her willingness to put herself at great risk, we were able to find the people we were looking for and carry their messages back to the United States. It was God's adventure and God was right—we were glad to be there, though I would never have chosen it myself.

Conversations about the trustworthiness of God and trusting God appear frequently and in many forms in spiritual direction sessions. It may be about others or ourselves. Trust questions arise out of human circumstances and contexts. They are not abstract considerations. "How can I trust God when I did everything in my marriage according to scriptural principles and now it has disintegrated?" or "Last week an eight-year-old boy was killed crossing the street. He loved God. I thought God rewarded people who were faithful." Tragic turnings of events often bring any and all trust issues we have with God to the surface. Let's listen in on a direction conversation.

Directee:	So tell me again why I'm supposed to trust God. I am angry and sad and cannot imagine why such stuff should be allowed. I wouldn't.
Director:	What's going on?
Directee:	Did you see the newspaper this morning? Front page.
Director:	No.
Directee:	A fifteen-year-old girl disappeared south of here. She'd gone out to bike on a back road and no one has seen her since. What is this country coming to? Neither kids nor adults can live ordinary lives without being concerned for their safety. I feel so bad for my kids. I had so much freedom in my childhood. Rode my bike all over town. Went to friends' houses without a thought in the world that someone might want to hurt me, kidnap me, or kill me. I am absolutely incensed.
Director:	I'd have to agree. This sounds worthy of your anger.
Directee:	You bet it is.
Director:	How do you think God feels about it?
Directee:	Good question. I wonder. If God is who I think God is, then God hates this stuff even more than I do. But if God hates this, why is it allowed?
Director:	What do you think about that? No, what's it like when you pray about this?
Directee:	I can't say I've done much of what I think of as praying yet. I've been hollering at God ever since I picked up the paper. I am disturbed about this young person who has disappeared, and it has made me even more anxious about my

sixteen-year-old son and where he goes and what he does. We've been working hard on allowing him the amount of independence and responsibility he seems ready for. How are we supposed to do this in such a crazy world? Now that's something I have already been praying about. A lot.

Director: What's that like?

Directee: I feel like I stand before God next to this fresh, developing young man and ask God to be Tom's guide and shield, to protect him, but even more than that, to help him learn what it means to be and become God's person in the world. I pray often about my part and ask for wisdom, patience, and a sense of humor for my wife and me.

Director: How does that seem now?

Directee: Not adequate.

Director: What do you mean?

Directee: I am beginning to wonder what influence the prayers of parents have on what happens with their kids. We have a fair number of friends whose kids are reaching way out of bounds of what their folks would like to see. As I sit here listening to myself, I get the idea that maybe God is nudging me toward something different in the way I pray for Tom.

Director: Oh.

Directee: I hadn't quite realized how much of the time I come to God talking endlessly, telling God what's going on in my world— my wife, the kids, my job—and praying about any and everything. Everything that interests me. I know God listens. But I'm beginning to question what God thinks about my prayer itself. Not just about how God will answer the prayers, but if this is the way God wants to be with me right now. I guess I'm feeling like I need to pray about my prayer more. I can't say I know what that means, maybe I can tell you more about it next time. I wonder if it could make a difference in how I pray about the fifteen-year-old who disappeared down south or about my son. I'm still riled. I can't see that talking about it further would be particularly helpful right now. I guess I'd like to try praying about it.

The holy one who is God invites us to trust the Spirit each moment of each day in all situations, relationships, and experiences. Spiritual direction can help us notice where we do and do not trust God. Describing ourselves and our sense of God honestly can affect our prayer and behavior and invite us toward greater dependency on God's love, mercy, and action on behalf of others and ourselves.

Spiritual direction encourages us to invite the Spirit to expand our trust. When we notice how we feel about our own or others' trustworthiness, spiritual direction brings us back to focus on our relationship with God.

At times we recognize what keeps us from trusting God more by identifying and praying about whatever hinders our trust in ourselves or others. The particular blocks we experience in human relationships have their counterpart in our relationship with God. Sometimes we focus directly on trust in God by praying and talking about it in direction meetings, and, on occasion, we are surprised by glimpses of ways our trust in God has developed and deepened.

We hope to trust in God with growing abandon, be less controlling and more willing to live in godly freedom. Participating in spiritual direction is one way to continue nourishing this development. In seeking direction we are looking for a relationship that will help us remember, listen to, and follow the trustworthy one who is God.

Trusting Ourselves

We also need to think about the quality and extent of trust we have in ourselves, because trust of God and of self are intertwined. In this context I do not mean trusting ourselves as opposed to trusting God, but rather trusting that the redeemed human self can perceive and follow God's desires and trusting our willingness and capacity to hear and respond to God. God invites us to rest, confident that when we remain in contact, God will let us know everything we need to know. Scripture contains many promises to that effect including Psalm 32:8, which says, "I will instruct you and teach you the way you should go; I will counsel you with my eye upon you" (NRSV).

It is a challenge to distinguish between when we are to trust our perception of what God intends and when we need to look again. Sometimes "we know that we know that we know this is God," with a kind of trust that feels like a gift. We trust our perceptions. At other times, we see that we are quite fixed in our attachment to particular interests and agendas. Then we are wise to doubt our ability to hear or see what God wants and do well to prayerfully question our motives and intentions.

At still other times we recognize that we are so confused that our best possibility lies in describing and offering ourselves and dilemmas to God and ask for mercy and grace. But when we are truly closed in on ourselves, it is unlikely we will recognize our condition and pray this way.

Then we simply have to rely on God to bring whatever is needed to our attention. No matter what our circumstances are, it is easy to become so involved in trying to decipher and control all that affects us that we forget about trusting in the loving providence of God, or about trusting "God in us" (Col. 1:25–27).

We may be too self-trusting or not trust ourselves enough. When we are too self-trusting we may think that our perceptions and interpretations are accurate simply because we seek God. Then our recognition of the limitations of our being only one human person can escape us. Too much trust in ourselves can cloud our willingness and ability to see how radically dependent on God and other people we truly are.

But on the other hand, most of us can also point to occasions in which we now see we did not trust ourselves enough. We knew what was appropriate at a particular time but did not act on what we knew. We may blame others or ourselves or circumstances, but no matter whom we blame, we wish we had possessed the courage to make other choices. We may not have thought much about the role of God's empowering presence in the midst of it all. It is easy to get tangled into thinking everything depends on us, forgetting about God in us, and not be secure enough about what we feel and think to trust ourselves and act.

We may not have thought much about the possibility that our trustworthiness was growing because of God's life in us. What are the effects of grace on human personality? Do people have the potential to be wholly God's, wholly good, or at least to be moving in that direction? What does it mean to be a new creature in Christ? Scripture says, "Delight yourself in the LORD and he will give you the desires of your heart" (Ps. 37:4). Might this suggest that our deepest desires will be changed by God as we cooperate with God's Spirit? When we allow and even invite our authentic desires to surface and bring them to prayer, to God, we see things in a new way and we see new things. The Holy Spirit often shows us the goodness of God reflected in our own personalities and helps us learn more about when and where to trust our deep sense of God, of life, and of what is called for.

One way to consider trusting ourselves, trusting God in us and God with us, is to learn from our own history by looking in a prayerfully detached way at ourselves during an earlier time in our life and inviting God to speak to us. We go back with a sense of prayerful openness and ask God to remind us of a time when things seemed clear and compare our present experiences of God, prayer, ideas, situations, and responses. We recall our experiences of God—how God seemed to us, how God was with us, what God taught us, and how things worked out. We are still the person we were then, but we have grown and changed. Sometimes when life seems unusually confusing, it is helpful to dwell imaginatively in a remembered, clearly graced moment or season of life and view the content and quality of our present relationship with God from that vantage point. Let's listen to a direction conversation.

Directee: How do I trust myself, let me count the ways. Not a long list. Sometimes I get sidetracked by my sense of having missed what God intended in a particular instance, and I forget the countless times I have heard God accurately and responded with action.

Director: What seems important about that now?

Directee: Oh, I think I am giving myself a bad time about financial choices. And I am sure that I am slow to understand.

Director: How is God a part of your thinking on this?

Directee: I can't say that I've invited God into this discussion yet, because I am not especially pleased with myself.

Director: Why does that give you pause about inviting God in?

Directee: I don't like always going to God with what I think I should be able to figure out on my own.

Director: Who else?

Directee: You've got a point there. Well, aside from the present dilemma, I guess I'm beginning to remember some things. A few years ago I knew that God wanted me to give money to certain people for a trip to Israel that they could not afford at the time. It seemed like the trip could have a significant long-term effect on their work. They were people in lay and ordained ministries that depended heavily on contributions. Their salaries are adequate but do not include resources for a trip like this. I felt somewhat uneasy, because I did not want them to feel awkward about it. I did not want it to change our friendship, and yet I knew it was God.

Director: What happened?

Directee: It worked out amazingly. No one was offended by the offer. It was possible to keep it private so it remained between them and me. The trip was all that I hoped and the graces from it are still overflowing to them, to others who were on the trip, to their ministries, and even to me.

Director: That sounds a lot like God.

Directee: Yes, it does to me too. I have no illusions about it being my idea, but I also know that I did hear and respond, and that God was happy, and I was happy. I guess that could give

| Director: | me some confidence about the present situation. This time it's about changing where I give support. I don't like to stop giving where I have been, but I am feeling drawn to give in other places. |

Director: Could you talk a little about the new places and what motivates you?

Directee: That's easy. In fact, it's hard to stop talking. I'm interested in an inner-city camp ministry for kids that needs money. They have a great program. I'd like to see some youngsters get a different view of human beings and at the same time be introduced to the possibility of a relationship with an unconditionally loving God. They need the connection and the hope.

Director: You're really excited about this.

Directee: Yeah. I think about it quite a bit, and I pray about it. I care about these kids. I think God cares more than I do. I am willing for whatever God tells me to do.

Director: That sounds like a good place to be.

Directee: Now that I listen to myself, I guess I'd have to agree with you. It seems more okay to trust myself to hear the Spirit—and to trust God—that when I pursue this and continue to pray, it is going to be okay. And I am not so worried about the other organizations as I was. If this is where God is leading me, then maybe God will take care of them too.

Although in some measure we will always be beginners, our beginnings can be at new places and at new chapters. We are developing sensitivity to issues of trusting God and ourselves through our spontaneous and considered responses. We are learning to trust more in God who is in us and who also walks alongside us.

Trusting Others

We carry our trust development one step further when we consider spiritual direction, showing our willingness to trust others. We are interested here in a specialized kind of trust. We desire to trust the Holy Spirit at work in and through another person and to accept that they are open to God and that God can use them on our behalf. Although a spiritual director may have many natural gifts, trusting in their competency or expertise is not our main objective. Instead, we seek to trust God in them, and in the Holy Spirit through them. The most helpful qualities they have to offer us are a heart surrendered to God and a willingness to listen to God with us.

Living alongside others who openly practice faith influences us. Scripture says that cooperation among believers is as necessary and significant as interconnectedness among parts of the human body (1 Cor. 12:12–14, 18, 26–27). Life is filled with examples of people working together, contributing their diverse giftedness, and trusting each other enough to accomplish something worthwhile. However, the trust required to let someone else glimpse our soul is of a different kind. Such trust is closer to who we are than to what we do. Spiritual direction depends on people with varieties of giftedness cooperating with the Holy Spirit and one another. Although our ultimate trust is in God alone, we learn and deepen our trust in God through interactive, interdependent relationships.

God speaks to us in ways that take our uniqueness into account. This creates the need to pray and consult with others who will help to discern God's heart and mind as we examine our experiences and ideas. Using other believers as a standard against which to measure ourselves is one way we already trust the Holy Spirit in others. That is why we are able to accept Scripture as the Word of God. We trust the Holy Spirit's activity with the writers of Scripture, so we trust Scripture. Our trust is evidenced by our ongoing reference to and use of Scripture as a guide and standard. We also trust the Spirit's life and effectiveness in more recent historical persons including contemporary believers whom we know and respect.

I am grateful for people who have influenced me from the time of my birth until today. Some I know only through their writings. Others I have personally encountered. If I were to make a list, it would be a lengthy one including family members, friends, counselors, teachers, professors, pastors, ancient and contemporary authors, and musicians and artists. I appreciate the people who have allowed me to participate in their lives from the inside out and the outside in. I have been influenced by people with whom I have laughed, cried, sung, talked, studied, argued, and prayed, friends who like to walk on a beach in every season in any kind of weather, friends who read and friends who don't, and friends who share my love of animals. Many of these people love God and appreciate similar things. Some of them love God and look at life through very different eyes. Some are not particularly drawn to God but are still gifts of God in my life.

We experiment with trusting God by trusting people we can see, hear, and touch. But all of our encounters with trust do not turn out as we would have liked or chosen. Most of us have had difficult experiences of misplaced trust. Some people have leaned heavily on others who taught them inaccurate or incomplete "Christian" ideas or practices or behaved toward them in ways that turned out to be unhelpful or seriously abusive, sometimes in the name of Jesus. These kinds of memories might give people pause when they consider spiritual direction. Of course, we have all been disappointed and disappointed others in areas of trust. We are part of the human family.

Sometimes, if we have been wounded, we hesitate to trust a particular person again or even a different person under a similar set of circumstances. Trusting another person with our story always carries some risk with it, and unless we believe God will use our openness for good and growth, it is senseless to reveal ourselves. However, in order to participate freely and derive benefit from spiritual direction, we need to be willing to explore trusting another person, God, and ourselves. Spiritual direction provides for such exploration in a grace-filled context.

Exploring Trust Possibilities

When two people come together for spiritual direction, they are not seeking to build interpersonal trust as much as to trust the Holy Spirit together. Therefore, the trust that develops through direction is both similar to and different from that in relationships based solely on human qualities. Expanding possibilities are present because developing trust with God is the shared meeting ground and goal rather than interpersonal relationships or exclusively human agendas. We see a small arena of life. When we open that arena to God and to trusting God, we are often amazed at where things lead. Life opens into experiences and situations we would never have expected.

When we look closely we see that we have trust preferences. Some of us trust God more easily than we trust either ourselves or others. We have seen so much of what we would describe as flawed, destructive, hurtful human interaction that it is difficult for us to trust anyone with a human face, including ourselves. This causes some of us to reach for God, but others have been so shaped by human failures that it is difficult to imagine a faithful, loving God. Some of us are independent and realize that we have come to rely on ourselves so completely that we may not want to depend on either God or others.

People respond to life's challenges in diverse ways. Clyde talks about his faith journey this way: "God and I are doing fine. It's like this holy someone is alongside me all the time, so I'm pretty easily attuned to God and me; we're a happy pair. But I do not have the same kind of trust of God in or through other people and am not quite sure why. Rationally, if God is willing to be my companion in this way, it does not make sense that I don't recognize how God communicates with others. I know I need help to break out of my closed system. I might discover some surprises."

Hal says, "I've come to trust in myself even though I realize I miss things. I've been disappointed so many times with other people that I am wary, and I just don't seem to engage sufficiently enough on my own to figure out what I believe about God."

Jan describes herself this way: "I listen to and abide by other peoples' ideas, feelings, and opinions more often and completely than I do to either my own or what I perceive to be God's."

It is helpful to identify whom we trust most easily and why we hesitate when trusting God, ourselves, or others. Some people discover that their trust issues are in the past. They notice that they are still reliving and trying to rework situations that did not turn out as they had hoped. Others are caught by wonderful memories of long ago. They remain engaged with the past. They have difficulty focusing on the present and remaining open to possible joys and challenges of this specific time in their life.

Terry says, "There's this unresolved friendship that still eats at me after several years. I am afraid to open the door even to God about it, but it crosses my mind fairly often." Sandra muses, "For me it is a business deal in which I am convinced I was taken advantage of by people from my church. I still have questions about how God was there." Charles remembers, "About ten years ago God and I had an incredible closeness. I was involved in a charismatic church and the worship was glorious. It seemed like there were no hindrances to being open to God and sensing the Spirit's presence. I miss that and think about it a lot. I ask what God might like to do with that and where God is now."

Some people trust more easily when thinking about the future—what might be or could be or will be. The past and the future are important; we are influenced by every moment. But only one particular moment at a time is available for our participation—this one. When our life energies are gathered around portions of the past or possibilities for the future, we cannot be fully attuned, awake, or aware to the given grace of God with us now.

Everyone has growing edges in all aspects of trust. In the journey of faith the Spirit's first invitations are to a God who draws and teaches us in ways we can understand. Eventually we are called to trust God, whom we perceive to be more than we can ever comprehend. It seems as if God beckons us, like Abraham (Genesis 12), to follow directions to destinations we cannot envision, except for the step we are to take now. When we entrust all that has passed and all that will be into God's care, we are more open to the heartbeat of each now—and to God.

God's Trust

We are so much more likely to think about our trust than to think about God's trust, that if this section had not been included, you might not have even noticed the omission. But one of the great gifts of spiritual direction is recognizing over and over how God trusts and entrusts us. God entrusts us with bearing God's presence, voice, values, and actions in the midst of a beleaguered world.

I began thinking about this several years ago when my mother came home after a Magnetic Resonance Imaging exam (MRI) and said, "I wonder who God decided to trust with the information necessary to help people in this way." Since then similar thoughts have crossed my mind when healing insights or other kinds of discoveries have taken place. My mother's musings came to me again when I noticed an article written by the man who invented the MRI in which he described his persistence and driving desire through many years of struggle to develop a noninvasive, diagnostic medical device.

This is a dramatic example, but I am convinced there are endless examples, great and small, of instances in which God entrusts people with information that will allow them to reflect God in the world. A woman spoke to me recently about coming out of a huge grocery store on a holiday eve. Every parking place was filled. Customers walked through the store with long lists and baskets piled high. There was a festive mood but also a sense of urgency as people tried to complete more tasks than could be accomplished. When this woman finished her shopping, she walked out to her car, loaded several bags of groceries into the back, and clamored in, ready to be off to the next task. But something stopped her. She sat quietly for a few prayerful moments and then noticed a shopping cart in the empty space next to her. A woman's overstuffed purse with lists hanging out the top sat in the top basket of the cart. The owner was not in sight. "Thank you, God, for slowing me down enough to notice and giving me the opportunity to care for someone's valuables." She went into the store with the purse, handed it to a clerk behind the information counter, and left with joy that God had trusted her with this task. She said it reawakened her awareness of God's trust of her. Small turns bring divine gifts.

God invites human cooperation in initiating and completing all that God desires. Through the incarnation (Christ's life, death, and resurrection), we are empowered to live like Christ. A part of God's incarnational availability is entrusted to us—to people who listen, desire to be open to God's voice, and are willing to act for God's sake in the world. God entrusts us with particular relationships, ideas, tasks, and hopes through all the stages of bringing them to life. It seems as though God entrusts all people with some things that only they can recognize and bring to reality. God invites us to cocreate through dependency on God and a willingness to do our part.

Trusting the Process of Spiritual Direction

Authentic spiritual direction requires us to trust God, another person, and ourselves enough to speak honestly about our Divine/human love relationship. It also provides opportunities to recognize the ways God trusts and entrusts us.

We may be quite convinced of our need and desire to trust God, others, and ourselves but have some reservations about our trust in the process of spiritual direction. Voicing our questions, taking them into our prayer, and discussing them with others are ways of asking God to bring whatever is needed to our attention. As we seek, the Holy Spirit will guide us as we think about whether God is inviting us to take part in spiritual direction as a directee, director, or both.

Do not expect trust to appear suddenly and in a state of completion. Trust grows gradually as we venture forth, little by little, with God and each other. As our trust grows, so will our willingness and courage to speak and listen with greater freedom. Seeing things more clearly is often one of the fruits of our growing trust.

The underlying question for anyone thinking about trust and spiritual direction is this: "Is the Spirit asking me to depend on God's love more deeply by trusting another person enough to talk with that person about my relationship with God?" In chapter 6, "Selecting a Spiritual Director," I will describe appropriate spiritual directors, people you might think about trusting in this way.

Reflections

As you reflect on and pray about what draws you to spiritual direction, you may see your trust history more clearly. The Holy Spirit can use anything that surfaces to enhance growth and help you recognize present possibilities with God. If painful memories arise, it may be an indication that God is inviting you to resolution or healing.

Approach the following questions with a gentle, prayerful openness.

1. Draw a lifeline, divide it into five- or ten-year segments, and consider how you have trusted others, God, and yourself. Whom have you trusted and how has that worked out? Place the initials of particular people along the line. What do you notice?

2. What in your history raises questions about whether you should trust yourself? others? God?
3. What encourages you to trust yourself? others? God?
4. What do you think and feel about your own trustworthiness?
5. Do you see yourself as a predominantly trusting or untrusting person? How might that influence your participation in spiritual direction?
6. How and when has God trusted you?
   I trust God most fully when . . .
   If I trusted God more I would . . .

5 | Preparing for Spiritual Direction

The first service that one owes to others in the fellowship consists in listening to them. Just as love to God begins with listening to His Word, so the beginning of love for the brethren is learning to listen to them. It is God's love for us that He not only gives us His Word but also lends us His ear. So it is His work that we do for our brother and sister when we learn to listen to them.

Dietrich Bonhoeffer[1]

Spiritual direction is: "A covenant friendship between Christians in which one assists the other in the discernment of God's presence and the contemplative living out of God's call." The term *covenant friendship* implies the importance of relationship as core of the Christian life. We all need help from others in order to listen to and respond to God. Unaided, we often misunderstand and misinterpret our deepest experiences. Caught up in the whirl of events, we forget God or push the spiritual pilgrimage into the recesses of our lives. That fact emphasizes the importance of understanding spiritual direction as a relationship, a "covenant friendship" between two Christians.

Howard Rice[2]

My soul, wait silently for God alone, for my expectation is from Him.

Psalm 62:5 NKJV

Spiritual direction takes place within the context of ordinary life, and many considerations influence our participation, including our expectations, awareness, willingness, self-concept, and perceptions about sexuality. Reflecting on these influences before we begin spiritual direction can prepare us to be more intentional about our practice.

Expectations

Carl expects to receive significant insights and assistance from spiritual direction because friends have told him about some of their experiences. Susan is somewhat ambivalent about entering direction but feels as though she should because she has been asking herself a lot of questions and pondering why God seems to be with her sometimes

80

and not other times. She would prefer to work it out alone, but she also wonders if meeting with a director could help.

When I first considered spiritual direction, I questioned whether a director would see into my heart as if I were transparent, and I did not like the prospect. I did not know much about spiritual direction and wondered if I would control what we discussed or if a director would structure our time together. I was uneasy about the possibility of someone seeing aspects of myself that I was not ready to disclose or had not recognized, and yet I knew I wanted other eyes to help me pay attention to whatever God wanted to develop in and through me. I asked myself who was really going to be in charge: God, the director, or me?

Expectations are how we think something will be. They are not necessarily a reality, but we often treat them as if they are. They consist of ideas and imaginings based on our own history. Expectations include what we carry in conscious and unconscious memory and can influence our present anticipations and behaviors. We combine these memories with present information and consider how the future will unfold. Our expectations help us prepare to respond to anticipated and unanticipated future circumstances.

We have and act on conscious and unconscious expectations, often without giving the expectations themselves much thought. Where do our expectations come from: Scripture? other people? ourselves? God? cultures and subcultures? the media? other spiritual sources? Do these expectations come from a single source or a variety of sources? We can learn many things about ourselves and God's interactions with us if we stop to consider the source, content, and tone of our expectations and their influence on us. Because the focus of spiritual direction is our relationship with God, it is helpful to consider expectations that impinge on that relationship.

We come with a set of expectations every time we worship, pray, study Scripture, or serve God. We may anticipate that God will teach and bless us or perhaps think it is unlikely that we will sense God's presence. We may think that our absence of feeling will confirm our suspicions that we are not doing things right or the right things in our relationship with God. We may expect to be confronted with uncomfortable information about the inadequacy of our understanding, love for God and others, or service in God's name. Sometimes we are apathetic or bored, expecting no sense of being touched by the holy, because our relationship with God seems formal or dead, with little or no real communication. At other times, whether we anticipate nurturing, correction, or nothing in particular, we believe we will be open, willing, and able to hear God. In some circumstances we expect that we will withdraw out of fear, awe, or our own obtuseness from anything that is unmistakably from God. We are often surprised.

We may wait for long periods of time to say something to God or do what we believe the Spirit invites because we fear what will result from our actions or God's response. At times we are so conditioned by what is past that we have difficulty recognizing the open potential of the future.

Scripture-based expectations are centrally important. However, we need to recognize that these expectations are shaped as much by how we interpret Scripture as by what Scripture actually says and intends. Due to the complexity of both Scripture and ourselves, we should carefully interpret and apply Scripture. We need to continually examine, pray about, and seek growth in the way we read, hear, and act on God's Word. Chapter 11, "Scripture," includes extended discussion of these subjects.

Expectations about spiritual direction are present amid our other expectations, and anyone we go to for spiritual direction will also have expectations. It is good for directors and directees to consider how their individual and shared expectations about God, human nature, Scripture, and spiritual direction could enhance or hinder effective direction. No matter how we pay attention to expectations, it is essential that we do so prayerfully, including God in our exploration.

Anytime we consider doing something new, we naturally have some fears. Allowing fearful expectations to surface is helpful because then we are more likely to bring our fears into prayer and ask for help. This kind of preparation increases the likelihood that when we do choose spiritual direction we will feel more settled and trustful about our involvement. Some people who are considering spiritual direction may express fearful expectations such as the following.

Directees may:

fear appearing inadequate. They may have suspicions or convictions that when they begin to talk about their spiritual life they will feel deficient and embarrassed by their own shallowness.

consider if a spiritual director will judge or criticize them because they are already evaluating themselves negatively.

think they might feel awkward, appear self-centered, or look as though they are taking themselves too seriously.

fear losing their independence or that a director will tell them what to do in their relationship with God. Deeper still, they may fear losing some personal control over their lives. Anything that makes us feel we are giving up control can be unnerving even when we remind ourselves that we are depending more on God rather than another person.

think they could be introduced to unfamiliar ideas.

suddenly discover they feel shy.

wonder if they will reveal things about themselves they have never discussed with anyone or if they will reveal more than has been their practice. They may fear feeling uncomfortably exposed if they speak freely to someone about their prayer and relationship with God.

feel more accustomed to sharing either negative or positive information about themselves and fear they will have to share some of each in a spiritual direction setting.

fear they might discuss concerns they have been avoiding and speculate about where that could lead.

What other fearful expectations come to mind?

Many of our fearful expectations about spiritual direction are rooted in our attachment to our ideas about ourselves, our self-concept. When we acknowledge our attitudes, however, speaking about them can be freeing. Such recognition often marks the beginning of new inroads of grace and healing.

Expectations usually abound on both sides of any undertaking, and if we are feeling drawn by the Spirit to consider spiritual direction, we may have some hopeful expectations as well. They, like the fearful ones, will include a range of realistic and unrealistic anticipations. When people consider spiritual direction they often hope they will:

discover answers to some of their questions of God and about God.

develop a relationship with someone who is serious about their desires, intentions, and actions in relationship to God.

be with someone who is "like them."

become more spiritual, holy, pure, and godly.

be challenged and encouraged in prayer and other spiritual disciplines.

receive healing.

feel blessed.

have someone else share the responsibility for their life with God.

What other hopeful expectations come to mind?

These lists include expectations that may open us to God or close us into ourselves or our agendas. It is difficult to categorize expectations permanently in either direction. Some may be harmless or helpful at one time and detrimental at another.

Expectations about spiritual direction flourish before and during the relationship. We think we know what we would like it to be, and we recognize some of our fears and hopes, but we do not know what will actually take place. Seeking spiritual direction implies a willingness to acknowledge that we do not know everything and probably do not even know everything it could be helpful for us to know. If we want to come to the Holy Spirit for direction, neither the director nor the directee can rely on a planned agenda or guess at their responses. The Spirit of God invites us to come in trust, believing that the Spirit will draw us into growing intimacy with God and enable us to respond to life out of this growing relationship.

In contrast to most areas of our lives, participating in spiritual direction calls us to a certain freedom from expectations—freedom to be open to whatever appears without having to speculate about it ahead of time. This open conversation is a way of trusting God with the past, the present, and the future and believing that the Holy Spirit will reveal whatever is needed. Rather than saying we have no expectations, however, perhaps it is more accurate to say that we shift from having expectations of each other or ourselves to hoping more in God. Our questions revolve more and more around being responsive to whatever the Spirit might bring to our attention rather than speculating about our own speaking, listening, or responses.

Awareness

Awareness is one of many things that influences our expectations. We are bombarded with stimuli every day. Some capture our focused attention and others remain in the background. We have said that people who come to spiritual direction want to be more aware of who God is and what the Holy Spirit is saying to them in the present. They want to pay full attention to the present rather than dwelling on their past history or what God is doing in and with others. God is always offering love, forgiveness, renewal, and guidance, but our awareness of God's presence and actions fluctuates. At times we are gratefully attuned to God's loving involvement with us. At other times we feel distant from God, even though we may try to convince ourselves that this is not the case.

It is usually not adequate for us simply to decide to listen to God more intentionally. By itself, such a resolution does not guarantee our ability to pay sufficient attention in an ongoing, consistent way. God's desires for us and our longings for God meet many challenges. Some of them are rooted in deep ambivalence. Our human hearts contain a mixture of ought to, want to, and hesitancy. We have many ideas about what is right for us. We want to follow God and cooperate with the Spirit, but at the same time a part of us would prefer having our own way and resists surrendering ourselves and our plans to God. Sometimes we struggle with God and sometimes we struggle with ourselves. When we choose spiritual direction, we are asking God to help us be attentive and open to the Holy Spirit's words and ways and to enlarge our desire and capacity to hear and follow. Let's listen in on a direction conversation that begins with awareness.

Joan looked at her journal in the morning to consider what she wanted to talk about in the afternoon's spiritual direction appointment. She was not sure where she would begin, but she had several possibilities in mind, including her gratitude about projects she had completed. She stopped at the mailbox at the end of the driveway and opened a letter. Suddenly, the likely topics for the afternoon's session changed.

The previous day, a friend had invited Joan to be in charge of a project. Joan knew she was not gifted in administration, but other parts of the project interested her, and she wanted to please her friend. They had settled on April 10.

God had been extending Joan's boundaries in so many ways that this opportunity seemed quite logical. Then today a letter arrived inviting her to attend a celebration in another city on the same day. Joan had initiated the celebration, not knowing the date it would take place.

Now, on the way to her appointment, she noticed she was feeling pulled in different directions, that she had strong feelings and opinions, and that she was not clear about what God was inviting. All the way to the direction session she thought about her options. After a few minutes of quiet prayer with her director, Joan started the session by describing her situation.

Director: What happened? What did you experience? What would you like to do?

This seemed routine. These were the normal questions any friend who knew her and her values might have asked. They looked at the questions from many angles, but nothing became clear. Finally, they decided to let this unresolved dilemma rest a while. But something was different. Now, Joan's story and all she had noticed and was feeling about the situation had become a part of the director's prayer as well as her own.

They talked about the completed projects. Joan spoke about how effortless one project had been. It felt like doing nothing because it flowed out of her gifts. She talked about her anxiety surrounding another.

Director: What does this say to you?

Directee: I hadn't been paying very close attention to myself and all
at once I saw that I felt defensive. I had thought I was past
that, and it caught me off guard. I felt like I was more than
a little off balance. [The director waits without speaking.]
It was right after this that my friend invited me to be part
of her project, and I made a commitment to her. By this
morning I was already feeling like I needed to do this
because of how important it seemed to her. I wasn't sure
about my qualifications for the project and something
wasn't settling. Then I began to feel like I had accepted more
than I realized without consulting myself or God as intentionally as I might have.

Director: That's interesting. I have to be careful not to just give you
my opinion about this. You'll have to take it into your own
prayer to explore. I know when I'm feeling overly responsible that's a signal for me to slow down, look around a little, and see what's going on.

In the light of this discussion, Joan noticed that she had scheduled
too much for the days ahead. This new venture would require time and
care and could not be sandwiched into an already full schedule. She was
embarrassed by her haste to say yes and the need now to admit she was
not suited for the task. She knew she had to say no quickly so that her
friend would have ample time to make other plans.

What part did spiritual direction play in this process? It provided
someone to listen to her story with a discerning ear, someone to ask her
questions, and someone who would pray as she listened.

Joan also gained insights for the future.

Director: Were there any aspects of this experience that caused you
to think about general patterns in the way you approach
things?

Directee: Oh yes. It's pretty easy to see that I made the commitment
to my friend at a time when I was out of balance—more out
of balance than I knew. I had recognized that the setting
was emotionally charged for me but had not taken into
account how it might be affecting me. Not a good time to
take on anything new. I'd like to remember that for the
future. Perhaps this was uncomfortable enough to help me
get the message. I surely hope so. [The director waits without saying anything.] One of the good things about this was

that it was so unsettling that I had to address it. The letter
brought it front and center in a way that might not have
happened so early in the proposed project with my friend.
I am thankful to God for that. Maybe it wasn't accidental
that everything came together so that it got my attention
on my way here. Once again, I feel protected by God and
that feels good.

No matter what we notice, it is comforting to know that we are not
ultimately in charge and that the Spirit can break through our blindness. Sometimes we see what is needed when we are alone; sometimes
a spiritual direction conversation reveals other aspects. Sometimes
insights come from the director and at other times the director becomes
only a prayerful presence who enables us to speak the words we needed
to hear. This directee was struggling with whether God was inviting her
to do something outside of her usual boundaries. Eventually the Spirit
confirmed her uneasiness. The experience clarified some qualities about
her responsiveness and the use of her energies. Once the matter was
decided, Joan discovered she was no longer weighing options and moved
peacefully into previously planned activities.

Willingness

Willingness is the opposite of willfulness, being full of our own will
and ways and the satisfaction in being self-made or self-controlled persons. Willingness to be aware and willingness in general are prerequi-
sites for spiritual direction. Willingness is a chosen position of vulnerability that recognizes we are ordinary human beings in need of God's
love, companionship, and guidance. It includes our acknowledgment
that we are not all we would like to be or all that God hopes for us and
points toward our desire to hear and follow the Spirit's invitations even
when it means giving up our ways in favor of what we perceive as God's
ways.[3]
When we are even a little bit honest, we recognize that our measure
of willingness varies depending on what is being asked of us and by
whom. Some of God's opportunities seem to offer pleasurable outcomes.
Surrender to these requests is easy. But there are times when the Spirit
invites or simply takes us into unfamiliar territory either inwardly or
outwardly. Then we may feel decidedly uneasy about following. God's
love and intentions are larger and farther reaching than we realized.
They extend beyond the kind of people we are used to and the kinds of
problems, possibilities, and joys that are familiar to us.

Evelyn Underhill writes about some unexpected outcomes of willingness toward God.

> We see that plainly in the Saints; in the quiet steadiness of spirit with which they meet the vicissitudes and sufferings of their lives. They know that these small and changing lives, about which we are often so troubled, are part of a great mystery; the life that is related to God and known by God. They know, that is, that they, and all the other souls they love so much, have their abiding place in Eternity; and there the meaning of everything which they do and bear is understood. So all their action comes from this center; and whether it is small or great, heroic or very homely, does not matter to them much. It is a tranquil expression of obedience and devotedness. As Ornan the Jebusite turned his threshing floor into an altar, they know how to take up and turn to the purposes of the Spirit the whole of life as it comes from God's Hand. St. Bernard and St. Francis discard all outward possessions, all the grace and beauty of life, and accept poverty and hardship; and through their renunciation a greater wealth and a more exquisite beauty is given the world. St. Catherine of Genoa leaves her ecstasy to get the hospital accounts exactly right; Elizabeth Fry goes to Newgate, Mary Slessor to the jungle, and Elizabeth Leseur accepts a restricted home life; all in the same royal service.[4]

Scripture and our own lives are filled with examples of the Spirit's invitations to be and to do more than one would have thought possible. Moses, David, Abraham and Sarah, Esther, Mary, Paul, John, Peter, and countless others were called by God to walk unfamiliar ground. They were often directed along a different life route than they expected or called to go where they would never have chosen. Their lives unfolded in ways they could not have foreseen when they first gave their willing hearts to God. In some measure everyone is called by God to aspects of life they could not have anticipated.

Most of all, Jesus embodied radical willingness when he became the loving incarnation, the God/human. The history and eternity of humanity would be different if Jesus had not embodied the desires of God. Choosing to surrender natural human preferences in favor of God's desires characterized Christ's life and culminated in his death and resurrection. The call to willing surrender and self-offering is part of God's work within the Trinity as well as in human beings (John 8:29; Heb. 10:5–7).

As we mature in faith, our willingness is tested, expanded, and refined. We become more conscious of our limitations and turn to God. The necessity of God's grace becomes clearer as we become more attuned and accurate in our recognition of our dependence on God and less sure of anything that causes us to describe ourselves self-righteously. At times, when confronted by the less-than-ideal behavior of others, we may recognize that we are capable of similar actions and give thanks to God for helping us avoid unwelcome pitfalls. Scripture instructs us to be holy as God is holy, yet we increasingly realize the impossibility of holy behavior unless it is brought about by the Spirit's empowerment and our willing responsiveness and cooperation. Many people use spiritual direction as a window through which to notice and attend to their own expectations and expressions of willingness and willfulness.

Self-Concept

We all have ideas about ourselves—about who we are, why we are as we are, and what God might have created us to be and do. These and other perceptions about ourselves are together called our self-concept. Self-concept is not permanently fixed but rather dynamic, fluid, and changing. It is easily influenced by physical patterns of sleep and nutrition and our level of health and wellness. When faced with a similar set of circumstances, we can respond in different ways based on whether we are exhausted or rested, hungry or well fed, sick or healthy. The ways we get along with people who are important to us and our present life experiences also strongly influence our perceptions and opinions of ourselves.

At times we may not realize we are being dominated by what we think of ourselves and that we are acting in response to our own negative and positive evaluations of our thoughts, feelings, and behaviors. We may become startled or embarrassed when our attachment to our idea of who we think we are is challenged. Someone or something exposes where we do not yet express the fruits of the Spirit, and we see our self-centeredness and self-preoccupations. We notice that we are more self-centered than Christlike. Our sense of deficiency can make us feel uncomfortable or defensive or sometimes just newly awakened to our need for divine help. Other times we are surprised by our own grace-filled responses that surface in unforeseen ways. They encourage us to trust in God's continuing influence.

The problem of self-concept is not so much that we think of ourselves; it is more that we think of ourselves so much. We think of ourselves more often than we think of others or God and frequently give our interests priority.

Many spiritual direction conversations revolve around self-perceptions.

Directee: I've been doing some work that has evolved in a very different way from my usual pattern, and I'd like to talk about it in this spiritual direction session. I have some ideas about why this might be and would like to know how it seems to you.

Director: Okay.

Directee: I was invited to speak at a church service, in fact, three of
             them at a large church. That's not something I'd normally
             say yes to. I am not a preacher. I have been okay with teach-
             ing groups of about twenty. But it seemed as though God
             was inviting me to do this new thing. As the date drew
             nearer, I decided to visit the church a couple of times to see
             what it was like. I wondered how I would be received when
             I saw that my style of presentation was dramatically dif-
             ferent from what they were used to. But it still seemed like
             God was asking me to do this.

             About a month ahead of time a rough draft of the talk
             came to me. That's early for me. After I went on a retreat
             the talk changed some. Writing it was really easy. Ideas
             and refinements came to me and I'd add them from time
             to time. It was a long, slow preparation, and every detail
             seemed important. The talk was ready a couple of weeks
             ahead of time. Then a friend prayed with me about it. We
             sensed God was doing something, but neither one of us
             knew what.

             I was not nervous before, during, or after the talks . . .
             maybe a little before the third one. But that wasn't about
             the talk itself. I was just noticing my physical energy level
             and realizing I was tired. The whole point of my recount-
             ing this is that the entire process seemed almost effortless
             from beginning to end. And that really felt different.

Director: What do you make of it?

Directee: I'm a little hesitant to say, because I don't want to be imag-
             ining things. But it felt to me like this was something God
             wanted and that all I was asked to do was listen and fol-
             low and God would do the real work. I had hoped to go to
             a special event in the afternoon after the talks, but I had a
             strong impression that God wanted me to stay home so
             that something could be completed, almost like there were
             things still carrying over from the morning. I cannot say
             that I heard anything—no voices or anything like that—
             but I did have strong impressions. It would have felt as if
             I were going my way rather than God's if I had not
             remained at home in solitude. When I was out for a walk,
             the words popped into my head, "My yoke is easy and my
             burden is light."

Director: What do you think about all this now? How is it in your
             prayer?

Directee:	This is where I start to feel a little uncomfortable. If I'm honest I'd have to say I believe God has more for me to do in that setting, or at least more work in the same genre—work in which God opens a way and my part is to listen and follow. It felt like some kind of call or endorsement that is still mostly hidden.
Director:	What part isn't hidden?
Directee:	It's clear that the whole thing was God's idea, and I have a sense that I did what I was asked to do. But beyond that, I really don't know, except that I think God used the talks in ways not known to me.
Director:	Is there anything you sense that God is saying to you now?
Directee:	Just wait.
Director:	How does that seem? Waiting?
Directee:	Surprisingly peaceful. I say surprising because I am usually so impatient about finding out what's coming next. But this isn't that way. I'm quite content to let things unfold whenever and however they do.

Persons who choose to be directees are willing to become less invested in their own way, hoping to hold their preconceptions about themselves and everything else less tightly and gradually to be less interested in themselves or their self-concept and more interested in God and God's ideas.

Directees seek to acknowledge their changing self-concepts and open themselves to God's interventions. In other words, the goal of spiritual direction is not to assist directees in strengthening the ego but in more fully surrendering the ego to God. Directees do not privately control and define the growing, changing self and self-concept, nor do they surrender them to the director. Instead, they give them fully and freely to God.

Sexuality

Contemporary use of language is not always clear, and dictionary definitions of the words *sexuality* and *gender* have not caught up to the ways they are presently used. In some writings, *sexuality* and *gender* are used interchangeably to denote all aspects of biology and what it means to be a man or a woman.

In this discussion, however, sexuality encompasses our way of being in the world embodied as male or female persons. The term *sexuality* refers to the concrete way we live in and experience the world as body-selves.[5] The term *sex* is connected to biology-related considerations including libido and procreation. The term *gender* refers to one's sex and how we have been socialized within our particular culture, what we have learned is accepted behavior for men and women. Our ideas about what is feminine or masculine are defined by culture.

All people including directors and directees are aware of sexuality as an ongoing part of who they are (embodiment) and have definite ideas about what it means to be a man or a woman (gender). In fact, we cannot avoid perceiving and interpreting everything through our male or female lenses. Every human relationship has sexual aspects simply because we are sexual beings (sexuality). Spiritual direction is no exception.

Spiritual direction is an intimate relationship. We speak about what is most important to us. Sharing essentially personal feelings and thoughts is similar to sharing our bodies and at times can seem even more intimate than physical communion (sex). We are whole persons with a body, mind, emotions, and human spirit. It is not possible or healthy to separate or compartmentalize parts of ourselves; every aspect of being human affects every other aspect.

We often feel received, understood, and loved by God in new ways through a spiritual director and are aware of a director's acceptance and appreciation of us. Open lovingness with God promotes sensitivity to open lovingness on the human plane. The opposite is also frequently true; when we are touched deeply by human love, we become more receptive to Divine love. Authentic love of any sort overflows. Directees often discover that their deepening love for God, creation, themselves, and others influences everything including their appreciation of sexuality, sexual behaviors, and gender considerations.

Because we are human, love stirs our bodies as well as our emotions. Some directors and directees are sensitively attuned to their own sexuality and sexual responsiveness. They are comfortable with their sexuality, affirm the goodness of being a man or a woman, welcome their sexual responsiveness, and are committed to responsible, loving expressions of their sexuality.

Others may be overly hesitant regarding their sexuality because of messages they heard as they were growing up. They may have a history of sexual trauma or abuse. Sexuality may appear dangerous, and denying their sexuality may seem a reasonable way to protect themselves. Exploring ideas about sex and sexuality may be a fearful prospect or an attractive temptation that unnerves them. When such people begin to realize how radically God loves them, however, at some point they are also likely to ponder that God is the one who created them as male or female. Sexuality is God's idea. They may begin paying attention to the particular ways they express their masculinity or femininity and make that a part of their prayer. Day-to-day living is also influenced. Many directees say they are experiencing an increasing enjoyment and freedom as a woman or man loved by God and in their ability to love others.

Topics involving sexuality come up in spiritual direction sessions. At times one or both individuals will notice deepening awareness of their interests related to sex, sexuality, or gender. Sometimes their heightened sensitivity is related to learning how being a man or a woman colors their relationship with God. They may see ways that their gender influences prayer, language, and their response to God. Sometimes they are learning about masculine and feminine qualities within themselves and how God might be inviting them to recognize and express these qualities. They focus more intentionally on what it means to be a man or woman who is loved and called by God. When the Spirit invites them to pay closer attention to gender-related perceptions, they may also be drawn to explore the fatherhood of God, how God is like a mother, and how God is beyond gender considerations.

Ideas about gender may not seem as threatening as reflecting on sexual behaviors or feelings that arise when directees become more aware of their sexual responsiveness. When they become aware of their sexual stirrings, they may encounter questions about appropriate expressions and behaviors. Some people notice that at times they become sexually aroused when they participate in prayer and meditation. Spiritual direction offers them a place to consider this, pray about it, and process what it might mean. These and other sexual matters are legitimate questions, but when people are unduly fearful, they may be drawn to pay more or less attention than is warranted at a particular time. Most people tend to judge sex-oriented thoughts and attractions as negative or positive as soon as they appear, depending on the context. They may not have considered the possibility of addressing sexual interests by openly acknowledging them and offering them to God in prayer. It is fairly common to either suppress sex-related stirrings by pushing them away as too dangerous or to move toward acting on them. Paying direct attention to them with God can open us to the protection and guidance of the Spirit, cause us to ask for grace and wisdom, and deepen our trust in God.

Our interest here is the same as with every other subject that surfaces in spiritual direction: "What is the Holy Spirit inviting us to hear, notice, do?" Sometimes the Spirit of God brings up particular subjects because our fears prevent us from living wholeheartedly. Or God may desire to show us that when we listen to and follow the Holy Spirit, God will protect and help us in areas that are confusing or have caused difficulty in the past.

Expectations, awareness, willingness, self-concept, and perceptions about sexuality influence how we enter into spiritual direction and with whom. These aspects provide fruitful avenues to explore and open to

God in prayer whether or not we sense God inviting us to a spiritual direction companionship.

Reflections

1. What do you expect about and from God?
2. What helps you notice your expectations?
3. Under what circumstances do you seem blind to your own expectations?
4. What do you usually do with expectations you notice?
5. What are the sources of your expectations about spiritual direction?
6. What helps your awareness and what hinders it?
7. What have you been surprised about not noticing related to yourself? others? God?
8. What do you seem to notice easily about yourself? others? God?
9. How do willingness and willfulness show up in your personality? in relationship to God? in relationship with other people? in relationship to yourself?
10. Make a list of words that describe how you thought of yourself at the following ages as far as they apply to you. It can be fun to go beyond your present age and consider what you hope your self-concept might be in future years.

    5
    10
    15
    20s
    30s
    40s
    50s
    60s
    70s
    80s
    90s
    100

11. How is your sexuality a gift?
12. What do you notice about your comfort level related to your own and others' sexuality?
13. What kinds of questions about sexuality might become part of your prayer and topics for discussion in spiritual direction?

Selecting a Spiritual Director | 6

The church itself is a spiritual director. It tries to connect your story with God's story. Just to be a true part of this community means you are being directed, you are being guided, you are being asked to make connections.

The Bible is a spiritual director. People must read Scripture as a word for themselves personally, and ask where God speaks to them.

Finally, individual Christians are also spiritual directors. A spiritual director is a Christian man or woman who practices the disciplines of the church and of the Bible and to whom you are willing to be accountable for your life in God.

Henri Nouwen[1]

Likewise every good tree bears good fruit, but a bad tree bears bad fruit. A good tree cannot bear bad fruit, and a bad tree cannot bear good fruit. . . . Thus, by their fruit you will recognize them.

Matthew 7:17–18, 20

How does someone select a spiritual director? In many ways the process is similar to the ways we choose a counselor, a mentor, or a friend. Anytime we seek a meaningful relationship, we need to be intentional. When we search for a spiritual director, we also have the opportunity to hold our own ideas gently and to recognize God's. The Holy Spirit is the one who brings people together for spiritual direction. Our task is to discern when we should take part in direction and with whom. Prayer is the primary pathway for our search.

Sometimes God answers our prayer simply and directly and there is little exploration, planning, or activity on our part. At other times God guides us through a process that is an essential preparatory prelude to spiritual direction during which many of our questions and desires are clarified. However the process takes place, our fundamental questions are, "What is the Spirit saying to me about spiritual direction, and what is the next step I should take?"

Everyone has gifts and limitations. We need to pray and think about which qualities in a spiritual director seem important to us and consider theological background, understanding, and interpretations. We need to discover what we think about various concepts by asking questions such as, Who is God and what is God like? How do people experience God? What does it mean when Scripture says people are created in the image of God? What are the effects of sin? What is the role of Scripture? What is prayer? What provides opportunity for deepening in relationship with God?

We also need to pray about and reflect on what we hope for in spiritual direction and how our director's prayer and faith may influence us. What is the director's background and ours? What degree of sameness would make us feel at home? What amount of difference would benefit and challenge us? Should we choose a layperson or a pastor? A man or a woman? Someone of the same or a different denomination? From our own or another church?

Many people do not engage in such extensive questioning. The timing is right for them, and spiritual direction is the next natural step. When people have a seemingly endless number of questions, it may indicate that they are overly anxious or pushing themselves into something they are not ready for. At other times, asking questions is important and helpful and is characteristic of the initial phases of learning about an unfamiliar area.

Tom thinks he would like to talk to someone who is a member of his church because he knows their theological language and interpretations are similar. Jim prefers to speak to someone outside of his church. He feels he can better trust someone who would not be influenced by knowing the circumstances and other people in his environment.

There are advantages and disadvantages connected with anyone we might choose as a spiritual director. The rest of the chapter explores specific things to consider when making this choice.

Similarities and Differences

If we choose a spiritual director who is very much like us, we may feel received, accepted, and understood almost immediately. Such a choice may make spiritual direction itself more comfortable. But, paradoxically, when a director is too much like us, we may feel too transparent. Sometimes such a person seems to know intuitively what we think even before we say much. If we are very similar, we may encounter many possibilities for meaningful discussion. Yet such a situation also makes it easy for us to become diverted from listening to God. The director may be inclined to give his or her best advice rather than depending on God. We may be less likely to recognize shared blind spots that are influenced by our similarity.

Conversely, if we are too different from each other, this can affect our capacity to hear and interpret each other accurately. What seems evident to one of us may not be at all clear to the other. Language is subtle, and the same words may carry different connotations, implications, and expectations for one person than they do for another.

But it is not only theological language that is involved. Our use of language in general and our range of vocabulary, whether we are more or less naturally verbal, influence the words we use and how we interpret what we hear from others. I am not speaking here about spiritual direction terminology but about our general fluency. It can be intimidating for directors or directees to talk with others whose command of language is significantly beyond their own. This may distract them from listening for God.

We do not want to place ourselves in a direction relationship in which we feel defensive or have to grasp to understand what the other person means. We desire a relationship with someone we respect and appreciate and in which we can rest in the assurance that the other person affirms our relationship with God and the particularities of our faith and experiences.

Any two people will naturally be somewhat different from each other, and the distinctive characteristics represented by a particular direction pair or group will influence what is observed and discussed. The main thing is to identify differences that would make it difficult for us to tell the truth to someone and believe that the person is also open to the guidance of the Holy Spirit. We pray that we will recognize a relationship that embodies the right kinds and amounts of similarities and differences.

We may identify many qualities that draw us to a particular person for spiritual direction, or we may recognize that we know very little about a person but still feel invited by God to speak to that person. Whether we think we know why a certain person is appropriate for us or not, God uses many surprises to deepen and encourage our life of prayer, faith, and service.

Sally is thinking about asking Sarah, who leads the Tuesday women's Bible study, to serve as her director. Sally appreciates Sarah's approach to Scripture, and she has learned that Sarah has experience with Scripture study and is interested in praying with Scripture. Sally is drawn to these practices, to Sarah's gentle down-to-earth expression of her faith, and to her sense of God's love for everyone.

John is praying about asking someone he perceives as quite different from himself to serve as his director. John calls himself radically extroverted and is looking for balance. He is drawn to a person who has been developing a life of quiet prayer for many years because he wants to awaken this side of himself. He wonders if God is inviting him to this now. John says a few years ago he was not even the slightest bit interested in these things but now wants to explore practices of quiet meditation and reflection.

The health of direction friendships depends on the freedom to express whatever God is inviting. The possibilities for authentic encounter and growth can be hindered if either person feels overly inhibited. This does not include the normal reticence we feel when describing personal failures, sinfulness, and incompleteness or when speaking about intimate experiences of grace. Some hesitancy naturally arises when talking about such subjects. At the same time, though, we should not always speak about our most sacred moments with God. As we participate in spiritual direction, we learn to honor the Spirit's leading regarding our conversations. At times it will not seem suitable to discuss our experiences with anyone other than God. Like any intimate love relationship, some aspects are simply cherished and not revealed to others.

There is a range of similarities and differences with which each person is comfortable. Some people delight in the challenge of variety, and others feel safer with people who have characteristics similar to their own. Acknowledging and respecting our preferences and bringing them into prayer can influence our choice of a spiritual director.

Theological Considerations

Everyone holds a mixture of true, partially true, and untrue perceptions related to God and persons—to theology. Some of our perceptions are carryovers from childhood. We hold others because we have not examined them in recent years, if ever, and are unsure what we think. Some we have studied and are convinced are true. Examining theological ideas is a more prominent part of some stages of the spiritual journey than others. But the Spirit of God may bring these matters to the fore at any time for consideration. Therefore, it is wise to choose a director whose theological presuppositions are compatible with ours.

Direction sessions should not deteriorate into theological arguments nor push people outside of where they believe truth lies. At times, however, God does challenge and enlarge people's views. It is important for directees to notice when they feel they are being jarred related to theology. They need to bring this into their prayer and ask for grace to discern if they are moving in a direction that is not of God or if they are being called to learn new things from and about God.

Gender Considerations

Those who have studied, taught, and practiced spiritual direction hold varying opinions about offering spiritual direction in same or mixed gender pairs or groups. Gifts and challenges exist with either choice. People who are considering spiritual direction need to explore their willingness to work with whomever God invites by bringing these possibilities into prayer.

When we are spiritually attuned and growing in our desire and capacity to recognize and respond to God's love, this deepening intimacy with God cannot help but affect all our human affiliations including marriage, friendships, and spiritual direction relationships. Although we desire to love God and others as we love ourselves, love that enlarges our hearts and boundaries is both wonderful and throws us off balance. Intentional, open spiritual sharing builds meaningful, interdependent friendships. Spiritual and sexual intimacy can become confused in either same or opposite gender relationships. We may not know whether we or the other person is trustworthy to set appropriate limits, and our sense of our own ability to enter into such friendships responsibly may or may not be accurate. We are more likely to exhibit caution in situations in which there are immediate sparks of attraction than when we sense nothing. But it is always wise to acknowledge our dependency on God and be prayerfully aware.

Let's listen in on a direction conversation in a retreat setting. The potential directee has come away for the day to pray and think about entering spiritual direction. When he arrived at the retreat center, the person who met him asked if he would like to speak with a director sometime during the day. He thought this seemed like a good onetime opportunity to explore some of his questions. He is meeting with a nun trained to give spiritual direction.

Directee: You know this is a new experience for me. I am a Protestant, and this is my first spiritual direction session.

Director: That's interesting. Let's begin with quiet prayer together. I'm going to light this candle on the table to remind us of the light of Christ, the presence of the Holy Spirit, and to invite us to offer ourselves to God for this time together. After a few minutes of quiet prayer you can begin talking about whatever you like.

She lights the candle and they pray quietly. The directee settles down and asks God for help. He takes a few slow, deep breaths and then opens his eyes.

Directee: Where to begin? I guess I'd like to use this opportunity to talk with you about choosing a spiritual director. I am in the midst of that process. That's why I came to the retreat center today. I have been sensing the Holy Spirit inviting me to do this for a while. I have been reading a little, writing in a journal, and talking to friends. Now I am at the point where I am satisfied that this is what I want to do and that it's something God is nudging me toward.

Director: What is there in this that makes you believe it is God's idea and not just something you'd like to do because it looks new and interesting?

Directee: I've asked myself that question. I do like to jump on all the newest spiritual bandwagons, and I've tried lots of things. In fact, I'd guess I'm one of the first in my group to spend any time at a retreat center alone just to be with God.

Director: How has that been?

Directee: Pretty surprising. My wife has been encouraging me to do this for about five years, and I've thought it was a good thing for her but that I'd be bored or it would feel like a waste of time. But that's not how it has turned out. I've been here three times in the last six months. I come for the day. When I come through the front door I am thinking about all the things I'm involved in and the first couple of hours are usually pretty busy. First I worry about what I'm not getting done at work by being here and feel like I should be doing something useful. But if I wait with myself through these and other challenges, I eventually settle down. I walk outside part of the day. I take my Bible with me and a journal. I talk with God all day and even try to listen now and then. By the end of the day I am surprised how my perspectives have changed. It feels like I have let go of many concerns. I return to my day-to-day, busy life refreshed and with a better sense of why I do what I do and how God is a part of it all.

One thing I'm praying about is whether God wants me to work with a man or a woman as my spiritual director. I've written lists of pros and cons for both and haven't come to any conclusions.

Director: How does God seem in this?

Directee: That's the odd part. I don't feel like that's the major issue for me right now. In fact, I wonder if it's a nonissue to God when I get right down to it.

Director: Why do you think this is so?

Directee: I don't know, but maybe it's because I've told God that the most important thing I want in a spiritual director is some-

one who can help me with my prayer. It seems to be changing and I am not sure where it's going. I used to use long
prayer lists and was disciplined about it. Now that seems
to have paled, and I'm asking how I'm supposed to pray.

Director: So in effect you've told God that you'd be satisfied with
either a man or a woman if it was clear that this was someone who could help you with your prayer?

Directee: I think so.

Director: It sounds to me like you are experiencing freedom—freedom to hear and follow the Spirit—and that you are willing to go in whatever way God invites even though you have
made lists of pros and cons. You are aware of having many
opinions about this and yet seem open to God. It sounds
like you are just waiting to hear how God will lead you. That
sounds like grace—not something you could create for
yourself no matter how much you ponder the possibilities.

Directee: That's comforting. This gives me hope that I will be able to
recognize the right director when God shows me. I think
I'll stop trying to sort this out for now and spend the rest
of the day enjoying God's company.

We need to consider our reasons for choosing a particular spiritual
director in light of why we are thinking about entering spiritual direction
and our ideas about what God intends. Sometimes we know we have significant issues with or about persons of the same or opposite gender that
are influencing our relationships with others, with God, and our prayer.

It is a good idea to bring our thoughts about working with a man or
a woman into our prayer. If we are feeling particularly lonely or longing for a sexually intimate relationship, we need to honestly discuss this
with God and pay careful attention to what comes to mind as we prayerfully explore our motivations for beginning spiritual direction. Much of
what is important here is not necessarily open to our view. It is wise to
ask God to protect and guide us. We may recognize that we need to pray
for a direction friendship in which we will not be diverted by sexual
desires from our intention to listen to God.

There are times when it seems right to work with a director of the same
gender, occasions when God guides us to participate in direction with
someone of the opposite gender, and instances when either way seems
appropriate. A director of the opposite gender may see different sides to
an issue and challenge us as we listen to and follow God. They will also
encourage us differently. Someone of the same gender, however, will
share gender-conditioned ways of looking at God, self, and the world.

Whether we choose a same or opposite gender direction friendship, we need to make the decision in the context of prayer. If the body of Christ is to benefit from the gifts of the Holy Spirit in all persons, women and men, men and men, and women and women need to be free to listen to each other, speak to each other, and pray and listen to the Lord together. Chapter 15, "Common Areas of Difficulty," includes further material about sexuality and spiritual direction.

Who Is a Spiritual Director?

In some ways every person of faith is a spiritual director. We pray for and encourage each other to notice grace and act on our experiences and ideas about God. However, some people discover that others frequently seek them out for conversation and prayer. They may gradually recognize that God is asking them to serve as a spiritual companion to others. They may participate and serve in the community of faith in many other ways including teaching, praying for others, committee work, speaking or writing, or organizing volunteers.

Authentic gifts of spiritual direction are called forth by God through other people. A person to whom God has given gifts for direction may not recognize their own giftedness until they respond to someone's request for prayer and conversation. Spiritual directors do not simply decide that they are or would like to be directors. They are not self-appointed and will not usually offer to serve as a particular person's director. But it is appropriate for them to offer themselves to God and others for the purposes of spiritual companionship in a general way.

There are probably many persons who have acted as spiritual directors but have not used that term in describing themselves. C. S. Lewis is an example of such a person. His teaching, books, and letters were filled with an attentiveness to the Holy Spirit rather than generalized advice giving. A letter he wrote to the mother of a ten-year-old boy is an example of appropriate direction for children.

Dear Mrs. K:
Tell Laurence from me, with my love:
1) Even if he was loving Aslan more than Jesus (I'll explain in a moment why he can't be really doing this) he would not be an idol-worshiper. If he was an idol-worshiper he'd be doing it on purpose, whereas he's now doing it because he can't help doing it and trying hard not to do it. But God knows quite well how hard we find it to love Him more than anyone or anything else, and He won't be angry with us as long as we are trying. And He will help us.
2) But Laurence can't *really* love Aslan more than Jesus, even if he feels that's what he is doing. For the things he loves Aslan for doing or saying are simply the things Jesus really did and said. So that when Laurence thinks he is loving

Aslan, he is really loving Jesus: and perhaps loving him more than he ever did before. Of course, there is one thing Aslan has that Jesus has not—I mean the body of the lion. (But remember if there are other worlds and they need to be saved, and Christ were to save them—as He would—He may really have taken all sorts of bodies in them which we don't know about.) Now if Laurence is bothered because he finds the lion body seems nicer to him than the man-body, I don't think he *need* be bothered at all. God knows all about the way a little boy's imagination works (He made it, after all) and knows that at a certain age the idea of talking to friendly animals is very attractive. So I don't think He minds if Laurence likes the lion-body. And anyway, Laurence will find as he grows older, that feeling (liking the lion body better) will die away by itself, without his taking any trouble about it. So he needn't bother.

3) If I were Laurence I'd just say in my prayers something like this: "Dear God, if the things I've been thinking and feeling about these books are things You don't like and are bad for me, please take away those feelings and thoughts. But if they are not bad, then please stop me from worrying about them. And help me every day to love You more in the way that really matters far more than any feelings or imaginations, by doing what You want and growing more like You." That is the sort of thing I think Laurence should say for himself, but it would be kind and Christian-like if he then added, "And if Mr. Lewis has worried any other children by his books or done them any harm, then please forgive him and help him never to do it again."

Will this help? I am terribly sorry to have caused such trouble, and would take it as a great favor if you would write again and tell me how Laurence goes on. I shall, of course, have him daily in my prayers. He must be a corker of a boy: I hope you are prepared for the possibility he might turn out a saint. I daresay the saints' mothers have, in some way, a rough time.

Yours sincerely,
C. S. Lewis[2]

Usually a director and directee know each other and have face-to-face meetings, but C. S. Lewis's letters to an American woman from 1950 to 1963, published under the title *Letters to an American Lady,* are letters of direction between two people who never met each other in person. And *Letters to Malcolm,* a book about prayer published after Lewis's death, is filled with spiritual direction. Many persons who have read these books have received helpful spiritual guidance even though none of the letters were written personally to them. They are not letters of spiritual advice so much as documents that enable the readers to recognize and respond to what God is drawing their attention to as they read.[3] I, along with thousands of other people, might consider myself a long-distance directee of C. S. Lewis.

When I thought about entering spiritual direction on a one-to-one basis, I considered what qualifications of a director were important to me. Most people do that in some way. The following descriptions provide a useful place to begin such a process, but we also need to remember that directors are ordinary human beings whom God uses in a particular ministry. If we anticipate that any one person will embody all the qualities that follow, we are looking for unrealistic perfection. Notice which qualities seem more important and inviting to you as you read the list of characteristics.

In regard to God, Christian spiritual directors:

believe in, seek, and have a deepening, ongoing love/faith relationship with the Triune God.

are committed to Scripture as God-given for faith and practice and seek to live according to scriptural principles.

are aware that God is the primary source of knowledge, truth, and love and that a director may be a carrier of these attributes.

seek to be aware of and open to notice the Spirit's presence. They make provision for nurturing their own contemplative ways of listening to God and do not separate reality into spiritual and non-spiritual categories.

desire to trust the Holy Spirit in directees, themselves, the spiritual direction process, and outward experiences and actions.

are convinced that God invites human beings into loving relationship and that God will guide those who seek Divine/human relationship.

believe that the Spirit gives grace to enable people to desire and respond to God's initiatives.

enjoy being used by the Spirit of God in spiritual direction and give God the credit for its fruits.

As people, Christian spiritual directors:

are persons of prayer who are committed to continue developing their own maturing relationship with God. They participate in personal prayer, Scripture study, service, a community of faith, and spiritual direction. Practicing spiritual directors continue to receive spiritual direction as long as they are giving direction. They desire to be like Christ—continuing to listen to and follow God.

pay sufficient attention to their own relationship with God outside of direction meetings in order to be attentive to God and directees during direction meetings for the sake of the directees' relationships with God.

have the ability to "bracket" material when they are in direction conversations. They are able to notice and let go of their desire to speak about their own experiences in order to focus full attention on God and the directees. They are careful that their own issues do not get mixed with those of the directees.

are called and gifted by the Spirit to walk alongside others in their intention to hear and follow God. This call is confirmed by others coming to them for conversations about spiritual life, prayer, and discernment.

are aware of their own gifted but imperfect humanity and need of God's grace. They are willing to share their vulnerability and ongoing need for God.

provide for appropriate means of accountability and supervision for themselves as directors.

are old enough to have experienced some of the confusion, sorrow, and joy of ordinary human life graced by God. Some people prefer to meet with a director who is chronologically older than they are. Others find this fades in importance when compared with a person's prayer life, experiences, and maturity in particular areas.

have a sense of humor. When people become overly serious or solemn, even about their spiritual life, they tend to close in on themselves rather than remaining open to God. Therefore, a sense of humor is helpful. Sometimes it is refreshing to be able to laugh when life is overwhelming or ridiculous. It is important for a director to have an open trust in God that invites and allows for laughter.

In regard to the process of spiritual direction, Christian spiritual directors:

are genuinely enthusiastic about growth in persons in the way that is right for each person and congruent with Scripture. They do not espouse a set pattern to which all must conform. They respect and appreciate the individuality and uniqueness of persons created by God and desire to cooperate with the work of the Holy Spirit in directees.

encourage directees to discern God's intentions and make their own decisions.

depend on the Spirit's leading in the direction relationship and want to listen for God rather than be guided by agendas set by themselves or directees.

are able to accept, care about, and affirm people. Spiritual directors are able to speak the gospel and proclaim the forgiving, renewing life of Christ that is available to all.

are discerning about the readiness of directees for particular opportunities in prayer, study, Christian disciplines, and service.

are sufficiently grounded in God so that they are free to speak the truth in love. They are able to listen to whatever topics arise with-

out being overly threatened by the content and respond in prayer
and in seeking God with directees.

know that sometimes they may be drawn away from listening to the
Spirit when directees are describing intense negative, positive, or
unfamiliar experiences.

are committed to honor confidentiality and respect and appreciate
the willingness of directees to talk about their personal relationship with God.

act responsibly with and toward directees with the intention of loving them with Christ's love. Due to a director's sense of responsibility to God concerning directees' well-being and development,
they may at times refer directees for counseling or medical diag-
nosis or assist them in finding another director.

No one spiritual director possesses all these characteristics in the same
measure. Directees need to pray and think about which qualities seem
more important to them. Some people write in a journal about the particular characteristics they hope for in a director as a way of placing their
ideas clearly before themselves and God. As they pray about these characteristics for a few days or weeks, directees often say the desire for certain qualities grows or diminishes.

Some of our desires in any relationship are healthy and appropriate.
Others suggest we are trying to take control and protect ourselves from
serious engagement in the ways in which God is calling us. Through
reflection we may see that we have been looking for someone who is perfect, a notion we need to prayerfully dismiss. The intention of spiritual
direction is to be free to let God direct, guide, and teach us. When we
think we know whom we should ask, it is time to begin or continue dis-
cussions with that person. Sometimes the first person we ask turns out
to be the right one and sometimes that person does not.

Preparation of Spiritual Directors

As we said in chapter 1, "What Is Spiritual Direction?" the Holy Spirit
is the primary teacher for spiritual directors, who are called and gifted
by God to offer spiritual direction. Some directors have had formal education in spiritual direction, but not all have. There are numerous educational programs in the United States for spiritual directors, and short-
or long-term study leads to certificates and advanced degrees. Credible
programs include experiential as well as academic requirements.

Ideally, students accepted to these programs have been directees and
perhaps even directors for a period of time, sometimes for many years,

before they sensed God's call to pursue formal training. None of the legitimate programs of study guarantee that a person will become a spiritual director after completing the course. The Holy Spirit is the one who calls forth and confirms ministries of spiritual direction. However, study can help directors clarify and deepen their understanding of the ministry to which God is calling them. Through study, others discover that prayer and additional information about direction help them recognize that they are not called to be directors, that God has other plans for them. Spiritual Directors International maintains a current directory of spiritual direction preparation programs that can be obtained by writing to them or through their web site.[4]

Many fine directors have little or no formal education in spiritual direction. Spiritual direction is one of the gifts that overflows out of a life of prayer and listening to God. Some people who are well suited to offer direction may not be familiar with the term *spiritual direction,* even though they have been listening to and praying with whomever God sends.

If we are interested in meeting with a particular person, it might be helpful to know what education or experience that person has had regarding spiritual direction. At the same time, we should not choose formal education as the determining factor in either a person's suitability for the ministry of spiritual direction or whether we should ask that person to be our spiritual director. We learn more by asking how people became spiritual directors and by listening to how they speak about their sense of God's calling and preparing them to offer spiritual direction. We may want to inquire about how spiritual directors arrange for their own accountability, how they provide for supervision, and how they nurture their spiritual life. It is most important to ask, "Is the Holy Spirit drawing me to this person for spiritual direction?"

How Do We Find Spiritual Directors?

Spiritual directors are among us within every denominational heritage. Some of them are already using their gifts. Others are waiting for an invitation from a potential directee. Henri Nouwen's response to the question, "How do we find spiritual directors?" is a helpful one to consider at this time when many people are discovering the ministry of spiritual direction and looking for spiritual companionship. Nouwen wrote:

> The first and nearly spontaneous reaction to the idea of a spiritual guide is: "Spiritual guides are hard to find." This might be true, but at least part of the reason for this lack of spiritual guides is that we ourselves do not appeal to our fellow human beings in such a way as to invite them to become our spiritual leaders. If there were no students constantly asking for good teachers, there

would be no good teachers. The same is true for spiritual guides. There are many men and women with great spiritual sensitivity whose talents remain dormant because we do not make an appeal to them. Many would, in fact, become wise and holy for our sake if we would invite them to assist us in our search for the prayer of our heart. A spiritual director does not necessarily have to be more intelligent or more experienced than we are. It is important that he or she enters with us into the Scriptures and the silence where God speaks to both of us. When we really want to live a life of prayer and seriously ask ourselves what the prayer of our heart may be, we will also be able to express the type of guidance we need and find that someone is waiting to be asked. Often we will discover that those whom we ask for help will indeed receive the gift to help us and grow with us toward prayer.

The openness and the honest seeking of the directee are of primary importance to both individuals in a spiritual direction relationship. It is also the search and openness of the directee that calls forth and creates the power and gifts of the director.[5]

It is interesting to notice the truth of this quotation as it has been lived out in recent years. People seeking spiritual direction, individuals who are following God more intentionally in prayer and being asked by others for spiritual direction, and formal education programs for spiritual directors have significantly increased in number.

How do we look for a spiritual director? On the practical level:

Speak to friends or acquaintances who are participating in spiritual direction.

Ask for suggestions from a minister or denominational headquarters.

Explore possibilities at retreat centers, monasteries, and seminaries in the area.

Look on the Internet (see suggestions in the bibliography).

Perhaps my experiences with spiritual direction will aid you in your search. I have been involved in many short- and long-term direction relationships. The first relationship I can identify as a spiritual direction affiliation began informally in the late 1970s. When a friend and I began studying prayer and spiritual direction, we realized that what we called prayer ministry was what other Christians called spiritual direction. We also realized that the time seemed right for both of us to look for spiritual direction companionships outside of our friendship.

I gathered more information by reading and talking to others. I prayed, wrote in my journal, and thought about the qualities that were important to me based on my perceived needs and hopes. I also considered the type of person God might choose for me. Then I began to explore places where direction was offered and looked at descriptions of ministering organizations and people.

In time I decided to call for an appointment with a Roman Catholic man who was a member of the Jesuit order. Based on the information I read about him, I sensed he was called to spiritual direction and I discovered he had been offering direction for several years. I also learned about his ministries of teaching and leading retreats. His interests seemed compatible with mine. Then I prayed about the possibilities.

Though I made the decision based on prayer and the description of his interests, relationship with God, and ministry, it still felt like a leap into the unknown. I was uneasy at my first appointment because of expected theological differences, because he was a man, and because I was not sure what to expect. Our first conversation was challenging, stretching, and interesting. Afterward I realized I had been nervous but that in spite of my anxiety we had been open together to the Holy Spirit and to what God intended.

It became clear almost immediately that our backgrounds were not as important as our trust in God and expectation of the Holy Spirit's participation with us. I also noticed a sense of quiet confirmation that seemed like God's blessing. My spiritual director and I prayed and worked together for two years through many ordinary and surprising opportunities. When he moved to another area of the country, we parted.

My second intentional direction friendship developed almost a year later. From time to time, I prayed about the absence of regular spiritual direction in my life and asked God, "If? Who? When?" I approached a mature Baptist woman who had a prayer ministry as a possible director, even though I knew she was not familiar with the term or the concept. I asked her to read materials about direction so that she would understand exactly what I was hoping for and could think and pray more specifically about the possibilities. When we met together to talk, pray, and consider what God might be intending, it was clear it was not the right time for us to participate together in spiritual direction. She said she wondered if the Spirit was inviting her through our process together to seek a director for herself. Even though the answer was no to the question I was asking, the experience was helpful and positive for both of us.

During this time without a spiritual director, I felt invited by God to set aside one day a month with God at a retreat center and to spend the day praying, reading Scripture, and writing in a journal. I felt called to more solitude and silence than had been my custom so I could listen better to what God was saying and teaching me. On one of these days I had the opportunity to meet with a Benedictine sister and was surprised when that initial meeting developed into a new direction friendship. I continued to set aside one day each month and to meet with my director for an hour in the afternoon. This direction friendship, too, lasted a few years before responsibilities took her to another city.

After these two relationships, I longed to find someone whose life was similar to my own, perhaps a woman, married, Protestant. I again prayed about the situation. A few months later I asked a woman to serve as my spiritual director. I asked her for a nine-month commitment, thinking that might be enough time to accomplish some specific goals about which I desired prayer, discernment, and support. We were together for several years before I felt drawn to participate in the Ignatian Exercises and sought someone who was trained to guide me through this journey with Scripture and prayer.

God has guided, comforted, encouraged, and blessed me through many years of spiritual direction companionships as a directee. I have spoken with men and women, Roman Catholics and Protestants, and trained and untrained directors.

In the final analysis, a wide variety of persons can serve as spiritual directors as long as their deep intention and call is to listen to God with others. Perhaps the most important thing to do as we select a spiritual director is, ask God.

Recognizing an Appropriate Spiritual Director

We have already said it often, but perhaps we cannot say it too often—from beginning to end the intention of spiritual direction is discernment of God's presence and leading. Therefore, we desire a direction relationship that helps us with discernment.

The entire process of seeking a spiritual director is prayerful, some of it worded and some of it in offering ourselves to God without words. God rather than ourselves or our questions is the center of interest. The Spirit may guide us quickly and unmistakably to an appropriate spiritual director in answer to our specific prayer. Identification of the right spiritual director may occur without our anticipation of it, as when I met a director on a retreat and realized it was an unexpected beginning. In these circumstances, we often know that such a direction friendship is appropriate, although we would have difficulty describing exactly why this is so. Such direct awareness is often characterized by a sense of God's love and a kind of peacefulness.

When we act on this knowing and begin meeting with a spiritual director, the reality of our participation will either confirm or challenge what we thought we perceived. Knowledge from God is confirmed by external circumstances and outcomes and by congruence with Scripture. Sometimes circumstances send us back to reexamine what we thought was appropriate. For many people a process of extended reflection and prayer is important because it brings additional information to light. Some people find writing in a journal helpful. Others may choose to talk with a third party.

When discernment is given regarding an appropriate spiritual director, whether it is after a short or lengthy search, at a time when we expected it or not, within or outside of a spiritual direction meeting, we may feel an appreciation for God's providence, faithfulness, and care for us. For some people this sense of Divine blessing helps them trust God enough to continue with spiritual direction.

The First Meeting

Prior to the first meeting with a spiritual director, it is a good idea to think and pray about what we want to discuss. Which questions and ideas stand out from those we have been examining? We may know many things about the person we will be meeting with and even know some of the reasons why we are thinking about choosing that person as our director. We should communicate some of these thoughts to the director so that the director has a better understanding of why we are coming to him or her in particular and what we are seeking.

Some spiritual directors have questions they like to ask potential directees and may ask them to fill out an application form in advance. Other directors ask directees to write a short spiritual autobiography and send it to them before their first conversation. This can help directees reflect on their own spiritual journeys, where the Spirit has led them thus far, and their hopes for spiritual direction. Having this kind of information ahead of time enables directors to listen to directees with some understanding of their history. Some directors, however, prefer to begin the first meeting without this kind of background because they want to see what God will bring to their mutual attention in this first meeting.

The first session is often a time in which both persons ask God to show them whether they are to participate together in an ongoing spiritual direction companionship. The first conversation is usually not the time to plunge into the most intimate concerns of prayer and life. But it is a good idea to begin somewhere in the middle with subjects that are of true importance. Both people need to communicate sufficiently about themselves and their faith so they can get a true reading of the possibilities for their work together. Occasionally, God surprises us with recognition that a particular relationship immediately seems right and we feel free to speak openly about whatever comes to mind even in the first meeting. But even this kind of spontaneity needs to be gently taken into our prayer.

The discussion will evolve as the hour progresses. Even in an exploratory session, we want God to order our time together and we desire to hear the Holy Spirit. A relaxed, open, conversational environment is conducive to our listening. We hope the Spirit will guide which topics arise and how they are addressed. It is a bit like learning to ride a bicycle with stops and starts, exhilarating moments and scary ones.

Some people become anxious and find it difficult to relax at a first meeting. But there is no need for undue concern. God knows our hopes, fears, and frailties, and also our desires. We may want to look good to ourselves, the director, and God, and this may influence what we say. Yet God is still sovereign, faithful, and able to bring about whatever is needed.

First meetings are usually marked by a mixture of peace and discomfort. We may feel vulnerable. Just the idea of considering this kind of commitment can unnerve us. The content of our first conversation may open unexpected avenues. Perhaps we feel unsettled about the process or the director, or our expectations may have been quite different from what is taking place. We may even feel bored. Whether we feel predominantly calm or unsettled, we still need to continue to ask whether God is inviting us to establish a spiritual direction companionship with this person.

Sometimes strong interior unsettledness, without any sense of peace, is an indication that this relationship is not right for us. We need to ask ourselves, "Could I relax enough with this person to be genuinely open to God? To my own heart? To this person?" A part of our discomfort may come from knowing that we cannot predict what will arise or what the Spirit might say to us through spiritual direction. This can be unsettling even when we love God and are sure of God's love for us. We need to ask, "Is this a discomfort to which God is inviting me? Does this kind of discomfort draw me closer or push me away from openness with God?" God-given discomfort is confirmed by a deep peacefulness even while we are aware that we are not relaxed on the surface. It is a kind of "settled unsettledness," a holy peace that is present in the midst of a wide range of possible human experiences, thoughts, and emotions.

During the first meeting it may become clear that a spiritual friendship with this person could help us develop a deepening relationship with God. We arrange for future meetings and set an evaluation point within a few months. Or for a variety of reasons it may become clear that the Spirit is not drawing us to this relationship. It is different from what seems called for now. God uses these encounters to teach and guide both directors and directees. The decision not to pursue a relationship can be just as God-given as the decision to pursue it. There is grace in either yes or no. More than one meeting, though, is often required before both persons are sufficiently clear about what God intends.

Is This the Right Relationship?

It is difficult to describe what makes a spiritual direction companionship seem right because we are dealing with inner reality—our sense of God's invitations to us; our willingness, desire, and freedom to hear the Holy Spirit; and our resistance. We need to ask, "Could this person be a friend in God, a friend of the heart whom I could allow into the place where I dwell with God?"

Reflect on a three-way conversation with Jesus and this other person. Does this seem like a good gift or is there discomfort in the conversation? If we are uncomfortable, what is the source of our unsettledness? Do we feel we have interrupted a private conversation between the Lord and the other person? Do we feel invited to share their friendship, teaching, and experience? We may realize that this man or woman is not the particular friend of Jesus we are called to be with at this time. If it feels Jesus is out of place in our conversation, we need to look carefully and move slowly. We may be drawn to this person for reasons that have little to do with our love and relationship with God or with spiritual direction.

Christ has many faithful followers, and all uniquely embody and express their relationships with God. Is this the particular friend God is beckoning us to walk beside? Some expressions of Christ in other people seem inviting and some seem threatening. Most human relationships contain a mixture of both. Noticing whether someone could be a friend in God brings all necessary elements into one question.

Reflections

1. What do similarities and differences mean to you when you think about entering spiritual direction? Describe your sense of appropriate kinds of similarities and differences and how they might influence your willingness to trust God with this other person.
2. How and what do you pray about in relationship to finding a suitable spiritual director?
3. How do you wait for God related to spiritual direction? Do you feel invited by the Holy Spirit to actively seek someone by making phone calls and inquiries, or do you feel you should wait until God guides you to someone or brings the right person into your life?
4. What is on your list of hoped-for qualities in a spiritual director?
5. When you pray about asking someone to be your spiritual director, whom does God bring to mind? Write a list of the names.

Where do these individuals align with the qualities you have just listed and where do they differ?

6. Looking at your list, what items are surprising or new to you? Which would you not have put on such a list two or three years ago? What does this tell you about your faith journey? Does it seem to point toward any clear next steps?

7. Which of the qualities on your list are qualities that you possess in some measure and which do you feel you do not possess? What does that say about the kind of person you believe God is inviting you to? Does this description confirm what you have been thinking or invite you to consider a different kind of person than you have been thinking about until now?

Shaping the Spiritual Direction Relationship | 7

My experience and that of others has convinced me that if God is in my felt need for spiritual direction, then it is safe to assume that God will assist me in finding the resource I need. It is also safe to assume that God will invite into spiritual direction with me the person I need to be my spiritual director.

Rose Mary Dougherty[1]

There is a time for everything,
and a season for every activity under heaven.

Ecclesiastes 3:1

Spiritual direction relationships are shaped by many factors including length of commitment; frequency and length of spiritual direction meetings; settings for meetings; payment; spousal, friendship, and other kinds of relationships; responsibilities of directors and directees; and how spiritual direction relationships come to an end. Each of these areas contains elements that merit examination before a person begins the practice of spiritual direction.

Length of Commitment

It is customary to schedule a meeting or two to explore whether God is inviting a particular spiritual companionship. Both people should pray about and consider their sense of God and grace in the relationship. If the two people feel they are compatible, they likely settle into a working pattern for nine to twelve months. When both people accept the relationship itself and are committed to its intended purposes and duration, they are free to move beyond the questions about whether they should engage in spiritual direction together and can focus their attention and hopes on God.

Carole and her director have agreed to meet monthly from September to June. Gary is beginning spiritual direction early in January and hopes to see his director once a month until July. Julie knows the summer ahead will be a time of transition, and she is seeing a director who will be available through the summer. Her director has decided to take a month's break after the summer.

Many directors take a break of a month or two out of each year. During the break, whenever it comes, both people pray about and consider whether to return to the direction relationship for another period of months.

Even with established guidelines concerning the intended length of a direction commitment, either person is free to terminate the relationship at any time. It is important, however, that neither one departs hurriedly or without mutual discussion and prayer. Some difficulties will naturally arise as they do in every human relationship. Yet both people should make every effort to honor their commitment to engage fully and remain in the relationship for a period of time. Spiritual companionships are entered with prayer and care and deserve the same treatment at the end. A commitment to spiritual direction includes a willingness to listen to and stay with each other even when the relationship becomes difficult or confusing.

When we encounter complications in a relationship with a spiritual director, they may reflect struggles in our relationship with God. Sometimes when we want most to withdraw from direction, we should pray, wait, wrestle, and continue to participate in the relationship as a way of remaining available to God. We should consider beforehand what we will do if we feel like ending the relationship.

Sometimes a directee or director may abruptly decide that a relationship should come to an end. This decision needs to become the focus of prayer and honest discussion. Both people need to examine prayerfully their reasons for separating and the specific characteristics of their willingness and willfulness in response to how the Spirit is leading. A section at the end of this chapter, "Ending Spiritual Direction Relationships," and chapter 15, "Common Areas of Difficulty," further address potential problems in direction relationships.

Frequency and Length of Spiritual Direction Meetings

Direction pairs and groups decide together about the frequency of spiritual direction conversations. Some people schedule a few meetings fairly close together at the beginning of the relationship. Others prefer to establish a pattern they will follow throughout their relationship. Monthly direction appointments are most usual but not necessarily right for everyone. Some people establish a pattern of less frequent meetings or make appointments as needed. Individual circumstances vary.

Tom sees his director every two or three months and calls for a time when it seems appropriate. Karen sees her director two or three times a year when she is on retreat. The frequency of meetings is a matter for prayer. What is the Spirit inviting here? The sense of what is right needs to flow out of prayer and reflection and a prayerful understanding of God's leading.

Even while affirming this kind of freedom, it is apparent that choosing to meet with a director once a month has some advantages. By establishing a regular pattern of appointments, we make direction an ongoing part of our journey. Making the commitment to meet monthly with a director may be an important aspect of our intentionality to listen to God.

Spiritual direction appointments usually last from fifty to sixty minutes. Longer meetings may encourage a tendency to waste time. Time limits assist both directee and director in discussing what is genuinely important. Even though we have decided to take part in spiritual direction, sometimes we would rather avoid discussing and praying about what needs attention in our relationship with God. We prefer to discuss anything other than our areas of genuine confusion, pain, or resistance, or even of unexpected grace. A limited amount of time helps us come to terms more quickly with why we have established this relationship—to listen and give attention to the Spirit.

Setting for Spiritual Direction Meetings

The specifics of physical surroundings are more important for some people than others. No matter what level of significance we give to the setting for direction, however, it is important that we feel welcome. We select and prepare a room that is comfortable and private, where we will not be interrupted or overheard by others, and therefore, can speak openly. We arrange to forward calls, turn off the phone, or choose a room without a telephone. We want to protect the time and place for spiritual direction just as we guard our time and place of personal prayer.

Some directors prepare a place for spiritual direction in the same way they create an environment for quiet time with God. They choose objects that remind them of God's presence and love such as framed passages of Scripture, a cross, an icon or picture of Christ, a plant, or a lighted candle. A delicate mobile of fish fashioned from twigs hung from the vaulted ceiling of my office for many years. During direction conversations, I would often notice its movement in the slightest breeze and remember that I was depending on the unseen movements of the Spirit of God. I felt less inclined to respond out of my fear that nothing of significance was happening. These kinds of preparations help both director and directee.

At the beginning of a direction appointment, we usually need a few minutes to shift our focus more intentionally toward God and away from whatever we have been doing and thinking about. Once we have chosen the space for our spiritual direction meetings and are both satisfied with the arrangement, entering that place becomes part of our intentional way of attuning ourselves to listen to God.

Tony meets directees at an office in a church. Kate sees directees at a center for spiritual renewal where six other directors also have offices. Lorraine and Janet have set aside places in their homes. John and Dick offer direction at a retreat center. Sue and Carole do what they call "coffee cup direction." They meet their directees in a quiet coffee shop in the middle of the afternoon and say that even if there are others around, it is amazing how God uses this setting. Jim notices that some of his directees like to walk while engaging in a direction conversation and that walking outside together encourages a natural flow of prayer and conversation.

Some directors and directees feel protected in a setting where other people are present, even if they are on the other side of a door. Others prefer a place where they are truly alone because they feel a greater sense of freedom to speak authentically. Wherever it is, however, the direction environment should be a kind of holy ground that feels and is safe.

Payment for Spiritual Direction

Spiritual direction is a gift from God. Therefore, any discussion about fees for spiritual direction needs to take place between two people who are both aware of this gift.

Payment for spiritual direction is a subject of much discussion among spiritual directors. Their ideas about fees are related to how God has drawn and prepared them and the ways they are responding to God's call. They make decisions about any kind of payment according to what they sense through their prayer. Here's how several directors describe their arrangements.

Director 1:   Spiritual direction seems to be the center of my call to ministry. I have studied and participated in direction for many years. Offering spiritual direction is full-time *work* for me. I see several directees each week and receive payment that supports my ability to devote myself fully to the ministry of direction.

Director 2:   From beginning to end my call to give spiritual direction has been marked by the Holy Spirit. I believe that offering direction is my way to serve God. I think of myself as using divinely given gifts for God and for God's life in others. I support myself financially through other means and see a few directees each month.

Director 3: Our retreat center offers spiritual direction as a part of ongoing ministry. We offer individual and group direction. The payments received help to support the ministry of the center but do not cover our costs.

Director 4: Spiritual direction is new in our church setting. We feel that it is important to charge a fee. It seems that directees take the matter of direction and making space for deepening their love for God outside of the direction sessions more seriously when they make a financial contribution.

Director 5: Every now and then someone calls for spiritual direction. Sometimes we converse on the telephone or even by e-mail. At times we arrange for a face-to-face conversation. It seems like it is God's idea and timing whenever and however it works out. There are no fees involved.

Director 6: We are part of a group spiritual direction arrangement that has a facilitator. We are grateful that someone guides the process with us. We have an agreed upon financial arrangement that provides for the facilitator's time.

Director 7: Several spiritual direction groups meet one Tuesday evening a month at our church. Everyone begins together with Scripture and prayer and about twenty minutes of quiet prayer to prepare ourselves for spiritual direction. Then we move into our direction groups of three or four people for the remainder of the evening. Each of the small groups has a facilitator. There is a set fee to participate that covers costs associated with the evening.

Director 8: We are part of a small spiritual direction group. One of us prepares the space; the others bring a simple meal. We eat together in silence and then each of us has a half hour for spiritual direction. The cost? Time set aside and a willingness to prayerfully listen and speak, waiting for God.

The central idea with which directors and directees struggle is that the Holy Spirit is the one who really gives spiritual direction. God gives gifts of discernment to directors. We ask if it is right to charge for what God freely does and gives. The usual way this dilemma is addressed is by saying that direction fees are not given "for" spiritual direction in the same way one pays for counseling. When people do make contributions or payment for spiritual direction, they are not paying for the session per se, nor for advice or counsel. They are making a contribution to help support a particular ministry. Many people need to receive payment in order to set aside the time to offer direction. If they did not get paid, they would need to seek a paid position of another sort. Payment is a way of supporting an ongoing ministry rather than paying for services.

When payment is part of a direction arrangement, most directors take a directee's ability to pay into account and make provisions including sliding fee scales or scholarships. In this way, no one is turned away due to limited financial resources. There is often no charge for spiritual direction when it is part of a ministry that is supported by other means, and pastors do not usually expect or receive payment for direction from members of their congregations.

Even when direction is financially free, it is costly for both persons in other ways. It is costly in emotional energy, time, care, intentionality and willingness, and in continuing prayer and surrender to God. It is challenging and stretching to directors as they make spiritual gifts of discernment available to others. Both directors and directees give and receive. Directors often speak about having a sense that their call to offer spiritual direction is a kind of sacred entrustment. They sense the Holy Spirit inviting them to offer direction, and this call and their experiences with directees deepen their respect, care, and appreciation for God's life and love extended to all who seek God.

The sense of costliness of spiritual direction makes some people hesitant to participate. They wonder whether it is appropriate for them to spend significant time, money, energy, and care on themselves and their relationship with God. They may even question whether it is all right for them to set aside a half hour a day just to be with God. People feel the pressures of limited resources and speak about clamoring voices within and without that tell them many things are more important than supporting their spiritual life. Pursuing any Christian discipline, however, has countercultural aspects. When we seek and hear God more clearly, our values often shift from prevailing cultural norms. This, in turn, influences all our relationships. In the end, therefore, spiritual direction is not for ourselves alone. It is part of our call to be God's people in the world. Whatever the costs are in time, money, energy, and care, they are far less than the benefits that flow out of listening to God.

Distinguishing between Spiritual Direction and Other Relationships

Many people who consider spiritual direction recognize they are already involved in relationships that seem to overlap the territory covered by direction. These relationships include:

marriage	study groups
counseling	prayer groups
pastoral care	support groups
discipling	one-to-one friendships

These kinds of relationships may include aspects of spiritual guidance. God can speak to us through all relationships and situations, so it is not unusual that we are already using our affiliations with others in some ways for discernment and paying attention to God. We might question how a spiritual direction companionship would differ from these relationships or how our participation in spiritual direction could influence the nature of our other relationships. Some of these differences become clearer when we think about our present relationships and notice how we spend our time with various people.

- What are the goals of each of your relationships (socialization, study, work, prayer, discernment, support, encouragement)?
- In regard to an individual or a friendship group, how do you act in the relationship concerning setting explicit and implicit goals? Do you consider the purposes and possibilities inherent in relationships or do you tend to let relationships develop without thinking much about their purposes?
- Which goals seem clear to you and the others, and which are less clear?
- Which of your goals are fully shared with other members of these groups, and which are not?

Differences exist between talking about God with family and friends and intentionally choosing to listen to God in spiritual direction. Participants in a spiritual direction relationship are very deliberate at the outset about the goal of being available to listen to God and each other. This is the central purpose of the relationship. Many other relationships arise out of life circumstances rather than out of clear decisions to develop one kind of relationship over another. The main difference is the focus and level of intentionality toward prayerful discernment.

Even when we decide to see one person on a scheduled basis for spiritual direction, we continue to pray and process information with trusted others. This is to be expected. We might even say that we are part of a network of spiritual direction. We may feel drawn to speak to a spiritual director at a conference or a retreat even though we regularly participate in ongoing spiritual direction. It is important to have a central commitment that we believe is invited by God but also to recognize that the Spirit continues to invite us through many resources and persons. Asking one person to listen to God with us in spiritual direction seems to enlarge our awareness and capacity to recognize God's interactions with us in other contexts and with other people.

On the other hand, it is not appropriate to seek spiritual direction from persons other than our director because of disenchantment, ambivalence, or defensiveness. We need to remind ourselves that we are seeking God through direction, not primarily wise human advice. If we notice we are pursuing a number of people, hoping to hear the Holy Spirit speak, it may be an indication that we should intentionally turn to God through prayer, Scripture reading, and solitude rather than to another person. Sometimes we need to ask ourselves what we are truly seeking and what we are trying to avoid.

Discussing Spiritual Direction with a Spouse

If we are considering spiritual direction and we are married, it is a good idea to talk about it with our partner. We may describe our sense of God's invitation and discuss whatever seems helpful. If we are unsure about our ability to describe spiritual direction adequately, we could suggest that our spouse peruse the first chapter of this book or one of the books or web sites listed in the bibliography.

We usually choose to marry people who are not exactly like us. Spouses differ from each other in many ways. We may or may not share Christian experience and belief. Even when we do share the same faith and its values and traditions, we are likely to need and choose different ways of growing in our faith. Some of our choices are affirmed by our spouses. They may consider other choices threatening. Despite how they may react, we should not become secretive about what we do because this cannot help but raise uneasiness in our partner. It is important to talk openly about possible spiritual direction friendships in whatever manner seems appropriate.

What we need to discuss is influenced by whether our spiritual director is of the same or opposite gender. Our personal history, whether we are naturally attracted sexually to people of the same or opposite gender, the present climate of our marriage, and the reasons we are considering spiritual direction all influence what we should pray about and discuss with our partner.

Some people ask whether spouses should serve as spiritual directors for each other. In the context of life together it is natural to act as spiritual guides to one another at times, especially if we share similar spiritual hopes. We may talk about our relationship to God, pray together, and serve together. However, most couples discover that when one or both of them sense God's invitation to spiritual direction, they wish to speak to someone outside the marriage.

Married couples are necessarily deeply involved in each other's lives, and it is next to impossible to be fully objective when trying to listen to God with our spouse. We have too much invested in anything the Holy Spirit might say to our mate and are affected by what we hope for our partner. The major intention of spiritual direction—listening to God as clearly as possible without distracting influences—can be easily compromised.

Many couples participate in prayerful discernment about joint decisions and intentionally nurture their love of God together as well as individually. Their interaction becomes a special part of the network of relationships that influences them. Spiritual guidance networks include everything and everyone that enable them to recognize and respond to God.

Our networks are unique. Susan's network includes her husband, Sam; a spiritual direction relationship with Jean; trusted friends in groups at work and church; special lifelong friends of the heart, some near and some far away, with whom she keeps in touch through face-to-face meetings, phone calls, e-mail, and letters; her pastor; immediate and extended family members; onetime direction opportunities on retreat days, seminars, and short-term educational settings; and whatever arises out of the circumstances of her life.

Cal's network is smaller but just as important for him. It includes a man with whom he has been friends since high school; his wife, Karen; their family and church affiliations; and a spiritual direction group that includes two men and two women.

Considering a Friend as a Spiritual Director

Friends may have some of the same difficulties as married couples in being lovingly detached spiritual directors for one another. The strength of the friendship bond and level of personal investment may hinder their ability to hear God clearly with and for each other. But there are times when direction companionships with friends seem appropriate. If God is leading friends in this way, they should set aside specific time for direction conversations and alternately assume the role of director and directee.

I began talking about spiritual direction with a friend before either of us knew much about it. We called it prayer ministry. We were involved in a healing prayer ministry and were learning about prayer as we walked alongside many people. God was opening our awareness in new ways, and we began discussing our numerous questions. We pondered healing and Scripture, Jesus and the Holy Spirit, many varieties of prayer, our desires and God's desires. We were being drawn to love and serve God. It became clear that the Spirit was offering and inviting us into God's love in new ways. Our love relationship with God was becoming more central. First my friend directed me. As our friendship grew, our spiritual direction conversations became more mutual.

In a reciprocal arrangement, participants may schedule back-to-back sessions, but it is usually more satisfying to separate these sessions by a few hours or days. Directees need to focus on their role as the directee without having to think about directing someone else immediately before or after their own session. Also, time spent in solitude and silence before and after a direction conversation makes it possible to pay closer attention to their own heart and to God.

Some friends find that when they are with each other often and share numerous social encounters, it becomes more difficult to remain sufficiently objective in spiritual direction together. They may need to prayerfully discern which mode of relationship God is inviting for a particular time and choose one or the other—social friends or spiritual companions. However, others discover they are able to interact in different ways at different times. When they set aside a special time for spiritual direction, they experience a sense of freedom to hear and respond to God and each other that makes true spiritual direction possible.

There are many differences between seeking God's guidance through spiritual direction and seeking the advice of a friend. Both are valuable. Participants in spiritual direction seek to discern and continue to pray about whether the qualities that enhance spiritual direction are present in a particular relationship.

If God is inviting direction within the context of a friendship, God will also help us function effectively there. As a general practice, however, it is usually easier to maintain proper and healthy boundaries, avoid complication, and speak freely when spiritual direction relationships are established outside of social friendships.

Responsibilities of Directees and Directors

Direction partners make a commitment to attend to their relationship with God both within and outside of the direction hour. Directees always retain responsibility for their own relationship with God. At no point does that responsibility shift to the director. Directees grow in discernment as they prayerfully determine what their spiritual practices will be and take responsibility for their own participation. Intending to respond to the Spirit's guidance, they choose how, where, and when they will pray and be involved with Scripture. They decide how God is calling them to function in the body of Christ in worship, prayer, study, and service. Directees prayerfully discern what God is asking of them and decide how they will respond.

Spiritual direction is not a system for surveillance. Directees are responsible for their own authenticity with God, themselves, and their director and for willingness to address whatever the Spirit brings to their attention. But when they communicate with a spiritual director about what they are and are not doing, they can better recognize their motivations and blind spots and consider adjustments. Sometimes directees set impossible or ill-fitting goals that need to be altered. Even though they speak to a director about these things, the heart of their relationship with God always remains between them and God.

Directors commit themselves to pray, listen, and respond honestly with directees and consistently nurture their own relationship with God. Directors usually provide for accountability and supervision for their practice of spiritual direction. They ask directees for permission to speak with a supervisor if necessary but in a way that disguises the directee's identity.

Directors pray for and with their directees in and outside of direction sessions. Ongoing prayer is so foundational to the possibility and process of spiritual direction that if prayer disappears, so does true spiritual direction. Directors pray for directees and directees pray for their directors. The direction relationship itself becomes part of the prayer of both in whatever ways God seems to invite.

Ethical, moral behavior according to scriptural standards is the intended norm for spiritual direction. Directors and directees make important commitments to each other as well as to God. They enter into a two-way confidentiality that facilitates openness and builds trust. Speaking about intimate details of our relationship with God often makes us feel vulnerable. We need to know we are protected from becoming the subject of conversation with others. Both persons accept responsibility to notice and talk about moral or ethical questions when they arise.[2]

Directors and directees grow to appreciate each other and God in each other, but spiritual direction companionships are not primarily social relationships in the sense of sharing activities outside of spiritual direction meetings. Both parties choose to preserve the lovingly detached quality of their relationship as an open place to listen to God.

Ending Spiritual Direction Relationships

Spiritual direction relationships do not last forever. Each direction relationship has a life of its own. It begins, grows, and develops, and in time it fulfills its purpose. Some direction affiliations are onetime meetings. Others last for many years. When we begin in direction we schedule a time to evaluate whether to continue, often in nine months to a year. Sometimes we decide to meet for a longer period of time until we complete a project or meet a goal. A time of transition may also call for a longer life for the relationship. But even when this is the case, it is helpful to reevaluate roughly once a year whether a particular spiritual direction companionship is still God's idea.

Listening for the Holy Spirit includes paying attention to when it is time to end a direction relationship. Through personal prayer, reflection, and direction conversations, we may sense that God is calling us to something new. Perhaps the Spirit is inviting us to a new direction companionship or to a season away from direction.

Our present direction relationship may seem important because we are still hearing God through our prayer and interaction together. But in our listening we may recognize that God wants something else for us. When a direction friendship has become special to us, we may find it difficult to let go. We may want to hold on to something that feels adequate or familiar. We may feel uncomfortable ending a relationship in which we have sensed God's presence and blessing. We need to bring our sense of loss or sadness into our prayer and allow ourselves sufficient time to pray, process, and prepare for God's new initiatives. Then, when we are ready, it is more likely the change will seem like the next, right step.

At times we feel drawn to move on because the direction relationship itself no longer seems appropriate for a variety of reasons. When we are feeling dissatisfied in our present arrangement, we are right to question our motivations for wanting to leave and to test them in prayer and waiting. The original intentions of the relationship may have become blurred. Perhaps the relationship has moved toward counseling or social friendship. Perhaps we have grown in ways that could be encouraged more fully by a different person. Perhaps we are interested in participating in other kinds of prayer or spiritual disciplines.

One or both persons may have become so deeply invested in the relationship that it is increasingly difficult to listen objectively to what the Spirit is saying. Or directors may know their directees so well that they are limited in their ability to see new things that God is inviting. Sometimes directees become overly dependent on directors rather than growing in dependency on God.

Regardless of our reasons for wanting to end a direction relationship, we need to discern what the Spirit is saying. Listening for God and to God is not always comfortable. Sometimes we prefer not to listen. Yet prayer and discernment are called for whenever we consider leaving a spiritual direction companionship. This may be a short or lengthy process. Directors and directees pray together and alone, reflect on their motivations for continuing or ending the relationship, and ask the Holy

Spirit for guidance. We want to identify and describe our hopes and fears and our reasons for staying or leaving as clearly as possible. We may immediately recognize surface reasons, but we also need to bring the stirrings at deeper levels into our conscious prayer and consideration. We want to tell God, ourselves, and each other the truth about what is transpiring and notice where the Spirit leads.

In any direction relationship there are moments when either or both persons would rather not continue. The desire to leave a relationship can come from within ourselves, from other persons in or outside the relationship, or from spiritual influences. Some of these are from God and some are not. Sometimes we desire to leave spiritual direction when we are getting closer to our real issues with God. Hence, we need to seek discernment and avoid hasty decisions. Consciously or unconsciously, we become less sure about whether to trust God or our own instincts, and a part of us would rather flee than confront what we believe the Spirit is bringing to our attention. We need to allow adequate time for God to reveal what is prompting our desires for change. Through prayer and discernment we seek a place of peace where we sense God's presence and care and are clear about our next step.

When a separation is called for, director and directee need to remain together long enough to complete whatever seems appropriate. We may experience joy, sadness, or fear. When direction has been meaningful, we may eagerly anticipate the next opportunities God will provide for us because we are convinced of the goodness of God. Or we may wonder whether we will ever again be able to experience such spiritual intimacy and freedom to love God and grow in Christ with another person. If the direction relationship ends over a disagreement or anything that feels like a betrayal, we may fear we will have difficulty allowing ourselves to be vulnerable in another spiritual direction companionship.

Grace is operative through all possible sets of circumstances. At the end of any important relationship, we likely possess a mixture of thoughts and feelings ranging from joy over the gifts experienced with the other person to deep sadness or even grief at our parting. Again, we are invited to look to God, to invite the Holy Spirit to guide and comfort us, and to ask the Lord to help us take the next step. As we respond to God's loving presence, grace is always available.

Reflections

1. How often would you like to meet for spiritual direction?
2. What aspects of place seem important to you?

3. How do your attitudes about and history with money influence your ideas about paying a spiritual director? Are you likely to take direction more seriously if you pay? What are your reasons for not paying? How does this seem when you pray about it?

4. How important is it for you to see someone for direction, and how will you discuss this with your spouse or other significant people in your life?

5. As you read about the responsibilities of a director and directee, what invited you and what caused you to hesitate?

6. What kinds of arrangements made at the beginning of a spiritual direction companionship could facilitate a satisfying end to the relationship when that seems appropriate? What provisions for ongoing assessment could be helpful?

7. How might your personal history of ending relationships influence your perceptions, thoughts, feelings, hopes, fears, and prayers at the end of a spiritual direction relationship?

8. If you are participating in a spiritual direction relationship, how would you describe the relationship and how God has used it in your life? Where have you
   sensed grace?
   noticed your blindness?
   been called into deeper love and service of Christ?
   struggled mightily?
   been moved or changed by God?

9. What is the primary reason for ending this spiritual direction relationship?

10. Have you or are you grieving about leaving a spiritual direction relationship? What does it feel like you are losing?

11. What do you sense God is calling you to next?

Spiritual Direction Conversations | 8

It is a good rule of thumb for spiritual directors to ask themselves, What truly constitutes our spiritual concern here? . . . What things are getting in the way of our simple, humble intention towards the working of the Holy Spirit in this person's life? . . . Spiritual direction should deal primarily with those qualities that seem most clearly and specifically spiritual, those that reveal the presence or leadings of God, or evidence of grace, working most directly in a person's life. Thus, it is to be expected that spiritual direction will give primary attention to such things as the directee's inclinations in relation to personal prayer life and other ascetical practices like fasting and simplification of life; to senses of God's presence, absence, or callings; to experiences of fundamental meaning; to personal longings for God; and to the multiplicity of factors that seem most to help or hinder freedom for fullness of living in God's reality. . . . All of life's experiences can appear legitimately in spiritual direction, but they need to be seen in the light of spiritual concern, and at all costs they should not be allowed to eclipse that light.

Gerald G. May[1]

For where two or three come together in my name, there am I with them.

Matthew 18:20

Our attitudes, the subjects discussed, the roles we establish for directors and directees, and the flow of spiritual direction conversations reveal how we are listening to and resisting, following and pulling away from God. Spiritual direction is influenced by everything that has meaning for us—whether we are sad or happy, stressed or relaxed, in healthy or troubled relationships, feeling productive and content or not. Our demeanor substantively shapes what is possible during spiritual direction conversations.

The kind of listening and speaking we want to nurture flourishes best in a low-key, informal environment in which we can relax and remain receptive to God. But that is not always possible. Sometimes we arrive for spiritual direction feeling troubled, excited, or intensely involved in the experiences of the day. We may be full of strong, active thoughts and feelings that seem to work against us at first. Our efforts to curtail our racing thoughts may only distract us further. It is helpful to acknowledge our condition and simply place our churned-up self into God's care. Some of the most beneficial direction conversations take place when we are acutely aware that we need to depend on God in order for anything worthwhile to occur. We invite the Holy Spirit to be with us as we are rather than as we would like to be.

Although we speak about the recent past and reflect on implications for the future, focusing on the present is most important. We want to be fully available to God and to each other when we are together. Our willingness to let everything else that interests us fade into the background significantly influences what we are able to hear and see. (It is embarrassing to realize how seldom we pay undivided attention to anyone or anything.) This quality of attending presence with God and with each other is the foundation of spiritual direction conversations. All topics arise within this context, which is dedicated to listening to God.

Spiritual direction offers a unique perspective in which we seem to walk alongside Jesus or the Holy Spirit, who is our close companion. We ask to observe ourselves in a caring but gently detached way. We want to see what needs attention, and we want to hear what God is saying to us. We also want to notice if we are too hurried to listen to the Holy Spirit or even to our own best advice. We hope that being attuned to God during spiritual direction conversations will help us be more awake and available to listen to God in daily life.

The attitude or atmosphere of direction is as important as its content. Are we hurried, wanting to get through our direction session, or does it seem like a gift that we are reluctant to see come to an end? How are our attitudes during direction representative of the way we live? What mix of hurriedness and savoring characterizes our days? Our alertness to God and each other fluctuates during the course of an hour. We may take mental or conversational side trips. Sometimes we get derailed.

The following dialogue is an example of a direction conversation. Dave described an experience with God, and his feelings and responses drew him and his director toward the mysteries of God. Then they shifted from awe and appreciation to analysis, looking at Dave's experience from many angles. It was not long before they became entangled in the depths of psychology and lost the sense of delight with God with which Dave had entered the hour. They were still talking about God and God-related material, but they had moved toward intense examination and away from the qualities of prayerful conversation.

Director: I think I owe you an apology. I was so interested in your description of your experience that I moved out of my own sense of prayer and listening to the Spirit. I drifted into analyzing what is beyond figuring out. It feels like we went on a strong side trip. What do you think?

Directee: Yes, I'd agree. However, I did have a lot of questions so the analysis seemed helpful when we began. But when our probing took the focus in a completely different direction, some of the aliveness seemed to dim. I lost my sense of how sacred it really was and my sense of God's presence with us, which I was so conscious of when we started. That makes me feel a little sad.

Director: Is there some way that seems right for you to respect your experience and continue to enjoy it with God?

Directee: I think maybe journaling and private prayer are better for me than talking about it now.

Director: That sounds right.

Directee: Thanks for ending the sidetrack. It felt like a huge relief to get out of that dissecting mode. It almost felt like someone or something wanted to distract me or diminish my sense of how intimate and deeply affirming my experience was with God. I am grateful for how God was with me. I don't ever want to forget how that felt.

Director: Maybe we could be quiet for a few minutes, return to prayer, and see what God has in mind. You can reopen the conversation when you are ready.

Topics of Discussion

Directees most often choose the topics of discussion. Choosing what to talk about is one way of communicating what has meaning and significance for them and their readiness for specific topics. It takes courage, willingness, and the right timing to speak out of that place where they are friends with God—out of their heart.

Directees talk about numerous facets of their Divine/human relationship. They talk about their experiences with God and their ideas about God, when they sense that God loves them and when they wonder if God has forgotten or dislikes them. They describe where they are aware of grace and where they feel they are at an impasse or are confused, angry, disappointed, or sad. Directees talk about prayer and many other ways they seek God. They speak about what they do to encourage their own love, willingness, and desire to listen to and follow God.

Directees talk a great deal about prayer in spiritual direction because their first priority is to pray about whatever they are noticing, learning, questioning. Prayer is the way they intentionally open and offer themselves to listen to and respond to God. Directees also speak about anything that has meaning for them and that can help them notice how God is a part of every aspect of their lives. They speak about:

> God and themselves as the Lord's person, child, daughter, son, follower, servant, beloved friend, disciple.
>
> the characteristics of their prayer and relationship with God.
>
> their sense of God's love and their desire to respond with ever growing love.
>
> their sense of having no feelings in relation to God or negative ones.
>
> God and Scripture and themselves—which Scripture passages seem to be speaking directly to them and how they are responding, and the pattern of their reading and study and ways of interpretation.
>
> God and their relationships with others—what the Spirit is teaching them or asking of them through relationships with family members, friends, and associates, people they get along with and people they do not. Matters related to sexuality, gender, and sex also become part of direction conversations (chapter 5, "Preparing for Spiritual Direction"). Chapter 15, "Common Areas of Difficulty," includes material about ways that sexuality can become a distraction in spiritual direction.
>
> God and organizations—churches, schools, workplaces, and social groupings.
>
> God and work—God's work, their work, others' work.
>
> God and the world.

When directees listen for the Spirit's invitations, they often sense what needs to remain in the private intimacy of their love with God and what they are to talk about. Anything that prompts directees to listen to and consider God can become part of a spiritual direction conversation.

The Flow of Direction Conversations

Directors pray before directees arrive, asking to be awake to the Holy Spirit's presence and to put aside any personal concerns. Directors pray in whatever ways seem appropriate related to their own circumstances. This often includes prayer acknowledging any expectations they have for the hour ahead and offering them to God. Through prayer directors place themselves at the Holy Spirit's disposal.

Most spiritual direction sessions begin with shared recognition of both participants' desire to hear the Holy Spirit. Sessions may begin with prayer, including silent or audible prayer by one person or both, or a Scripture reading that sets the tone.

Then the directee begins the conversation. Some direction partners plan for a few minutes of silence after the directee has finished telling his or her story before the director responds. Either person may ask for a quiet or audible prayer interlude whenever it feels appropriate. Appreciation for insight and for God may evoke prayers of gratitude. If the partners feel anxious, confused, or blocked, they may want to pause to pray—to ask God to show them what their feelings indicate, or simply to offer themselves again to God.

Sometimes we build defenses against the Holy Spirit and work against ourselves because we are ambivalent about wanting to see what God is revealing. Even when we speak about important topics, they are not always what we most need to discuss, and we know it. We try to do the best we can and then trust God's grace. Whether what we talk about is central or peripheral in our relationship with God, our willingness to speak with another person about it and welcome God's presence and perspectives seem to be all that is required.

At least a part of us wants to be free to acknowledge and move beyond our limited desire, biases, and resistance to recognize and follow God. The action of starting where we are able to be authentic, no matter where that is, opens the way to our hearts and increases the likelihood of hearing the Holy Spirit.

During any direction conversation, both persons move in and out of attention, prayer, and listening to the Spirit and each other. We sense our own wanderings. Some of this is the normal fluctuation that occurs during any conversation. At times, however, our wandering indicates avoidance of what we need to discuss or hindrances that distract us from our deepest intentions to hear and follow God. We are influenced by our inclinations to take charge and by numerous other distractions—things that catch our eyes or ears or thoughts and draw us to other matters. When we see ourselves moving off or that we have been away from our sense of God or the other person, we intentionally offer our hearts and attention to God and the conversation and ask for grace to reenter the dialogue.

From beginning to end, true spiritual direction is most dependent on God's love for us and God's desire to be the way and show the way.

The Directee's Role

Directees who are anticipating a spiritual direction session find themselves in an interesting dilemma. They may be thinking about something that is going on with God that is of particular interest to them but at the same time know the primary goal of direction is to address what the Spirit brings to their attention. They want to address their questions and also remain open to the Holy Spirit's leading.

Whatever vitally interests us may or may not be what God knows we need to notice and discuss. Our willingness to listen to God and speak authentically is our part. God does the rest.

Sometimes recalling a story and telling portions of it to a director reveal a great deal about our relationship with God. We may remember that we received healing, help, or guidance through previous direction conversations when we spoke about topics we had no plans to address. At other times the questions we attempted to surrender by not discussing them became the ones the Spirit drew us to in ways we could not have anticipated. The issue in not setting an agenda is one of relinquishment. It is not so much about particular subjects we will or will not discuss as it is about inquiring whether we will trust God to provide for us in spiritual direction. Sometimes it is easy to invite the Holy Spirit to order the time and sometimes it is difficult.

Directees usually speak more during direction sessions than directors. After prayer, directees begin talking. Their words represent what their relationship with God has been like since the last session. Sometimes directees describe their sense of aloneness, wondering whether they are still cooperating with the Holy Spirit as fully as they might because they have little or no sense of God's presence, grace, or peacefulness. At other times directees are conscious of being in close companionship with the Lord. They may have discovered or rediscovered concrete evidences of God's love, presence, and provision.

Whatever directees speak about becomes a window through which they hope to see what God is saying and becomes a place to begin. The Spirit of God can steer their prayer and conversation to where they are in need of divine leading, teaching, restoration, comfort, or guidance. The Holy Spirit is able to draw directees to where they need to be through even small amounts of willingness and surrender on their part. Sometimes they are surprised by what they hear themselves saying. The following direction conversation is an example of a directee talking about a special experience.

Directee: That was an incredible vacation. It felt like we were present in the midst of the creation of the world. It was more than I could have anticipated and felt like a direct answer to prayer. You probably remember when my mother was dying and I was physically and emotionally exhausted from walking alongside her, helping where I could, and I asked God if we could go on a real vacation when it was over. But this opportunity came out of the blue. I read in a magazine about a comet that was supposed to be the only one visible in my lifetime. It would only be visible from Hawaii, Australia, and a few other places I thought I had no chance of visiting. I told God about how much I would love to see that comet but never imagined I would.

But God knew better. What a surprise. My husband received an award that included a trip to Hawaii. So we were there—on top of the Haleakala Crater on the island of Maui at 3:00 in the morning looking at a spectacular stellar show and a comet visible to the naked eye. Through a telescope we could see the comet and its tail trailing across the sky. We saw countless stars. I cannot describe the vast beauty. This was followed by a sunrise that transformed the volcanic crater. Amazing. And as if that wasn't enough, the next day when we went snorkeling, a hundred dolphins came to swim with us.

Director: How did that make you feel?

Directee: Extravagantly loved by God. Grateful—and astonished. But why would God be so lavish? You know I've been trying to learn to be more careful about resources, and suddenly it's like God pulled out all the stops.

Director: Why do you think that might be so?

Directee: I don't know, but maybe God is trying to show me that it's not always right to conserve, that we should be lavish with some things—like love. And that it gives God pleasure to bless us. I know I did not do anything to deserve what felt like God's special attention. But I did enjoy it. When I get discouraged, I think about that day, which felt like God was near and we were celebrating with the whole creation. It helps me to remember God loves me and to open my heart and thoughts to God.

Trying to put into words what is beyond words helps us recognize heretofore unnoticed aspects of our relationship with God and triggers insights that seem different from those that arise in solitary prayer, Scripture study, or worship.

The Director's Role

Directors are prayer-listeners. They may listen for long periods of time without speaking or respond in a back and forth dialogue. There are advantages and disadvantages to both interaction patterns. When directees tell their stories without interruption, themes may become apparent that would not have been recognized as easily through a piecemeal presentation. Speaking at length without interruption can elicit new insights and possibilities. Sometimes, however, when a directee gives lengthy, detailed accounts, a director can become confused by the quantity of material. When a directee's story is long and complex, a back and forth dialogue may be better. Sensitive directors pray about the God-invited pattern of their interaction, which may differ from one session to another. Each direction conversation takes on qualities that are suitable for a particular time.

Richard Foster describes the director's role clearly when he says, "His direction is simply and clearly to lead us to our real Director. He is the means of God to open the path to the inward teaching of the Holy Spirit."[2] Directors listen, pray, and reflect on what directees communicate verbally and nonverbally and also look for what never seems to enter the conversation. Directors pray even while directees are speaking, sometimes about specific things but more often in a way of intentionally offering themselves and the direction conversation to God.

Some directors take notes. They write down what directees say or ideas that arise as they pray and listen. They may note questions they would like to ask later. By writing down these reminders, they are able to continue listening to directees without interrupting while also making sure they will not forget about these potential questions. They allow the questions and information to remain in the background in their prayer.

Because directors do not want merely to give their own opinion about what directees are saying, they will often plan for a few moments of silence before responding in order to pray and consider where God is taking the conversation. When spiritual directors notice they are moving toward an area that a directee has not mentioned, they pray about what to do. Should they pray only? Should they offer leading questions that could draw the directee into a new topic? Should they wait until the directee talks about it?

When directors speak, they mirror back to the directees what they think they are hearing as a way of checking perceptions. "From what I've heard it seems that this is what you have been saying to me. Is that right? Do you want to add anything?" Directors use many communication skills to help directees hear what the Spirit is saying. Directors' responses include what we have already mentioned: prayer, teaching, questioning, comforting, discerning, and guiding to and through Scripture. Directors help directees recognize how their prayer and life experiences are interconnected and to see how God is participating with them.

Sometimes directors feel strongly that God is asking them *not* to speak about particular areas. This may be because it is not yet time or the Lord is bringing the directee to new insights in other ways. Directors may not know why they feel hesitant, but they bring their sense of caution into prayer and wait for God. God's desired timing is essential. Waiting for the Spirit of God is not always comfortable. We often want to pay attention to an area as soon as we recognize it. But willing waiting is at the heart of spiritual direction. If directors open areas too soon, their observations could hinder a directee's developing dependency on God. Directors pray that their responses will enhance what is genuinely of God and that nothing will be said or done that could be harmful.

Spiritual direction is most effective when it is a nondirective process. Max Thurian, a monk of the Taize Community in France, says:

> Spiritual direction, which is non-directive, as it is known in psychological language today, is more beneficial to the directee. This technique calls for the director to listen and to refuse directly to intervene in an authoritarian and outright manner, so that the person in direction may more easily discover for himself by prayer and reflection enlightened by the Word of God, what the will of the Holy Spirit is for him. Christian spiritual direction does not seek to impose itself on a person and thus makes itself in the end expendable.[3]

Spiritual direction is a way of supporting and encouraging the faith journey. The issues, questions, confusion, or sense of God's grace that directees speak about arise out of the context of all areas of life. No matter what comes up for discussion, a director wishes to focus on how God is involved. "How are you praying about this? What do you think God is saying to you? How are you experiencing grace? What makes you feel or think that God is not present or does not care about this or about you?" Questions such as these are at the core of the director's role in spiritual direction.

Bringing Spiritual Direction Conversations to a Close

The characteristic qualities of the persons involved in direction, the consistency and characteristics of their prayer, their ways of working together, and the nature of the content they explore influence their time together and the outcomes of direction.

At the end of a session, directors may suggest Scripture passages or ways of praying or encourage directees to notice God's presence in daily life. They talk about whatever came to the forefront through their time together.

Direction sessions often end with prayer, which takes many forms: individual or shared, silent or audible. These prayers recognize the Holy

Spirit as the primary spiritual director and release directees and their journeys into God's care. After a direction conversation, the partners go their separate ways to discern and follow what they believe God invites and intends.

Reflections

1. Take a few minutes to quiet yourself and offer this time to God. Then look at the list of direction conversation topics on page 132. Write in your journal about particular areas, situations, issues, and relationships that draw you to prayer and that you might consider discussing in spiritual direction. Is there a kind of aliveness or interest around any of what you have written that makes you wonder if the Holy Spirit is prompting you to look at something more closely? What does this say to you?
2. What do you perceive about your own receptivity and resistance with God generally and/or about any of the particular areas you have written about above? Remember this is *neutral* information. Bring it into prayer and ask God about it.
3. What seems appealing or not appealing about
    telling your entire story?
    interacting through back and forth dialogue?
4. What questions do you have related to spiritual direction?

Three conditions are essential to the life of the group. Members must agree to commit themselves to 1) an honest relationship with God; 2) wholehearted participation in the group processes through prayerful listening and response; and 3) opening their spiritual journeys to the consideration of others.

Rose Mary Dougherty[1]

As iron sharpens iron,
so one person sharpens another.

Proverbs 27:17 NIV ILE

Some group spiritual direction is intentional and some is serendipitous. We worship with other Christians, hoping to hear a meaningful word from God that is particularly appropriate for us. We listen carefully for such a word through all aspects of the service: music, Scripture readings, prayers, preaching, and silence. We participate in study groups and classes desiring to understand what God intends for Christians generally and for us in particular.

Many congregations offer small and large group opportunities for study, prayer, fellowship, and support for people who are grieving or addressing addictions or other life challenges. Participation in groups offers opportunities for encouragement and building meaningful relationships. Such participation may also include aspects of spiritual direction.

We receive spiritual direction indirectly and informally through others by observing how they affirm and nurture their relationship with God in the midst of daily routines and challenges. We notice our own lives, behaviors, and practices and consider how they are similar to and different from what we observe in other people of faith.

Our family provides a kind of spiritual direction by both negative and positive examples. As we grow up in biological or blended families and live in dormitory, apartment, or other communal living arrangements, we are shaped and influenced by those around us. Family members, friends, and associates with whom we interact on a regular basis also influence us.

Spiritual direction is more likely to be part of group life, however, when attention is given to questions such as, "How does God or grace seem to be a part of this?" or "What do you suppose God thinks about what we are doing?" or "How does this seem when you pray about it?" There is some *intentional* focus on listening for the Holy Spirit.

Intentional spiritual direction can be an added dimension to the already familiar group ways of caring for our own and others' needs, hopes, and fears. Church committees and boards tend toward spiritual direction or group discernment when they structure helpful means for listening to the Spirit. One way to do this is to plan ongoing prayer during the meeting. One committee member prays silently for ten to fifteen minutes and then passes the prayer on to the next person. When a person is the designated pray-er, that person does not participate in the conversation but prays about whatever is taking place.[2]

Spiritual direction in groups is similar to one-to-one spiritual direction in all central aspects. The same open, prayerful attentiveness, willingness, and desire to listen with each other for God characterizes group spiritual direction conversations.

Who Comes to Group Spiritual Direction?

Group spiritual direction, like individual direction, is for people who express their desire and readiness for *more*—they long for more of God. They want to sense God's presence and enjoy a relationship with God that has a moment-by-moment aliveness. They may think that grace from God flows constantly toward them, but they wish to be more aware of it and to respond more directly. They are or would like to be intentional about their life with God, their spiritual journey, and their commitment.

Some of the same people we mentioned in chapter 3, "Who Comes to Spiritual Direction?" also take part in group direction. They include people who are feeling restless or challenged, in transition, looking for companions on the spiritual journey, having spiritual experiences that are different from what they've known before, exploring questions about discernment, dealing with a loss, or responding to information about spiritual direction.

But group spiritual direction is not suitable for everyone who is interested in direction because of the limited amount of time that is set aside for each person. When people are living through difficult seasons of life, one-to-one spiritual direction, counseling, or both may be necessary. Spiritual direction is not psychological therapy and spiritual direction groups are not intended to be therapy groups.

It is important for potential group members to think and pray about what is suitable for them at a given time. Sometimes responding to a simple questionnaire such as the one in the reflections section at the end of this chapter is a useful discernment exercise. Each person in a spiritual direction group needs to be the focus of the group's prayer and listening for a specified period of time and then to pray and listen to God and others. People who are in the midst of a crisis may tend to be overly self-focused and distressed and turn the conversation toward themselves even when it is someone else's turn. It is important for potential group members to be forthright with other potential group members to determine if group spiritual direction is what is appropriate for them.

The Dynamics of Group Spiritual Direction

What happens in group spiritual direction? The same things we have said about one-to-one direction—prayerful listening for how the Spirit of God is present and active, bringing our perceptions and interpretations of our experience to light, clarifying, asking questions, reflecting back to one another what we see and hear. Out of these conversations God brings comfort, restoration, renewal, healing, and energizing. The Spirit points toward resources and supports us in our desire to live lives completely open to God and helps us experience, express, and appreciate the generosity of God.

In both one-to-one and small group direction, we are sidetracked at times by trying to answer each other's questions or resolve issues rather than prayerfully opening ourselves to the Holy Spirit's presence and responses. It is both a disadvantage and an advantage to participate in a larger group. There are more people to take the group on tangential paths, but there are also more people available to recognize side trips and gently invite us to turn our attention toward God.

One of the essential aspects necessary for group spiritual direction is the willingness to adopt a more contemplative attitude toward ourselves, God, and each other. Rather than offering each other our best advice and experience, we want to hear what the Spirit of God intends. Direction groups offer a kind of sanctuary from the usual advice-giving stance people tend to take with each other and encourage everyone in the group to let go of managing themselves so they can be more available to listen to God.

Some people confuse spiritual *formation* groups with *direction* groups. A spiritual formation group can be used to support our spiritual journey by introducing us to a range of spiritual disciplines through teaching, experimentation with different ways of prayer, and other spiritual disciplines and reflection. A formation group may provide support, learning, and some measure of accountability, but it does not usually offer the contemplative quality of listening for the Spirit's presence and invitations in each person's life, which is the purpose of group spiritual direction. There are benefits and limitations to whatever kind of group we choose.

A spiritual direction group provides a place where people can meet with others who choose to be intentional about their spiritual life. Many people feel isolated in their quest for God and are grateful for opportunities for ongoing prayer and conversation with others who are interested in pursuing similar desires. Group spiritual direction can be a welcoming place to experiment with listening for the Holy Spirit with others. Being with other people who are also trying to explore their relationship with God can encourage us to recognize that we are not alone or peculiar. Speaking and listening to others speak about life with God often show us that we share a commonality of experience.

We hear about others' struggles, perceptions, ideas, feelings about God, and challenges in relationships with other people. Group spiritual direction can bring a humbling awareness that human life is fairly unpredictable—we have mixed motivations and limitations—and God comes to us, loves us, strengthens and guides us in remarkable ways. Listening to moments of grace in other people's lives can awaken us to God's presence and participation in our own.

The call to authenticity with God and others awakens attraction and reluctance at the same time. It can feel like we are giving up some freedom rather than moving toward greater freedom in Christ when we reveal our true thoughts and feelings. Yet I have discovered through my own experience and listening to directees that God is more likely to meet us where we are—where our hearts and minds are thoughtfully engaged and where our meaningful questions and feelings reside. Hiding from our difficulties, even with God, obscures many joys. And hiding our true self draws energy away from the present—energy that can enrich daily life.

Differences between Individual and Group Spiritual Direction

There are differences between individual and group direction that can be perceived as benefits, limitations, or simply differences. A one-to-one direction session is not for both persons in the same way. In one-to-one direction conversations both people listen to the Holy Spirit but for the benefit of one of them. Directors willingly set aside whatever interests, concerns, and questions they have about their own relationship with God to give attention to God and directees.

Some spiritual direction groups are guided by a facilitator. When this is the case, the person who is acting as the facilitator does not receive spiritual direction in the group. The facilitator structures the group's time together and sees that guidelines are observed so that the intended prayerfulness is supported and nourished. The facilitator helps the group maintain an open, prayerful environment and invites the group to prayerful attentiveness toward God and away from offering advice.[3] The facilitator is prayerfully available to listen to God and the members of the group but is not the spiritual director for the group. The group is the director. Rather than taking any responsibility for structuring the time, group members are prayerful listeners.

In contrast to this, in a group without an outside facilitator, group members take turns overseeing the group. All members also take a turn as the directee, and the entire group functions as the spiritual director for one another. Every group member participates in all three roles.

Group spiritual direction embodies a deep mutuality in God. We both give and receive direction and have a sense that we need and desire to do both. It feels good to make space for attending to what is most important to us. We may not need each other's advice nearly as much as we need each other's prayer and prayerful understanding and affirmation. When we are able to settle into a place where we feel loved and chosen by God, we are often able to notice what the Spirit of God is saying to us. The group's prayerful support encourages us to be less controlling and willing to depend more on God.

Another difference between individual and group direction is that the diversity of personalities naturally increases when more people are involved. Freedom to express ourselves fully in a direction group is influenced by the members of the group as well as how many members are in the group. Increasing group size limits in some ways and enriches in others. The more people in the group, the more personal concerns and needs, communication skills, human dynamics, and considerations of group life we encounter. This is a large topic that cannot be covered in depth in this context. The bibliography at the back of the book includes resources for small groups.

Group spiritual direction works best with three or four people. Three is large enough for diversity, and four is small enough so that everyone can still be the directee for twenty to thirty minutes. Some people tend to feel rushed if they have only twenty minutes to talk. Groups with as many as six members can work if group members each have only twenty minutes or if they speak about their life with God every other time. Such groups may choose to meet twice a month so each person has a turn once a month.

We might think that spiritual direction in a group setting would feel disjointed because of the varieties of topics presented by group members. In practice, however, it does not seem to work out that way. Group members decide what they wish to share through their own prayer and reflection independently of one another, yet they are often surprised to recognize a recurring theme throughout their conversation. It does not always happen this way, but whatever occurs seems to have a unity about it. Perhaps this reflects that everyone is inviting God's presence and intends to be open to the Holy Spirit. Listening to one another and the Spirit of God often awakens our awareness of our common humanity.

Because there are a number of people in the group, at times we are more or less attuned to what is going on with the directee. As a group we are giving this person full attention, but individually we will not experience exactly the same kind, degree, or quality of attention throughout the meeting.

The gifts of God's grace in and to others in such a group become lenses for recognizing the faithfulness of God present in our own pilgrimage. Sometimes when we are acting in the role of director we may receive direction. At times it is possible to be more open to God about some of our concerns when we are listening to someone else. We hear different things when we feel no need to protect ourselves or justify our ways of looking at God or our experiences. Through listening to someone else's story we begin to remember or recognize meaningful aspects of our story. We may discover that the Spirit of God is speaking to us or simply loving us differently because we are less self-protective and more receptive. When this happens in group spiritual direction, we thank God for touching us but then return to our role as a director by offering ourselves to the Holy Spirit and listening to others as they speak. This added dimension of noticing how the work of the Spirit in another member speaks to our own heart is a bonus of group spiritual direction.

Making a Choice Regarding Group Spiritual Direction

Group spiritual direction? Individual spiritual direction? Which should we choose? Or are we feeling called to participate in both individual and group spiritual direction for a period of time? Potential directees prayerfully explore the options. They may also consider whether they are being called to group spiritual direction or another kind of group that is characterized by discipling, spiritual formation, mentoring, study, intercessory or contemplative prayer, or a particular kind of support.

Spiritual direction groups may be short- or long-term. We may participate in a direction group as a onetime experience or decide to make a longer commitment of nine to twelve months. Sometimes there are appropriate ways to "try on" group spiritual direction such as at a retreat. This kind of opportunity may help us understand what group spiritual direction entails and discern whether God is inviting us to participate.

It is important for those who choose group spiritual direction to know what it is and how it differs from other Christian helping relationships such as discipling, mentoring, and pastoral counseling. Those who are interested can read and discuss chapter 1, "What Is Spiritual Direction?" Or one person can read this chapter and teach others about spiritual direction. Those who are interested in becoming part of a spiritual direction group need to pray about what they have learned and begin a process of discernment to clarify whether spiritual direction is something to which God is drawing them. They need to explore their hopes, desires, and motivations. The decision to participate in group direction needs to be an informed choice made in the context of prayer.[4]

Organizing the Group

There is more than one way to provide for group spiritual direction, but whichever way we choose should take the following factors into account. At the inception of the group, potential members need to:

agree to participate with each other in a spiritual direction group of three to six people for a set length of time at a particular place and at particular intervals (e.g., once a month on Tuesday evenings for eight months from 7:00–9:30 at church).

discuss what spiritual direction is and share expectations, intentions, and hopes.

agree to protect the confidentiality of what is shared in the group.

decide on any commitments they wish to make regarding prayer for each other or the practice of Christian disciplines.

arrange for leadership responsibility and decide how group spiritual direction sessions will be organized including:

- choosing a structure: a group in which one person serves as the facilitator, a group with a facilitator that meets with a gathering of several direction groups before meeting separately, an independent group that practices mutual spiritual direction with group members taking turns as the facilitator

- providing for a prayerful, welcoming environment

- determining the amount of time each person will have to describe what is going on in his or her relationship with God and receive the prayerful attention of the group

- identifying what kinds of feedback are appropriate and when

- discussing how they will acknowledge and invite God's presence and assist each other and the group to remain openly attentive to the Spirit of God and each other

- considering any other planning they think could support effective group spiritual direction

Many different arrangements for group spiritual direction can work well. The following pages provide three examples of group arrangements.

Joan, Susan, Sandy, and Carole decided to begin a spiritual direction group together after conversation and prayer. They learned about group spiritual direction through one of the members of the group, and they decided on a home-based group. When they come together, after initial greetings they serve a meal and eat in silence, perhaps with background music. The time of silence serves as a transition from the activities of the day to their intention to listen to God together. They usually allow for an hour of silence including the mealtime before they begin sharing. Their time together includes the following:

> They offer prayers of thanksgiving and petition in which they ask God to guide and order the conversation and reveal what they need to see.
>
> Each directee has thirty minutes, which she divides as she desires, to tell her story, participate in silent reflection, and hear responses. A clock is placed in front of the directee during her turn so she can monitor her use of the time. Directees usually speak for ten to twenty minutes before the group moves into a few minutes of silence and then responds.
>
> One of the group members facilitates by asking group members to be silent to consider what they might say and to pray. After a few minutes the facilitator invites the group to respond to what they have heard.
>
> When it seems appropriate, the group takes a short break between presentations, particularly if they sense they are tired from listening intently. They walk around, get a cup of coffee or stretch, offer what has transpired to God, and prepare to hear the next person.
>
> When everyone has had a turn, the group closes with prayer. Sometimes everyone prays, sometimes not. At times the group prays about specific situations that have been the topic of individual presentations or they gather around one of the group members and pray with and for her.
>
> They schedule their next meeting before departing. They do not meet unless everyone is able to attend. If an emergency arises and one member of the group cannot come, they reschedule.

Tom, Joe, Marilyn, and Karen are in a spiritual direction group that grew out of a direction group at a retreat. When they saw how the Spirit blessed them, they decided to continue meeting once a month for the next nine months. Their pattern of prayerful listening to presentations interspersed with silence and feedback is similar to that of the first group.

Except for initial greetings, social conversation is saved for the end of the direction session. They do this as a way to express their shared intention to use this group to encourage and support each other in their desires to hear and follow God. They know they could be sidetracked into many tangential conversations because their lives are full, interesting, and challenging. So they begin with what they came for and catch up on other news later.

They do not share a meal together, and they take turns serving as the facilitator. The facilitator begins the session with prayer, inviting the group to be open to the Holy Spirit, and keeps track of the time so that each person has an opportunity to speak. When all group members have had a turn, they pray together. Then they take a few minutes to talk about the general qualities and content of their time together, what the Spirit seems to be saying to them, and where they did and did not remain prayerfully attentive to one another and to God.

Don, Carl, Mike, and Sam are part of a spiritual direction group that meets as part of a ministry offered at their church. Several direction groups meet simultaneously at the same location. This year twelve groups are meeting from September to May. They all attended a one-day retreat that set the stage for the rest of the year. Each group is guided by a facilitator.

The evening begins with announcements and twenty to thirty minutes with the entire group, which is used as a starting place for the evening's direction sessions. The large group gathering includes Scripture reading, opportunities for audible and/or silent prayer, and perhaps a guided meditation—whatever the leader chooses as a foundation for the evening's groups. After the time together, the group members go silently to their group meeting places desiring to remain in the spirit of prayer with which they have begun. The groups usually contain four people, and each person has thirty minutes of the group's time. They follow a pattern similar to the groups already described, alternating presentations and silence. A typical time schedule for a group spiritual direction session might be:

5–20 minutes: Scripture reading, prayer, quiet time as a way of preparing to listen to God and each other

30 minutes for each directee divided as follows:
- 15 minutes for oral presentation
- 2–4 minutes of silence, prayer, and reflection before members respond
- 10 minutes of group feedback and conversation
- 2–4 minutes of silence, journaling, prayer

The pattern of silence, presentation, silence, feedback, and silence is repeated with each directee.[5]

Participants in one-to-one and group spiritual direction possess the same intentions, attitudes, and goals. Both modes of direction help us pay closer attention to how God is present and active. Individual and group spiritual direction are neither more nor less than the other; they are different forms of the same ministry. Sometimes the Spirit invites us toward one, sometimes toward another, and occasionally toward both.[6]

Group spiritual direction may make it possible to offer spiritual direction within a faith community in which many people would like to participate but few have identified that God is calling them as directors. Group spiritual direction can also seem a less threatening way for many people to be introduced to spiritual direction. Group spiritual direction provides a supportive context in which to learn more about spiritual direction and prayerfully ask whether God is inviting us to participate in direction as an ongoing spiritual discipline as a directee, director, or both.

Reflections

1. What attracts you to group spiritual direction?
2. Where do you talk about what is important to you? How do you provide for your own nurture? How much energy and commitment are you willing to invest in this group? Is it too much or too little, or does it seem the right amount?
3. Are there any circumstances in your life right now that are taking up large amounts of your time and energy? What are they? How might they influence your ability to share in a group without dominating it?
4. Have you previously tried to speak in a group about your relationship with God? How did that go? What experiences have you had with other prayer, sharing, and study groups?
5. Are you likely to be able to meet with this group according to its proposed schedule?
6. What are possible drawbacks to participating in a spiritual direction group?
7. Is the Spirit of God inviting you to group spiritual direction? What brings you to this conclusion?

PART 2

Subjects Frequently Considered in Spiritual Direction

Love (III)

Love bade me welcome: yet my soul drew back,
    Guilty of dust and sin.
  But quick-ey'd Love, observing me grow slack
    From my first entrance in,
  Drew nearer to me, sweetly questioning,
    If I lack'd anything.

A guest, I answer'd, worthy to be here:
    Love said, You shall be he.
  I the unkind, ungrateful? Ah my dear,
    I cannot look on thee.
  Love took my hand, and smiling did reply,
    Who made the eyes but I?

Truth Lord, but I have marr'd them: let my shame
    Go where it doth deserve.
  And know you not, says Love, who bore the blame?
    My dear, then I will serve.
  You must sit down, says Love, and taste my meat:
    So I did sit and eat.

George Herbert[1]

I have said this before and I would say it many, many times, for fear seriously constrains people who do not wholly understand God's goodness by personal experience, although they know it by faith. It is truly a wonderful thing to know by experience the friendship and the tenderness with which he treats those who go by this road and to see how he defrays, as it were, all the expenses of the journey. . . . That is the wonderful thing about this journey: one is given more than one ever asks or even dreams of desiring. This is absolutely certain; I know it to be true. If you should find it untrue, never believe anything else I tell you.

Teresa of Avila[1]

Thus the Lord used to speak to Moses face to face, as one speaks to a friend.

Exodus 33:11 NRSV

Directors and directees often pray about and seek to understand their experiences with God. We may wonder if that is possible. Interpreting Scripture can seem so much safer than attempting to interpret experience. People ask, "Am I supposed to experience God—to have direct encounters with God? Is this something I am willing to explore? What do I think God is like? What are my childhood and present pictures of God? What names for God are familiar to me based on my background?"

Our affiliations influence what and how we think about relationships, other individuals, and ourselves. But our thoughts about relationships and our experiences with others are not the same thing. This is also true of our relationship with God. We can think about God, observe manifestations of God in the world, watch others participate in the life of faith, or choose to communicate and interact intentionally with God.

We interpret our relationship with God through our mind. Our thoughts are influenced by turning our mind toward God in repentance, asking God to forgive and enliven us. Part of the newness made available by our surrender to God is freedom to think more like Christ. Of course, we are still capable of self-centered thinking and misunderstandings and misinterpretations, but people who are in a relationship with Jesus have a renewed capacity to recognize and cooperate with God's desires. We discover that we suddenly and gradually have new interests, perceptions, and opinions in many areas. Our minds experience renewing effects of grace (1 Cor. 2:16).

Many people pay attention to what they think about God and what they observe in other people of faith but pay little or no attention to their *direct experiences* with God. Such a relationship is more like sending and receiving letters rather than being in face-to-face contact. Directees are challenged to notice their own experiences with God rather than paying attention to only what they have read or heard from others.

Intellectual analysis is important but so are other aspects. We experience and relate to God as whole persons involving all our faculties: intellect, will, imagination, emotions, memory, and bodily responses. In chapter 14, "Christian Disciplines," we deal more fully with these factors.

Our Interpretation of God

We have an assorted collection of memories, ideas, and experiences. We have a mental picture of God and an interpretation of what we think God is like and how God feels about us. Ann Ulanov said,

> Picturing God must precede any speaking about God, for our pictures accompany all our words and they continue long after we fall silent before God. Images—the language of the psyche—are the coin of life; they touch our emotions as well as our thoughts; they reach down into our bodies as well as toward our ideas. They arrive unbidden, startling, after our many years of effort to craft them.
>
> We keep our pictures of God secret from each other and often even from ourselves. For what would others think if we talked of God as a stalking animal, sniffing us like prey, or as an alien, a foreigner whose breath is upon our face, or whose foot is on our neck? What of a God so palpable and near that only an abstract symbol can make it bearable? . . . What of God, as the psalmist says, with great wings under which we hide? Or God's grace like a large lap into which we crawl, a breast upon which we lean? Or God a warrior calling us out to fight? Or God as Jesus sitting in the back pew of your church?[2]

Dr. David Seamands has written extensively about how people's childhood perceptions of God influence their present responses to God. Whether these perceptions are welcoming or threatening becomes an important factor in adulthood. It is essential to uncover and address hidden feelings, ideas, and suspicions about God. For some, God is primarily a resident policeman or wrathful judge, a God with impossible requirements and demands. For others, the emphasis is on *my* God—God of my understanding, my success, my comfort, my nation.

We tend to remake God according to a number of distorted images, which is one of the reasons the incarnation is so important. Only when the Word became human was it possible for us to see a clear view of God "full of grace and truth" (John 1:14). Seamands writes, "Wrong conceptions/feelings about God lead to various kinds of spiritual problems. Some of the most common are: the inability to feel forgiven, the inability to trust and surrender to God, chronic doubt and problems with neurotic perfectionism."[3] The good news about God often becomes distorted through unhealthy interpersonal relationships, especially those that occurred during the developmental years of childhood and adolescence.

Carl's family had nothing to do with church or Christianity while he was growing up, and no one in the family talked about God. He sensed there were hidden secrets, and he knew not to inquire. He listened to other kids at school and wondered why some talked as if God were their friend, and others used the word *God* as a swear word.

Polly, who is now an adult, read all seven books of The Chronicles of Narnia when she was eleven and was enthralled by the stories. At that time someone asked her why she thought the books had been written. She said, "Maybe to teach people about God. But I hope not, because my family doesn't believe in God." This year she has been reading the stories to her eight-year-old and her own questions have begun to stir again, as they did when she was a child.

Tony is in his thirties. When he was a child, his mother always told him, "God is watching you. Even if I can't see you, God can. You'd better act right." Now he thinks about her words and smiles knowing she was trying to control him. But he also wonders, "Is there a God? Does God watch me? And, if so, what does God think about me? Does God like me?" Some days Tony doesn't like himself very much, but on the whole he thinks he's an okay guy.

On the other hand, many people have childhood memories of sensing God's presence, being taught about God, and knowing that God loved them and would always accompany them throughout life.

Karen recounts childhood experiences of faith with gratitude and pleasure. She says her family never had extra financial resources, but Karen remembers countless times when her father said, "God will provide." And God did. To this day she relies on the God who provides and enjoys telling her own stories about God's generous love.

Ralph talks about his family and how much fun they had in their church. The church welcomed everyone in the neighborhood and planned events that included people who did not come to their church, or any church, on Sunday morning. He remembers being told, "This is what God is like—inviting and welcoming everyone. This is what Jesus is like—inviting us to come to get to know him. We do not need to be afraid." It was natural for him as he reached teen years to run to rather than away from God with questions, because he was sure God would be glad to see him.

Barbara describes lying on a beach blanket with her mom and dad on summer nights, looking at the stars, and talking about what they saw and about God and heaven. Her mom said, "Look at everything God has made. We cannot begin to imagine what it will be like when we die and go to be with God. I think we'll travel to galaxies we cannot see. The Bible says, 'No eye has seen, no ear has heard what God has prepared for those who love him' [1 Cor. 2:9]. I wonder what it will be like." Barbara says these conversations shaped her attitudes and anticipations.

John says, "When I was a little person, I just seemed to know God was near me. I do not recall how I decided this was God, but God and I would have long conversations. I acted like God was my best friend. It is difficult for me to remember some of the nuances of that now, but I know I felt like I had my best buddy with me no matter what."

Most of us remember some good, some confusing, and some negative factors in what we understood about God when we were young. Many people begin to look more closely at what they have heard and explore what they believe when they reach adolescence and adulthood. Simplistic explanations are no longer sufficient.

Many unchosen factors in life, including aspects of our personalities and childhood, dispose us toward particular ideas about God. But there are also chosen aspects in our distorted views of God. At times we choose self-serving responses to God and others, hold on to bitterness and unforgiveness, or deliberately decide to ignore or act counter to what we believe God desires. Life situations may cause us to consider or reconsider who God is and how God participates in human life—particularly when evil seems to be stronger than good.

Rhonda says, "How do you expect me to think God is good? Our family has always gone to church, and now my eighteen-year-old daughter has disappeared. Why would God let this happen? Did God do it? I don't know. But I do know that I'm not sure whether I'll ever be able to forgive God for this."

Steven shakes his head in disbelief. "Last year they came to me one day at work and said, 'We're sorry but your job is being cut out in the next budget.' I had worked for them for twenty years and thought I was a permanent part of the group. They said, 'You'll be finished in a week.' And I was. Out on the street before I knew it. How can they do that? Here I am a year later still in a daze. Angry. Bitter. Thinking about what to do. Maybe I need to give them a taste of their own medicine. I've thought of myself as a Christian until now, but I just don't know anymore."

Bill says, "For a long time I've thought God wanted me to look for a different kind of work, but I haven't been able to bring myself to do it. I work at a casino. The pay is good, and I need to support my family. The only trouble is that every day I see people throwing their resources away, and I don't do anything to influence them to think about their choices. Maybe God will look the other way and not be too hard on me."

Our perceptions of God are challenged by life circumstances throughout our lives. It is important, however, to know what we think God is like if we are considering spiritual direction. Until we have a true picture of God and recognize that God is sheer goodness and grace and that God desires a relationship with us, we cannot experience a lasting spiritual pilgrimage. Augustine faced the dilemma of approaching God and stated it this way in *The Confessions:*

> Should I call on You for help or should I praise You? Is it important to know You first before I call on You? If I don't know who You are, how can I call? In my ignorance I might be calling on some other object of worship. Do I call on You, then, in order to know You? . . . It's settled: let me seek You, Lord, by asking for Your help in my life.[4]

Experience with God as Portrayed in Scripture

What does Scripture say about human experience and experiences with God? God created Adam and Eve and was with them in the Garden of Eden (Gen. 3:8). God created humans to be companions: sons, daughters, friends who are free to choose whether or not to listen to and cooperate with their Creator. God's desire for relationship with humankind did not change when they ate from the tree of the knowledge of good and evil, and God continued to speak with them.

God chose to identify more fully with humankind at a specific point in time by being born as a human, Jesus of Nazareth. The possibility of our being fully connected with God ensues from being in relationship with Christ. Our ability to recognize God's desire to be involved with us and the gift of grace that enables us to respond to God come from the Holy Spirit. Jesus said it was important for him to go away so that the Father would send the Holy Spirit to be with us always. Believers are the temple in which the Holy Spirit dwells (1 Cor. 6:19).

Many scriptural passages affirm God's desire and delight to be in relationship with people. Zephaniah 3:17 says, "The LORD your God is with you, he is mighty to save. He will take great delight in you, he will quiet you with his love, he will rejoice over you with singing." If God loves us and we desire God, somewhere along the way we will encounter one another.

Reflecting on people's experiences with Jesus while he was on earth helps us think about what it is like to experience God in a person-to-person relationship. People experienced Christ in many ways, as teacher, leader, storyteller, friend, confronter, asker of insightful questions, one who overturned religious systems, compassionate listener, helper, provider, healer, one who opened doors to new perceptions and life possibilities, a mystery, and Messiah, Savior.

A wide range of thoughts, feelings, and behaviors were evoked in people when they interacted with Jesus. Their encounters with him provided information that was important for their relationship with God and opened the way for new opportunities. Jesus invited people to follow God. Some did and some turned away. Most of the life-changing experiences people had with Jesus were perceived to be between two human beings, even though it was clear that God was somehow involved. We can consider and pray about how our own interactions with Jesus are similar and different from those we read about in Scripture.

Chapter 11, "Scripture," contains references to numerous encounters between Peter and Jesus that are like snapshots of their relationship. The first time Jesus encounters Peter, he guides Peter to a miraculous catch of fish and then calls Peter to follow him and become a "fisher of men" (Luke 5:1–11). Jesus invited Peter to move away from shore and drop his nets into the deep. People who are reading this Scripture passage may sense that the Spirit is inviting them to move out into the deep, to move away from how they have been accustomed to doing things, and to follow Jesus in a new direction.

When reading Scripture, we may become aware that we are interacting with Jesus in ways that are similar to what is being portrayed, and we may consider and pray about what God intends. We may identify with a text in unique ways because of our own questions or circumstances. We notice if we are more like those who seek God or those who draw back. Praying about rather than judging what we observe opens interesting opportunities for understanding.

It might be less confusing if these direct encounters with Jesus were the only way people have had contact with Divine love, but some experiences with God described in Scripture are quite different from these person-to-person interactions with Jesus. God interacted with humans before Jesus' incarnation, during Jesus' earthly life, and after Jesus ascended into heaven. Abraham, Moses, and others were visited by God's spiritual presence—God's Spirit without any sort of body, human, angelic, or otherwise. God spoke to them (Gen. 12:1–4; 13:14–17; Exod. 6:1–8). Sometimes God communicated Divine presence through physical manifestations such as the burning bush, the pillar of fire by night and the cloud by day that led the Israelites through the wilderness, the Shekinah glory in the tabernacle, and the Spirit that came as a dove and rested on Jesus at his baptism (Exod. 3:2–4; 13:21; 40:34–35; 2 Chron. 7:1–3; John 1:32–34).

No one questioned whether they had been visited by God in any of these situations. Nor did they seem to have difficulty interpreting what God was communicating. They understood what God intended even though their short- and long-term responses to these experiences varied. Scripture shows that God communicates plainly enough so that people who seek to hear God are able to recognize God's messages and respond. But many mysteries remain.

Jesus' experiences of God the Father are a slightly different kind of example of direct Divine involvement. To be accurate we would have to explore these encounters as experiences of God with God, but also God with a human person. God's presence was demonstrated spiritually and materially at Jesus' baptism, when Jesus was transfigured, through Jesus' ministry in which people were healed physically and spiritually, and during the crucifixion of Jesus (Matt. 17:1–5; John 1:32).

Christ's appearances after he had been revealed as Divine through the resurrection are yet another sort of God-encounter. Jesus appeared to the disciples at least three times. He spoke with them, ate, and showed them he was alive after being dead (Mark 16:12; Luke 24:36–39; John 20:21). After Christ's ascension, the disciples, other followers of Christ, and some who were not followers of The Way were visited by the Holy Spirit in ways they recognized as an appearance of God (Acts 9:3–6).

The examples mentioned so far have described experiences directly of God or with God—experiences of God as Spirit or voice or as a visible manifestation. Sometimes, however, God sends messengers in human or angelic form. Scriptural accounts describe visits by godly messengers to Abraham, Lot, Mary, Zechariah, and others (Gen. 18:1–5; 19:1; Luke 1:11–13, 26–28).

It can be both unsettling and encouraging to think about these encounters because such occurrences run against our inclinations toward rational understanding. But they also deeply affirm what we hope is true—that God loves humans, desires relationship with us, and will do whatever is required to communicate with and be in relationship with us. Jesus promised that God would always be present to love and guide us in the person of the Holy Spirit (John 14:25–26).

God's Presence

Spiritual direction is dependent on the ongoing presence of the Holy Spirit, who invites us into relationship with God. The Holy Spirit draws us to experience God as well as to reflect on God. The Spirit opens our understanding so that we are able to recognize God present in others and in the world. As we have already said, part of deepening our relationship with God involves learning to distinguish the voice of the Holy Spirit from other voices. If we accept Christ's teaching about the important role of the Holy Spirit, we will want to explore how we pay attention to the Spirit. How do we acknowledge God who is within us and alongside us through the Holy Spirit? How do we interact with the Holy Spirit so that we are attentive to God?

It is interesting to explore where our thoughts and words are and are not congruent with our practice. For instance, some people ask God to "be present." The early Christians often prayed, "Come, Lord Jesus!" But Scripture teaches and we say we believe that God is *always* present. In spiritual direction we do not try to convince or manipulate God to be present but acknowledge that the Holy Spirit is present because Jesus said God would never leave us. At times we pray to be able to *sense* God's presence, but it is good to remember that God is present whether or not we have any sense of Divine presence. In spiritual direction conversations we affirm, celebrate, and act on our belief that God is present and loves and guides us (Matt. 28:19–20; John 14:15–16).

Our perceptions and interpretations of the person and nature of God are central to spiritual direction. We are dependent on God's self-revelation through Jesus, Scripture, and the continuing presence of the Holy Spirit. We desire to be receptive to God, who is included in but not limited to what we perceive of God. We seek God but recognize that our searching would never be sufficient to actually find God unless God were seeking us. Human beings do not manipulate God. Any spiritual being or power that is subject to our control is simply not God. Scripture contains directions to pray and persist in praying, which implies God listens to and is influenced by our prayer (Luke 11:5–13). But we do not determine how God will respond.

Faith Life

Every person's experience with God is unique. Faith stories begin and develop in ways that are shaped by endless variations. Yet no matter how faith begins, somewhere along the way Christians are invited into fuller understanding, appreciation for, and relationship with one God who is expressed in three persons: God the Father, Jesus Christ the Son, and the Holy Spirit.

Beginning with Jesus

Some people begin an intentional relationship with God by turning away from self as center and toward God through repentance and faith in Jesus Christ as their Savior. Later, as they pray, study Scripture, and make life choices that flow out of their developing relationship with Jesus, they pay more attention to God, who is also the Father and Holy Spirit. Their intentionality with God starts from an awareness of God incarnate in Jesus and God's willingness to embrace human life for the benefit of humankind. While many people tend to focus on Jesus' incarnation as primarily a judgment of human sinfulness, others believe that Jesus' incarnation was also an endorsement of humanity, which was created in the image of God. This encourages them to accept their gifts and live to their full potential.

This relationship with Jesus begins in different ways and at different stages of life. Eight-year-old Sue became concerned about whether she and God were friends after a Sunday school teacher mentioned that she could choose to "follow Jesus." On the way home from church, Sue talked this over with her parents and decided she wanted to invite Jesus to be her friend and Savior. At lunch, they asked Sue if she wanted to talk to God about what she had decided. Sue prayed, and they did too.

Tom made a commitment to Christ when he was at camp during the summer between his junior and senior years of high school. He had been reading Scripture, praying, and talking about whether he was really a Christian because he could not remember any one time when he made a commitment to God. As he spent time outdoors and reflected on his life, he realized he wanted God to know about his love and appreciation and also how much he needed and depended on God. On one of his afternoon walks, Tom invited Christ to be Lord of his life. Then that evening as the campers sat at the edge of the lake, a counselor talked about throwing one's life totally into God's care—completely letting go of oneself to God. The counselor invited the campers to think about their relationship with God and suggested that if they felt drawn by God to make this commitment, they should choose a rock to symbolize themselves. At the end of the evening those who wanted to could throw their rock with all their strength into the lake, indicating they were giving themselves to God. Tom and many other campers stood along the lakeshore under the stars and threw their rocks. Tom said he had strong feelings of love for Jesus and God's love for him as he offered himself to God.

Roger, age forty-four, describes himself as grateful for his sense of being born again. In fact, he remembers a precise turning point, an opportunity that seemed to appear from nowhere when he was in great personal pain. God asked him whether this kind of life—one with so many destructive consequences flowing out of his behavior—was what he wanted. Roger realized that God was ready and willing to forgive him and help him make a new start. He particularly remembers Jesus telling him he would never leave him or forsake him and that he would make it possible for Roger to live differently and make better choices. Roger believed Jesus would be there to help him with the qualities of character he knew he lacked.

May, in her early eighties, watched a television series about Mother Teresa and began examining how she had spent her own long years. After taking a close look at what she had thought and done, she became depressed. May wasn't particularly hopeful that surrender to Christ would make much difference, but she knew she could neither forgive herself for the pattern of abusive behaviors she had chosen nor escape from her long-practiced self-centered attitudes without God's forgiveness and help. So she decided to give God a chance and almost dared God to "do something with this old lady." Her transformation was not instantaneous, but soon it was clear she was moving in a new direction. She began to pray alone and with others about her desire to be made new. She became interested in the Bible and alive to spiritual possibilities that had not interested her before. Her numerous infirmities even seemed to be affected. She experienced physical improvement in some areas, and her new attitudes toward herself, God, and others influenced the atmosphere around her. People were genuinely glad to be with her, which had not been the case for years. May's family faced significant challenges in forgiving May for her past behavior, yet changes within the family also began to take place.

Jodi was attracted to Christianity when she began reading the New Testament for the first time. She began to learn who Jesus was and what he was like, and she began to talk to him. His values and teaching were so different from those around her. Jesus based his life on listening to God the Father and was willing to be and do what God asked. Jodi began to be hopeful about her own life and asked Jesus to be her Savior and companion in life.

Many people say their faith journey began with Jesus. A relationship with Jesus becomes the doorway for recognizing God, who is beyond human comprehension, who creates from nothing, and who is uniquely present today through the Holy Spirit.

Beginning with God the Creator

Other people begin their Christian journey through God the Creator. They enjoy the natural world and enjoy looking at trees and lakes, mountains and creatures, the sky and changing weather. The world's beauty, variation, and life fill them with awe. Through their open appreciation of nature, some people begin to wonder and inquire about the origin of such order and beauty. They realize that what they have learned about evolution does not resonate with what they see in the world, nor does it settle in their own spirits as a satisfactory explanation. Nature is simply too splendid even at the microscopic level to be the result of chance alone (Ps. 19:1–4; Acts 17:24–28; Rom. 1:20).

They are drawn toward the mind and heart out of which creation has come: God the Creator. Their gratitude for these gifts of God draws them to God, and they begin to investigate. With or without religious tradition, structure, or grounding, they take steps toward God. At some point, as they follow the promptings of the Holy Spirit, they may become involved in intentional prayer and/or study. They may meet others who are willing to listen to them and participate in Bible study, prayer, teaching, and worship.

Jim identifies with this kind of faith beginning. He was an avid nature lover when he was a child but never seriously thought about God's involvement in creation until he was in his early twenties. After college he began a spiritual pilgrimage that eventually led him to Christ.

Mary Ann blamed cataclysmic natural events on divine wrath. She took a long time to explore whether God cared about the natural world and whether God was interested in or loving toward humans, herself in particular. She gained a new perspective on creation through her interests in ecology. As she began to appreciate the interrelatedness of every living thing and the complexity and beauty of it all, she was drawn to speak to "Whoever made all this." When she discussed her questions with others, they too expressed similar questions, and a small group began to meet. They talked, prayed, read Scripture, and looked for others who might interact with them without judging or insulting them. They needed freedom to ask and explore whatever came to mind and felt fortunate to meet Christians who were clear about their faith yet also willing to walk alongside those with questions. They allowed the process to unfold and did not force commitments. They respected God's timing in their lives and prayed about their questions.

Jim, Mary Ann, and others like them are often drawn by the Holy Spirit to recognize that God, the Creator, chose to become incarnate in Jesus. Implications of the incarnation begin to shape their understanding of God and their awareness that God invites them to a relationship with him. These kinds of people usually have many questions about Jesus that call for careful, prayerful response.

Beginning with the Holy Spirit

Other people are first aware of a still small voice for which they have no name. They may converse with this voice, not realizing that they are praying as they seek to learn from this holy presence. If they follow the guidance of the Holy Spirit, they are drawn through a series of God-initiated invitations to Jesus and God the Creator.

Tim says his relationship with God began with the Holy Spirit. He prayed and often had a sense of an ongoing dialogue with Someone who loved him. He felt cared for and helped many times before he set out on a deliberate search and began reading Scripture.

Carole knew the loving confrontation of the Holy Spirit. She was drawn to change intended courses of action on a number of occasions long before she associated Jesus with the one who guided her so clearly (John 3:8).

Susan was invited to a prayer-for-healing worship service by one of her friends. Susan did not consider herself a Christian, but she was curious about healing and had some physical problems that were not responding to medical treatment. She decided to go. At the meeting she learned about the Holy Spirit's (God's) desire for people to be whole, and she was puzzled, amazed, and moved by what she observed in others and what happened to her. Near the end of the evening, people were invited to come forward for prayer. At that moment Susan felt more hopeful about the possibility that God exists than she had in years and surprised herself and her friend by deciding to ask someone to pray with her. She says she is not at all clear about what happened during the prayer but that she felt received, accepted, and loved by God. It seemed as if something inside her softened. Now she is actively seeking God, reading the Bible, and asking questions.

Just as people come to faith in a variety of ways, people are also drawn to spiritual direction through their own personal history as individuals who are loved, called, and desired by God. In chapter 2, "The Heart of Spiritual Direction," we acknowledged that the Holy Spirit may invite us to seek spiritual companionship at any time. People who decide to enter spiritual direction may be exploring the possibilities of faith or growing in committed relationship with God. Our journeys with God begin before we are aware that God is reaching toward us. They continue when we awaken to God and are shaped by our responses.

God's Love, Our Response

Christians from every era have written about direct encounters with God in which they have been drawn into the love of God and been given insight. George Fox, a Quaker, wrote,

And one day when I had been walking solitarily abroad and was come home, I was taken up in the love of God, so that I could not but admire the greatness of his love. And while I was in that condition it was opened unto me by the eternal Light and power, and I therein saw clearly that all was done and to be done in and by Christ, and how he conquers and destroys this tempter, the

Devil and all his works, and is atop of him, and that all these troubles were good for me, and temptations for the trial of my faith which Christ had given me. And the Lord opened me that I saw through all these troubles and temptations. My living faith was raised, that I saw all was done by Christ, the life, and my belief was in him.[5]

The center of Divine/human relationship is love—God's love. The reality of this love rooted in God goes beyond our ideas and experiences of human love and expresses itself in surprising ways. Even though our understanding of Divine and human love is limited, we are able, with the Spirit's help, to differentiate authentic love from its counterfeits.

We are created and in-breathed to life by the Spirit and recognize God's love as "home." Therefore, when we experience this love, we long for more. Those who followed Jesus were drawn by the completeness of his embodiment of God's love even when they did not yet realize he was the Messiah. It was costly for Christ, who was God, to be the bearer and embodiment of such love. Our participation in God's love is also costly for us. Our connection with God's love is accomplished through the death and resurrection of Christ and our willingness to turn to God. The Spirit of God invites us to cast our lot fully with God. It feels as if we are risking everything when we invite God to be our all in all—to give God every aspect of ourselves. We are free to decide whether to release ourselves into God's love and care.

We may not yet be fully able to recognize or receive God's love even when we say we believe in God's love for us. It may remain only an intellectual concept. We may affirm our belief in a loving God but have had little direct experience of anything we would label as such.

Contemporary Christians have often lost sight of the radical nature of God's love. C. S. Lewis explained it well.

When Christianity says that God loves man, it means that God *loves* man: not that He has some "disinterested," because really indifferent, concern for our welfare, but that in awful and surprising truth, we are the objects of His love. You asked for a loving God: you have one: The great spirit you so lightly invoked the "lord of terrible aspect," is present: not a senile benevolence that drowsily wishes you to be happy in your own way, not the cold philanthropy of a conscientious magistrate, nor the care of a host who feels responsible for the comfort of his guests, but the consuming fire Himself, the Love that made the worlds.[6]

A clear view of our perceptions of God may become apparent to us when we see we have acted out of narrow self-interest. We cannot imagine that God could possibly forgive or love us again. Our hesitancy to reveal our true thoughts and needs to God may indicate that we do not yet see the consistency and unchangingness of God's love. We may catch ourselves thinking of God as the Holy One who loves us only when we are on good behavior and feel unloved when we fall short of even our own expectations. Perhaps our perception of God has not kept pace with our maturation in other ways and is still strongly shaped by our remembrance of a childhood relationship with a parent or other authority figure.

Sometimes we are surprised to see that we harbor distorted images of God that we thought we had given up long ago. These discoveries provide topics for prayer and encourage us to ask God to free us from misperceptions and enable us to recognize God beyond what we have known.

Spiritual direction can help us hear the message about God's love more clearly when we realize that another human being is accepting us as we are. We are telling the truth about ourselves and God, and rather than running away, this person is praying with us for God's full intentions for us. At other times we may not have any particular reason to think we might be out of favor with God but are unable to recall experiencing God's love for us. It is easy to forget the reality of God's love when other things crowd our lives.

Although we may attempt to analyze why we feel loved by someone, why we love them, or how love happens, we never seem to completely figure it out. Love is filled with mystery and unanswerable questions. We discover that our explanations are inadequate to express or convey much of what we experience. Love has the qualities of a sacred gift. At times we are not sure we can receive or participate in a deepening communion with God with vulnerability and joy because we do not think we deserve to be so happy. When we experience God's love, our awareness of our inadequacies in relationship and expression may seem to multiply. But then they become less consequential because we stop focusing on ourselves. God is love. God loves us.

Sometimes we experience God's love strongly, clearly, and deeply. We truly know God loves us. But many intense experiences of Divine love are fleeting. They seem to be over before we realize what is happening. We have been genuinely unselfconscious. When we are fully involved in loving and being loved, we are not thinking about or analyzing the experience.

However, not all our experiences of God's presence are so short. We may be aware of God's love for hours or days or even weeks or months when we seem to be dwelling in the Spirit and appreciating and responding to God. Our sense of an alive, deepening, intimate relationship with God may arise seemingly for no reason or after an increase in our willingness or assent toward God. Perhaps we have released our hold on self a little or consciously invited God to be our all in all even when the risks of such surrender seemed high. Sometimes the Holy Spirit increases our awareness of God's love and quickens a kind of joy in us when we assent to the Spirit's invitations even in small ways. Paradoxically, we may wonder why we do not feel anything, when it seems that God hardly notices a relinquishment that seemed consequential. Our ability to judge what is central or significant as we grow in Christ is limited. Much of what God does will always remain hidden.

The Holy Spirit may startle us by giving us glimpses of infinite love within us, around us, and in others. We may recognize God's presence in ways that seem exquisitely gentle or almost ferocious. When God opens the way to heaven's love, we are reassured that God's love is enough for all—all questions, all rebellion, all sinfulness, all people. It is wonderfully clear that we are not manufacturing feelings or thoughts or talking ourselves into anything. The love of God is truly apparent. We may discover that we have been given grace to love God beyond loving what God does for, in, or through us, or we may notice that we love more of what God loves and ask if this is evidence that the mind of Christ is being formed in us.

I can remember attending a healing service at which it seemed God poured love on everyone present. It was abundantly evident that the Spirit was present by people's experiences and expressions—softness, relief, tears, laughter, a sense of wholeness, and a sense of being utterly loved by God. No one wanted to leave. Although many experienced healing of relationships and bodies, inner healing and restoration of healthy emotions, these things seemed incidental because they paled alongside the reality of God's presence. People felt great gratitude, but their appreciation was first for God revealed as love and then for the fruits of that love.

We can feel embarrassed about our love relationship with Jesus, the Holy Spirit, God. We tend to have self-conscious feelings about deep love relationships. We feel vulnerable in them because we see that we are not able to cause such feelings or guess what we will do in response. We also see that because of this love we behave differently than we would otherwise and are sometimes surprised by our own actions. We may feel that we are being ruled by strong emotions, which is not entirely pleasant. Our illusions about being primarily rational are challenged. As much as we love being in love, we may also shy away from it, even when it is with God.

Sometimes our relationship with Jesus feels similar to being in love with another person. God's love and our own loving responsiveness can overflow in ways that make us enormously happy. Within our culture it is generally more acceptable to experience this kind of love with someone of the opposite sex than with God. What are we supposed to do when we feel so alive with God's love? What is the Spirit showing us? Asking of us? Could we possibly just enjoy it? What is going on? What does God think about this? Are we being called just to "be" with God, to stay near in loving adoration for a time? Are we being called to sit at Jesus' feet in love as did Mary of Bethany (Luke 10:38–42)? When we have someone with whom to pray and share our love of and for God, we can be free to experience such feelings and allow the Holy Spirit to shape us in love. It is also helpful to explore our questions with a spiritual director.

Any love experience can have unsettling, sometimes scary aspects. Although human love is rooted in God's love, and they have similar essential qualities, Divine/human loving encounters are at a different level. They can feel so much more complete than other experiences we have described as love.

Jesus was with the three disciples who were closest to him when he was transfigured, and they were overwhelmed and afraid when confronted by God's love for Christ (Luke 9:28–36). Often we, too, experience fear when God reveals eternal love. We may feel as if there are no walls—none of our usual defenses—between us and God. Although we may have thought nothing of ourselves was hidden from God, now we realize it in a new way. We sense God's presence, but still our finiteness is so clear. At times we think we would prefer to have some small covering or protection. Yet, we would not want to have missed such an experience. We desire to love God with our whole hearts. We see that God loves us and that the Holy Spirit invites us to receive more of God's love, to grow in our love for God and the things God loves, and to become more like Christ.

We know at least intellectually that by being a Christian we are in a loving relationship with God through Christ and receive God's love continuously. We are also aware of many things that are expected of believers. God reveals situations and people as they are in the light of perfect love, including us. Revelation of truth, which accompanies our sense of God's love, can be unsettling. Therefore, as much as we desire God's love, we also fear it, and our responses to God are not always wholehearted. We consciously and unconsciously try to hold on to portions of ourselves for our own jurisdiction. But God is persistent and desires our wholeness and holiness. As we continue to listen and offer ourselves to God, God continues to transform us.

Our Experience with God Is Not Always the Same

Our experiences with God change and so do our perceptions of them. Life circumstances open new areas for learning on a regular basis, and the Holy Spirit is present to love and guide us. What we knew and experienced of and with God in the past cannot be applied like a formula to today's circumstances. But this knowledge is helpful as a foundation. Our personal history with God contains experiences and information with which we can compare our present awareness and understanding.

God addresses and nurtures us through encountering us in different ways. The particular graces God is nurturing in us, such as trust or wisdom or gentleness, are elicited by the Holy Spirit and often indicate things to pray about and consider. Because of ongoing, continuous human development and stirrings of the Holy Spirit, God may actually seem different to us at different stages in our faith pilgrimage—near or far away, gentle or demanding. We may be conscious that at times God is inviting us to pay more attention to one person of the Trinity. At other times we may find ourselves drawn toward God, who is One. Sometimes it seems as though we share the cross and at other times we celebrate the resurrection. Paul described what it was like to be a trusting follower of Christ in a variety of circumstances (Phil. 4:11–13). We, too, are given opportunities to become more aware of God and God's presence and to grow in our love for and trust of God through a wide range of experiences.

But we do not always experience God's presence with us as loving, in spite of the fact that God cannot be unloving. Our behaviors, ideas, and self-centeredness can get in the way of recognizing eternal love. At times we accurately believe God is angry with us, and at other times such an assessment is incorrect. God does suffer when we wound ourselves and others, and God's intentions for us are diverted by sinful choices. God is rightfully angry, as are we when something we have created or someone we have treasured and loved is marred or destroyed. God's anger is not self-serving but is an aspect of Divine love, based on full knowledge of our potential. God desires for us to be godly.

We may struggle for months or even years with our anger with God and the circumstances of our lives or our feelings that God is justly or unjustly angry with us. Even in this condition we are experiencing God, but we are also feeling that we are at an impasse and may or may not enjoy what feels like an ongoing argument with God. Although such experiences may sound negative, they are a necessary part of our spiritual life. We are sorting through our perceptions related to our understandings and misunderstandings, experiences, clear and blurred interpretations, and struggles with God. We may prefer to have a different relationship with God than we have. We may be working our way through old material to prepare ourselves for whatever might be possible now. We are trying to pray and listen to the Holy Spirit. The angry fog may clear away all at once by grace in the process of prayer and recognition of our own barriers with God, or it may depart more gradually as we seek to be aware of God's presence, view, and counsel.

Sometimes we do not realize we are angry at God, and it takes another person to show us—a friend, pastor, or spiritual director. At one point in my faith journey, when I was struggling with depression after the death of a family member, I did not seem to be able to move myself out of the darkness I felt inside. I had been reading an autobiography of a minister's wife who struggled with depression. She was led to her pastor for confession and prayer. It was my first meaningful introduction to the Christian discipline of confession practiced in a life-giving way. I wondered whether I, a Protestant, evangelical woman who had never considered such a thing, could benefit from the practice. I was miserable enough that I did not have anything to lose. So I went to my minister and asked him what he thought about confession and prayer. He said he believed that Jesus invites us to confess our sin, and then he outlined a process to follow. The pastor asked me to set aside twenty minutes a day for the next week to ask the Holy Spirit to show me if there was anything I needed to confess—paying attention to five years of my life at a time. He asked me to write down whatever came to mind without evaluating it—great or small, petty or of greater consequence. I was to see him again in a week.

I returned with my list of things, some of which seemed embarrassingly petty and some I viewed as more serious. I asked the pastor what I was to do. He said, "Let's go into the sanctuary and kneel, and then I'd like you to read your list aloud to God." Ugh. That was an uncomfortable prospect. But I did it, and when I finished, he asked me if I had any idea how angry I was with God. I blurted out something about who wouldn't be angry after all the things that had turned out badly, even disastrously. The pastor counseled me saying that I could say anything to God from within the family of God—"God, I do not understand what is happening. I need help. I am totally exhausted, puzzled, afraid, devastated"—but that my behavior indicated I was standing outside the kingdom and shaking my fist at God, which seemed more like blasphemy. What was I to do? Return to prayer and to God and ask for forgiveness. Then the pastor placed his hands on my head and prayed. Something left me that I had not realized was there. It was as if a great cloud lifted. All the circumstances of life did not immediately right themselves or become understandable, but the condition of my own heart and life was unmistakably rinsed and set free.

The Effects of Individuality

God reaches out to all human beings, desiring a love relationship. However, we do not all experience God in the same way. Traditional psychology, the Myers-Briggs Type Indicator, and many other conceptual frameworks for looking at human personality testify that people differ from each other in significant ways. God has created us to be unique. We all have gifts and limitations that color our view of and responses to everything, including God.

Some people prefer to pursue their love relationship with God in solitude, and others prefer groups. Some people are more interested in large overviews, and others pay attention to details. Some are drawn to analytical, theological thinking, and others are more attuned to feelings and responses. Some people rush to conclusions, and others are more comfortable to wait for things to develop. Everyone needs to be able to use all of these approaches. At times one focus is needed and at a different time, another. But we still have preferences regarding which of these responses we choose first, and our preferences influence how we perceive and respond to God and everyday life.

Sometimes the Holy Spirit speaks in familiar ways and sometimes in unfamiliar ways. If we are primarily drawn to intellectual pursuits, we may find ourselves surprised by our own deep emotional responses when we are touched by God. Such experiences may draw us to appreciate God and enlarge our thoughts. If we are usually more sensitive to emotion, we may notice that we sense God's presence through intellectual insight. God often meets us powerfully in our "shadow" side—that which is hidden from our view or seems less developed. God reaches for us as God desires, stirring new thoughts and feelings and opening new horizons.

Historic Tensions in Christian Spirituality

Our views of faith and experience with God are also influenced by the particular traditions that are a part of our history. By reading the following list, you may notice what has been emphasized in your faith tradition. These topics continue to be discussed in Christian circles, and the answers we embrace influence what we perceive to be true about God and what we value.

What is more important, denial of self or appreciation of all of life as a gift from God?

What is more important, intellectual understanding or an experiential relationship with God?

What is the relationship between God's work and human work? How do God's initiatives, our responses to God, and evil influence human relationships with God?

Different Christian faith traditions value and incorporate some facets of Christian spirituality more than others. Which is most important?

contemplative—emphasis on direct, loving encounters with God

holiness—emphasis on personal purity and separation

charismatic—emphasis on the Holy Spirit

social action—emphasis on caring for marginal people

evangelical—emphasis on Scripture and preaching

incarnational—emphasis on life as sacramental and finding God
in the details of ordinary life[7]

Are all followers of Christ at the same level, or are some advanced,
holier, or privileged?

What is the role and level of importance of preaching, baptism, and
communion?

What is the place and appropriate interpretation of Scripture?

How much emphasis should be placed on the interior life and how
much on the exterior life?

How are the lives of the individual believer and of the community of
faith interconnected? Should one be emphasized more than the other?

Our understanding of what it means to be a Christian is shaped by many
factors. Learning about what other Christians have thought can deepen
our appreciation of the richness and variety of grace. It can also awaken
our willingness to be open to explore God's invitations in new ways.

Seeking to Experience God

When we are hungry to experience God's loving presence near us and
believe we are searching for God, it is important to ask ourselves whether
we are truly seeking God or pursuing spiritual experience. We do get
lonesome for God and can feel isolated and confused. But sometimes
our search is not as much for God as it is for spiritual adventure. Perhaps we are bored. We might like to see ourselves as important spiritual
persons and think a particular kind of spiritual experience is one of the
criteria necessary for others to view us in this way. Perhaps we would
like God to heal someone through our prayer or bring about instantaneous, major life changes in us or in someone else with whom we have
been praying more as a kind of witness to our supposed godliness than
as an overflowing of God's compassion.

If we criticize or attempt to dismiss these thoughts and feelings without prayer, we can push them underground where they may remain unresolved. It is freeing to bring them into our prayer and invite God to help
us. Because of our persistent, natural self-centeredness, we get diverted
by a variety of things.

Is This God?

I have said that experiences of God are not confined to expressions of
God that are fully explainable through intellectual analysis or under our
control. But it is unwise to assume that every unexplainable spiritual

experience is a God-experience. The spiritual realm includes many lesser beings, some whose intention is to do God's bidding and some who seek to do the opposite. The spirituality of an experience is not sufficient evidence for its godliness or its goodness.

Authentic experiences of and with God are congruent with what is revealed about the nature of God in Scripture. A spiritual encounter might feel loving and peaceful, but if what takes place is not compatible with Scripture, we must prayerfully, carefully explore the source and intention of the experience. Christians need to be discerning and not depend solely on their own feelings and opinions. Shared discernment is one of the important tasks of spiritual direction conversations. Chapter 13, "Discernment," addresses discernment in a more focused way.

Many people are aware of ongoing encounters with God. Others are not sure they have ever recognized an experience with God. Some persons mark few but important moments when they knew God was truly present—moments or seasons of conversion when they changed direction; crisis points; births and deaths; the beginning of a new path; encounters with pristine, magnificent, or devastated natural settings; solitude or illness.

Any experiences of God we might have will be initiated and tended by the Holy Spirit. They are not under our control as far as our ability to bring them into being. However, it is in our power to quench the Holy Spirit, to turn away from whatever experience of God comes to us, to be unwilling to receive, listen to, or be open to the Spirit. We are both relieved and nervous when we recognize that only God determines how we will experience God—relieved because we know we cannot judge accurately what kinds of experiences will draw us to more Christlike rather than self-aggrandizing behavior, nervous because we have some sense of our frailty in any one-to-one encounter with God. We recognize that God could destroy us by being more present or active than our human psyches could bear. We also know that our perceptions of God are influenced by our humanity and may be challenged by spiritual sources that are not God. We are rightfully aware of our mortality and vulnerability when we go looking for God.

Most of our lives are spent somewhere in between flight from God and complete agreement with God, between being keenly aware of or oblivious to God. Invitations to listen to God appear moment by moment. Sometimes we do not feel at all like God's beloved ones when we notice our responses to the Holy Spirit's leadings. We run, hide, withdraw, argue, bargain, or look for other ways. We feel put upon when asked to behave in particular ways, and our response is self-centered; we are more interested in doing what pleases us. At other times we are open, eager, and delighted with God and God's love, and we respond joyfully. We encounter day-to-day challenges as we become ready and willing for God and God's love to dwell in us and live through us. We are uncomfortable when we recognize our frailties and inconsistencies in our loving relationship with God. Yet the Holy Spirit works in and through God's love and ours to bring about genuine transformation.

What kinds of experiences of God can we expect? We have described many examples of human experiences with God, but they are only representative rather than all-encompassing. We realize that God continues to surprise, instruct, and invite us through Scripture, other people and relationships, nature and life, and, at times, our direct awareness of God present with us. In observing our experiences with God we want to recognize and resist anything that leads us toward self-inflation and cooperate with whatever encourages Christlike attitudes and behavior.

Reflections

1. What is your operative (as opposed to professed) picture of God at this time in your life? What picture or idea of God actually influences or affects your present behavior, feelings, and choices?
2. Is God distant or near? How do your ideas about what God is like seem to help or hinder your spiritual growth and maturity, your personal development, and your sense of self?
3. How have you experienced God? Describe in detail. What made you decide this was God?
4. What kinds of experiences with God are you longing for? Why? How do you pray about this?
5. How do the three persons of the Trinity seem involved in your experience with God? What does your history look like in this regard? How does your prayer reflect where you and God are now?
6. What about your relationship with God brings your gratitude to the surface?
7. What was God like as presented by parents, teachers, authority figures, and friends?
8. When you read the material about historic tensions in Christian spirituality, what did you learn about your background?
9. What have you discovered about God through your personal experience?
10. What insights and feelings do you have when you read your responses to questions 1–4?

We are to hear. All of us are. That is what the whole Bible is calling out. "Hear, O Israel!"

But hear what? Hear what? The Bible is hundreds upon hundreds of voices all calling at once out of the past and clamoring for our attention like barkers at a fair, like air-raid sirens, like a whole barnyard of cockcrows as the first long shafts of dawn fan out across the sky. Some of the voices are shouting, like Moses' voice, so all Israel, all the world, can hear, and some are so soft and halting that you can hardly hear them at all, like Job with ashes on his head and his heart broken, like old Simeon whispering, "Lord, now lettest thou thy servant depart in peace." . . . And somewhere in the midst of them all one particular voice speaks out that is unlike any other voice because it speaks so directly to the deepest privacy and longing and weariness of each of us that there are times when the centuries blow away like mist, and it is as if we stand with no shelter of time at all between ourselves and the one who speaks our secret name. Come, the voice says. Unto me. All ye. Every last one.

Frederick Buechner[1]

For the word of God is living and active. Sharper than any double-edged sword, it penetrates even to dividing soul and spirit, joints and marrow; it judges the thoughts and attitudes of the heart.

Hebrews 4:12

The Bible is an important source of information, understanding, and spiritual direction. Second Timothy 3:16–17 says, "All Scripture is God-breathed and is useful for teaching, rebuking, correcting and training in righteousness, so that God's servant may be thoroughly equipped for every good work" (NIV ILE). Directors and directees read, study, and use the Bible as an aid to worship, prayer, and attentiveness to God. Its texts are rich in material for meditation and prayer, provide guidelines for godly living, and invite us to pay quality attention to our relationship with God—the most significant relationship of our lives. The embodiments and expressions of what it is to be a Christian, a follower of Christ, are also rooted in Scripture.

Spiritual directors appreciate the Bible. They are also careful to help directees avoid worshiping the Bible rather than worshiping God.

173

In John 5:39–40, Jesus described this possibility when he said, "You diligently study the Scriptures because you think that by them you possess eternal life. These are the Scriptures that testify about me, yet you refuse to come to me to have life." Directees seek to use Scripture as a means of coming to God and learning about God but realize that Scripture is not God.

Every person who reads Scripture is challenged to understand and interpret it. The way people attempt to do so is based on their view of Scripture. People within the Christian tradition have viewed Scripture in three major ways.

1. Meaning comes through the author, who is inspired by God. Therefore, it is most important to understand what the author intended to communicate, to know what the writing meant to the author, and how it was relevant to the people for whom it was written. After understanding the author's meaning, we can reflect on its significance for us.
2. The text is predominant, and the meaning is in the text. The author may not necessarily have understood all that he wrote. In fact, he could not have known it all. God inspired the author to write certain things, and the text has a life of its own. The product, which is the text, is more important than what the author intended to communicate.
3. Meaning resides in the reader. Meaning is personal and changes according to what God wishes to communicate to someone at a particular time. What the text meant to the author and to those who read or heard the text at the time it was written is not as important as the meaning a reader becomes aware of through their own reading and prayers in which they ask the Holy Spirit to speak to them through the text.

Many people believe all three views have some validity. Some groups or individuals choose to interpret Scripture almost exclusively according to one of the methods; others use a combination of the three.

At times directees speak about scriptural texts that seem to come alive to them, that the Holy Spirit has impressed upon them. The following direction conversation is an example of this kind of use of Scripture.

Director: What has your prayer been like?

Directee: Well, I don't know that I'd exactly call this prayer, but I've been walking around feeling grateful because of something that happened when I was reading the Bible this morning.

Director: Would you like to talk about that?

Directee: Yes, I think I would. At first I was not sure if I would tell you or anyone else, because it seemed like such a personal thing between God and me, and I did not want to spoil it.

Director: I can appreciate that.

Directee: Other people talking about it would make me uncomfortable. That's one reason I'm thankful for our conversations. I know whatever I say becomes part of your prayer, but does not go farther.

I have been using a devotional guide with suggested Scripture readings. This week I am to read Psalm 24 every day along with a particular passage for each day of the week. It has been good. After the readings I pray and sometimes write in my journal. This morning I had been thinking that I was going to be sorry to see the work project I am involved in come to an end, because God has seemed so close. It's like the Holy Spirit is at my elbow, or Jesus. I don't know for sure which one. Anyway, it is comforting to be aware of God's presence and companionship. I was appreciating that, talking to God about it, and feeling a little sad. I do hate the thought of this work coming to an end, because I don't want to lose the sense of God's nearness. Then I glanced across the page at Psalm 23, and it was like the words shouted at me from verse 6. It says, "Surely goodness and love will follow me all the days of my life, and I will dwell in the house of the LORD forever." I laughed out loud. Of course, that is what God is like. How could I forget? Anyway, now I'm still savoring this project but also happily expectant about whatever comes next.

There is also a wide range of views concerning the role of Scripture in the lives of contemporary Christians. Many people believe the Bible is the *final, perfect authority* in all issues. Others believe the Bible is the *primary authority* for the church, but it should still be submitted to critical study. A third perspective concludes that the Bible holds the *living core of faith* and that the meaning of Scripture must be compared with what has been learned through reason, human experience, and church tradition. Finally, some people prefer to see the Bible as a *historical document* about the church's life and beliefs in the past.

Many ways of reading and interpreting Scripture become apparent in spiritual direction. When directees speak about their experiences with Scripture, they may be using the text very broadly or narrowly in any one of the ways already described. Yet they are generally trying to discern what God is attempting to show them through a particular passage. Nevertheless, it is important to consider what level of authority directors and directees ascribe to Scripture and whether they believe scriptural stories hold more weight than other stories.

Sometimes the Holy Spirit invites a director to encourage a directee to look at how he or she is reading and interpreting Scripture or to study Scripture in an intensive way. The director's primary role, however, is not to correct or critique a directee's way of interpreting Scripture. The director's role is to listen to the Spirit of God with the directee. As directors prayerfully listen to directees, they may sense that a discussion of methods of scriptural interpretation is not what God is most interested in at this time. When such a discussion is not God's idea, it is a diversion from what the Holy Spirit is inviting. The way that a directee is praying with or about a passage of Scripture or making life choices based on scriptural texts may be what is central at a particular time. The director and directee try to hear what God is inviting in their approaches to Scripture and its application.[2]

Language

The versions of Scripture we read, whether they are in original languages or translations in other languages, shape what we hear. Translations are colored by translators, who shape the presentation of the text. Their personalities, interests, prayers, and the times and cultures in which they live influence their work, even when they intend to remain objective and communicate only what is present in the original manuscripts. Normal cultural usage of language also influences the specific words a translator chooses to express what they interpret as the original intention and meaning. Language changes as culture changes. Some present-day translations are more attentive to generic and specific language regarding men and women.[3]

Descriptive language for God includes more than two hundred names for God. It expresses God's otherness and complexity and our inability to fully comprehend God. All scriptural names describing God contain information and meaning. None of them alone or in combination with all others can encompass the whole of God. Part of our prayer includes asking what name(s) for God the Holy Spirit invites us to use. Some names seem more meaningful than others. The names we use to address God during peaceful seasons in day-to-day life are often different from the names we use when we cry out to God in the midst of dire, wrenching situations. Most of us call God by different names at different times depending on our circumstances.

Some of the names for God used in Scripture are Yahweh, the Holy One, Counselor, Guide, Beloved, Redeemer, Teacher, Lord Jesus, Creator, Father, Mother, Abba, the Beginning and the End, Lamb, Defender of the Helpless, Healer, Comforter, I Am. In our prayer we use both scriptural names and personal names for God. We may also notice the various names God calls us such as my child, daughter, son, servant, follower, disciple, little one, or beloved friend.

Within spiritual direction the language that is used for God and persons is shaped by Scripture, our particular Christian traditions, and what the Holy Spirit is bringing to our attention. There is great variety in the way Christians express their relationship to God, who is one and also three. Direction conversations reflect the uniqueness of personal and denominational ways of speaking about and to God. Words carry meaning, which overflows into interpretations and nuances. Directors and directees often ask each other what significance and meaning they ascribe to particular words and phrases. Because of the impreciseness of language and the diversity of backgrounds, we do not expect that all people will use the same words or necessarily mean exactly the same thing when they use the same words. It is important to listen carefully and communicate clearly. Our language and expressions of faith change as we deepen and develop. They reflect our responsiveness to God. Scriptural texts contain much to ponder and pray about.

Interpretation

Christians have strong ideas and feelings about the Bible, and it is easy to become highly invested in the way a particular group of Christians understands and interprets Scripture. Scripture is so central to Christian thought, experience, and life that debates over its meaning and importance have separated Christians into numerous groups. Some groups of Christians believe that all people who are truly Christian will interpret Scripture in exactly the same way—as they do. They may teach that those who hold different views of Scripture are more estranged from God than people who do not know or respect Scripture.

Reading the Bible, listening through its pages to what the Spirit has said in a particular setting about being God's people, and reflecting on what the Holy Spirit is saying to us through Scripture now are important aspects of spiritual direction. We may hear, read, and respond to Scripture many times during a week in our personal prayer, meditation, and study, and in church through worship, music, preaching, and discussion. We cannot pay equal attention to all the Scripture passages we hear or read in a week or a month. We need to discern which passages the Holy Spirit is drawing us to read, pray with, and study. What is God saying to us through Scripture? Directees talk about specific passages and what they think God is bringing to their attention.

God does not lead us in ways that are incongruent with the overall teaching of Scripture. But the Bible may not address our particular questions. Then we reflect on scriptural principles and the goal of Christian life, which is to be like Christ, place possibilities alongside these, and ask to see what God intends.

Spiritual Direction in Scripture

Scripture is a significant resource for spiritual direction as we read and listen to biblical texts. But even when we appreciate Scripture as a source of direction, we may not have observed how spiritual direction itself is depicted in Scripture. Identifying places where spiritual direction occurs within the biblical texts gives spiritual direction credibility and validity.

First Samuel 3:3–10 tells the story of young Samuel, who goes to Eli during the night because he heard a voice calling him and thought it was Eli.

> The lamp of God had not yet gone out, and Samuel was lying down in the temple of the LORD, where the ark of God was. Then the LORD called Samuel. Samuel answered, "Here I am." And he ran to Eli and said, "Here I am; you called me." But Eli said, "I did not call; go back and lie down." So he went and lay down. Again the LORD called, "Samuel!" And Samuel got up and went to Eli and said, "Here I am; you called me." "My son," Eli said, "I did not call; go back and lie down." Now Samuel did not yet know the LORD: The word of the LORD had not yet been revealed to him. The LORD called Samuel a third time, and Samuel got up and went to Eli and said, "Here I am; you called me." Then Eli realized that the LORD was calling the boy. So Eli told Samuel, "Go and lie down, and if he calls you, say, 'Speak, LORD, for your servant is listening.'" So Samuel went and lay down in his place. The LORD came and stood there, calling as at the other times, "Samuel! Samuel!" Then Samuel said, "Speak, for your servant is listening."

Eli's instructions to Samuel were like the guidance of a spiritual director. He encouraged Samuel to identify himself as God's servant, invite God to speak, and then to listen.

Jesus is the ultimate spiritual director because of his intimacy with God, his Abba. Jesus listened and responded to others out of his attentiveness to the Father, out of his participation in the Jewish covenant community, and out of his knowledge of Scripture and Jewish law. But the Father's love and presence and the Holy Spirit's anointing were the most powerful influences in Jesus' life and the source of direction for others. The prophet Isaiah foretold that this would be so:

> The Spirit of the LORD will rest on him—
>   the Spirit of wisdom and of understanding,
>   the Spirit of counsel and of power,
>   the Spirit of knowledge and of the fear of the LORD—
> and he will delight in the fear of the LORD.
> He will not judge by what he sees with his eyes,
>   or decide by what he hears with his ears;
> but with righteousness he will judge the needy,
>   with justice he will give decisions for the poor of the earth.
>
> Isaiah 11:2–4

Jesus taught and offered direction to his disciples and others before and after the resurrection. In each case, he spoke to their personal situation within the framework of God's faithfulness and invited them to recognize God's loving presence and availability to guide and bless. Some of those stories are recounted in Scripture. At Jacob's well Jesus listened and spoke to a woman about her relationship with God and her human relationships. Jesus pointed her directly to God.

> It's who you are and the way you live that count before God. Your worship must engage your spirit in the pursuit of truth. That's the kind of people the Father is out looking for: those who are simply and honestly *themselves* before him in their worship. God is sheer being itself—Spirit. Those who worship him must do it out of their very being, their spirits, their true selves, in adoration.
>
> John 4:23–24 *The Message*

Luke 8:40–48 tells the story of Jesus and the woman with the issue of blood. It is a story of bodily healing, but it also involves elements of spiritual direction. The woman had struggled because no one could help her. In Hebrew society her condition made her unclean. A woman was considered unclean during her menstrual flow for seven days. On the eighth day she was to bring two turtledoves or two young pigeons to the priest to be offered as a sin offering and a burnt offering. Whoever had a continuous discharge, however, remained ritually unclean. All beds, chairs, saddles, and vessels used by such a person were unclean, and anyone who touched that person remained unclean until sunset.[4]

The woman who touched Jesus had not been able to touch anyone, even her family members, for twelve years without making them unclean. She probably touched the edge of Jesus' garment anonymously out of desperation. She believed Jesus could heal her and knew her condition made it unacceptable for her to approach Jesus directly. Jesus felt the power of the Spirit as it moved through him to her and asked who touched him. He could have remained silent, knowing someone had been healed, but his calling her to identify herself was crucial for complete restoration. Jesus publicly announced that she was whole, and therefore, no longer to be avoided. In the midst of everyone, he affirmed and blessed her, saying, "Daughter, your faith has healed you. Go in peace."

How was Jesus acting as a spiritual director? He listened to the Spirit and to the woman. By calling her to identify herself, he brought out into the open what she would not have spoken about. Spiritual directors often challenge people to speak about their true condition, to name their difficulties and seek God's grace. In the presence of the community, Jesus affirmed the woman as a valuable human being after she had been on the periphery due to her condition. Because of her contact with Jesus, the woman was healed emotionally, physically, and relationally. Spiritual directors encourage directees to seek God, who can bring them to wholeness.

Many encounters between Jesus and Peter contain aspects of spiritual direction and provide useful information for contemporary directors. During the storm on the lake, Jesus invited Peter to walk on the water. Peter accepted, took a few steps on the water, realized what he was doing, and began to sink. Jesus said, "Keep your eyes on me." Present-day directors often say the same thing. "Keep your eyes on Jesus."

The following encounters between Jesus and Peter also involved spiritual direction and serve as models for the ways present-day spiritual directors respond to directees.

- the naming of Peter (Matt. 16:17–19)

  Jesus called Peter to see something in himself that was not readily evident to Peter or anyone around him. As directors listen to directees and the Spirit, they help directees see aspects of themselves that may have been hidden.

- Peter's confession of faith (Matt. 16:13–16)

  Jesus asked Peter, "Who do you say that I am?" When Peter answered, Jesus said, "No mere man has revealed this to you." Directors ask the question, "Who is Jesus?" and confirm the sense of the Spirit acting in a directee's life.

- Peter told the Lord he should not suffer (Matt. 16:21–26)

  Jesus responded, "Get thee behind me." Directors sometimes give swift, challenging responses when directees make spontaneous statements without praying or thinking about them first.

- dialogue about forgiveness (Matt. 18:21–35)

    Jesus taught Peter about forgiveness. Part of spiritual maturity involves learning to forgive oneself and others. This growth can take place in spiritual direction.

- prediction of the denials (Matt 26:33–35; Mark 14:30–31)

    Jesus told Peter that he would deny him and encouraged Peter to pray that his faith would be constant. Directors sometimes recognize potential trouble spots of which they need to make directees aware. Directors need to be honest witnesses and companions in the face of these possibilities.

- the agony in the garden (Matt. 26:36–46)

    Jesus asked his disciples to keep watch with him. Directors may advise directees to continue watching with Jesus even if no great accomplishment or success seems to follow.

- Peter's denial of Christ (Matt. 26:69–75)

    Peter is running from the scene. He is afraid. Jesus appears weak. People need a director to help them remain open to God even when they are afraid and to help them see the Lord's presence and action in the midst of their circumstances.

- Jesus' appearance after the resurrection (John 21:1–25)

    Three times Jesus asked Peter, "Do you love me?" During this important moment, Peter asks about John. Jesus helps Peter focus. "That is not important for you. Your role is to follow me." Directors help directees pay attention to God and to what is important.[5]

When he was speaking to groups, Jesus often told stories—parables—to invite people to listen to and respond to God. He used parables to catch people's attention and to illustrate and clarify the nature of the kingdom of God. His audiences would have been startled by stories of a Samaritan hero (Luke 10:25–37), a justified tax collector (Luke 18:9–14), or a father running to welcome his prodigal son (Luke 15:20). These stories said, "Look, this is what God is like." Jesus used these stories to offer spiritual direction by challenging people to look more closely at what they believed and why, what their own experience of God was and how they interpreted their experiences with God. This is the essence of spiritual direction—encouraging people to listen to and follow God.

In Scripture we observe Jesus always listening for the voice of his Abba—in relationship to his disciples, other individuals, small groups, and crowds. Present-day spiritual directors attempt to function in the same way by listening to the Holy Spirit and responding to directees and others out of prayerful attentiveness to God.

After Jesus' crucifixion and resurrection he continued to teach and direct his disciples. His encounter with two disciples on the road to Emmaus models spiritual direction.

> Now that same day two of them were going to a village called Emmaus, about seven miles from Jerusalem. They were talking with each other about everything that had happened. As they talked and discussed these things with each other, Jesus himself came up and walked along with them; but they were kept from recognizing him.
>
> Luke 24:13–16

Cleopas and his friend walked with this man they did not recognize as Jesus, telling him all about Jesus' ministry and crucifixion. They spoke about their confusion related to the women's discovery of the empty tomb. Then the stranger (who was Jesus) reminded them of the prophets' teaching in Scripture about the coming of the Christ. The passage in Luke does not say how long they walked and talked, but it could have been several hours. When they stopped for the day, the stranger said he was going farther, but they convinced him to stay.

> When he was at the table with them, he took bread, gave thanks, broke it and began to give it to them. Then their eyes were opened and they recognized him, and he disappeared from their sight. They asked each other, "Were not our hearts burning within us while he talked with us on the road and opened the Scriptures to us?"
>
> Luke 24:30–32

Jesus reveals himself when he chooses—then and now. It gets a little confusing when Jesus is acting as a spiritual director and he is the risen but concealed Christ. He is behaving like a spiritual director when he is listening to their story and responding by using Scripture—pointing them toward Scripture to read, listen to, and meditate on. But it is not until they sit down with him for companionship rather than discussion that they recognize who he is. So it is quite often with directees. They get involved in analysis, thinking, pondering—but what connects them with Jesus more often is companionship—making time to be with Jesus— rather than critical thinking. People can proceed for a long time and be involved in conversation or other pursuits and not recognize that Jesus is alongside them. Spiritual directors invite directees to slow down and ask, "Where is God in this? Where is Jesus? Where is the risen Christ?"

Spiritual direction is present in Scripture implicitly and explicitly and was a part of the life of the early church. If you would like to know more about spiritual direction in Scripture and in the church, the notes are a good place to begin.[6]

Scripture in Spiritual Direction

Directors who are steeped in Scripture and recognize how God has used Scripture in their own lives are able to offer this knowledge for the benefit of directees. But here as in all other matters, whatever knowledge directors possess should remain in the background. It can be tempting to offer an answer from Scripture without consulting God—forgetting to bring the matter into prayer and asking for God's guidance before speaking with directees.

But the stories, events, and experiences of Scripture do speak to the entire story of humanity. They tell about God, who is ever present and active. It is important for directees to identify places where their personal life stories connect with God's stories. The stories of Scripture become a way of identifying where they are and where they might be going. They become a helpful framework that enables directees to see God, themselves, and their lives more clearly.

Spiritual directors often suggest certain themes in Scripture for reading, meditation, and prayer. For instance, the Exodus story is about "a way out." It starts with release from bondage, moves to wandering in the wilderness, and progresses toward entry into the Promised Land. It is helpful to know that after we have been freed from bondage it is normal to experience a period of wandering in the wilderness. Perhaps a man has recently left a difficult work environment. Once he has left the situation, he may question, "Why do I let other people treat me badly in a work situation? What might God be showing me through this particular event? Does God want to bring me out of this repeating cycle?"

The Exodus picture shows us we have a God who notices our circumstances—who is with us in all the moments of our journey. God is with us in the wilderness as much as in the deliverance from bondage and the arrival in the Promised Land—which is a place of new possibility and wholeness. The call of God to leave Egypt is a biblical picture that can help us whenever we leave a bondage of sorts and enter unmarked territory that feels like a wilderness. Reading and reflecting on texts such as this one and inviting the Holy Spirit to speak to us may free us to see aspects of our situation we had not noticed. It is helpful to see that God takes note of human groanings—not just the groaning of the Israelites but our groaning and the causes of our distress.

Many stories and moments in Scripture relate to our lives. Themes that frequently appear in direction meetings include the following:

Fruitfulness from barrenness—When everything seems impossible, there can be life (Hannah in 1 Samuel 1; Elizabeth in Luke 1).

Trust issues, personal significance and insignificance—"Are not two sparrows sold for a penny? Yet not one of them will fall to the ground apart from the will of your Father. And even the very hairs of your head are all numbered. So don't be afraid; you are worth more than many sparrows" (Matt. 10:29–31). The story of the Good Shepherd (John 10:11–13) encourages readers to believe God cares about them.

The lost sheep, the lost coin, the lost son—God values us, makes searching for us a high priority, waits for our response, celebrates when we're found (Luke 15).

Dealing with health-related losses—In spiritual direction, people are freed to tell their entire health story—physical, relational, emotional, and spiritual issues that surround and flow from their health—and offer it to God and ask for help in new ways (the woman with the hemorrhage in Mark 5).

Lake crossings and transitions—"Let us go to the other side" (Matt. 14:22–36). At times we feel we are on firm ground and are called to move through a season in which we are off balance, troubled, and fearful.

Jesus' baptism in the Jordan River—God the Father told Jesus, "You are my Son, whom I love; with you I am well pleased" (Mark 1:11). When directees recognize that God loves them wholeheartedly, it can make an enormous difference in their perceptions of life itself and of particular circumstances.[7]

Directors may encourage directees to read and pray with a particular passage of Scripture for an extended period of time. Sometimes directees pray to view the scriptural texts from the "inside out"—as if they were present at the event or scene described. They ask the Holy Spirit to teach them by showing them details of the event. What kind of day was it? Who was present? What were the circumstances? With whom do they identify most strongly in a particular scriptural story—God-seekers, bystanders, men, women, children, people who are in the center of the action or on the edge? How is God manifest in the story? What prayers arise in response to the Scripture? Directees read Scripture passages and ask to be taught by the Holy Spirit through the events as they were described in a particular time and place.

The following example shows how a particular passage of Scripture was used in a direction session:

Directee: Today I am thinking about something I have to do—actually in the next few days. I am really dreading it.

Director:	Oh?
Directee:	I have to deliver difficult news in my workplace. There is a whole group of people I have been working with for several years on an ongoing basis. In fact, they have come to depend on me a lot and we have grown into a warm, working community—almost like an extended family. Now, because of financial cutbacks, I have been told that I will not be able to spend nearly the amount of time with these people as I have in the past. The change is not what I'd choose, because I know they are developing wonderfully with my facilitating support. But I have been told this has to be done, and I am the one who will have to deliver the message. I think they are going to feel betrayed, angry, and hurt, and I just hate to be the one who triggers these emotions. I am afraid they will lash out at me—you know, shoot the messenger. It seems like it could be difficult.
Director:	You have said you think the news will be unwelcomed by others. How is it settling in your own spirit?
Directee:	Mixed. I can understand the pressures that are shaping these decisions, but I do not agree with the particular value choices that are being made. I feel like I am being asked to be a mouthpiece for a decision I would not have made. With the decreased funds, it will be impossible for me to be with them and do what I've done in the past without totally exhausting myself. We'll lose one or two full-time people and are still expected to cover the same responsibilities some way. They will probably be sympathetic about that, but the bottom line is that they are not going to get the same level of attention they have had.
Director:	You must be feeling some grief and concern.
Directee:	Yes.
Director:	The scriptural picture that's been coming to my mind the entire time you've been talking is of Jesus when he sets his face and goes toward Jerusalem. He knows what is called for and it is not what he would choose. But in this case he knows it is God's desire.
Directee:	That fits in some ways. It feels like I do have to plunge in and do this thing. I do not want to do it, and I am not looking forward to it. But maybe I need to pray about how God is really in this for me. Am I going with or against God by doing this? On one level, it seems okay because I can appre-

ciate why the decisions are being made and I know if this is what has to be that I'm the appropriate one to tell others. But I am still in conflict around the core values that make this change necessary. Jesus at least knew what the Father intended.

Director: Those considerations sound like a good place for your prayer to begin.

Directee: I agree. If I could lighten up about some of my own strong feelings, maybe I could hear more clearly what God is saying about the plan and my part in it. I'd like to be able to do whatever I do with the assurance that the Holy Spirit is inviting my role in it. Then, even if it's difficult, I know God will bring good out of it. And if I am not supposed to do it, then I guess God will help me know what to say to those who have told me I am the one. Our conversation gives me some specific ways to pray.

Director: You might sit with the Scripture passage and see if there is anything there for you or not.

The Holy Spirit often uses Scripture to reveal God's heart and mind and ours. Scripture addresses major themes in human lives. As we have said, Scripture contains what seems like an infinite supply. Jesus spoke about eternal life arising from within followers of God like an ever fresh, inexhaustible spring (John 7:38–39). Scripture is similar because it is open to the illumination of the Holy Spirit—a renewing source of God's availability. Inviting the Holy Spirit to bring appropriate scriptural texts to our attention is part of our continuing prayer.

Reflections

1. What is your experience and history with Scripture?
2. How are you presently using Scripture?
3. Are there scriptural texts that you seem to return to time after time? Which ones? What do you think this may say about the characteristics of your relationship with God?
4. What scriptural texts seem important to you now?
5. What would you like to discuss with a spiritual director about Scripture?

Prayer | 12

Prayer is an unnatural activity.

Bill Hybels[1]

Now,
O Lord,
calm me into a quietness
 that heals
  and listens,
and molds my longings
 and passions,
  my wounds
   and wonderings
into a more holy
 and human
  shape.

Ted Loder[2]

And I pray that you, being rooted and established in love, may have power, together with all the saints, to grasp how wide and long and high and deep is the love of Christ, and to know this love that surpasses knowledge—that you may be filled to the measure of all the fullness of God.

Ephesians 3:17–19

At times it is difficult to think about our prayer or to pray because of our feelings of inadequacy or defensiveness. We may have tried to figure out how to pray and seemingly failed so many times that it is difficult to remain hopeful and continue praying. But we are in good company when we feel this way, because our questions about our good intentions, our responses to God, and our development as Christians are part of the journey of faith. Even C. S. Lewis expressed concern about his spiritual life and its unfolding. He wrote to his friend Arthur Greaves, "I am appalled to see how much of the change which I thought I had undergone lately was only imaginary. The real work seems still to be done. It is so fatally easy to confuse an aesthetic appreciation of the spiritual life with the life itself—to dream that you have waked, washed, and dressed and then to find yourself still in bed."[3] In the matters of prayer we often feel this way.

I invite you to read these pages about prayer knowing that you are a beloved friend of God—remembering that God's love surrounds you. At times we are given glimpses of this kind of infinite love through other people. Is there someone who has loved you lavishly, even if it was only for a short while, at any time in your life? Are there people you have loved in that way? Are there people for whom you would graciously and happily do whatever is needed on their behalf, for them or with them? Perhaps you are even aware of their flaws, but even their particular limitations draw you to support, care for, and provide for them so that they might blossom and grow. That is the best way I know to talk about prayer, because prayer is about God's love for us. Prayer is about being taught and transformed by God's love.

No matter how much we talk about Scripture, faith, or experience with God, Jesus, or the Holy Spirit, unless we actually attempt to be available to God we are only considering some interesting ideas from a distance. Spiritual life is born and realized in prayer when we open ourselves to willingly hear and respond to Divine love. Prayer is where our relationship with God is explored, nurtured, and deepened.

When good actions such as worship, Bible study, or service are detached from our prayer, they can become dead. We have many ideas about how to continue what God has begun in us and can easily slip into taking charge of our spiritual nurture and development instead of seeking the Holy Spirit's way. Laudable attitudes and projects may be congruent with Scripture and our own goals, but unless we ask God to help us set priorities, order our lives, and guide us moment by moment, how can we hope for our actions to grow from God's intentions rather than from seemingly good ideas of our own? When we pray consistently we frequently notice it has a marked influence on our intentions and actions.

The opportunity to look more closely at prayer is one of the gifts of spiritual direction. Directors and directees spend a great deal of time paying attention to the prayer of the directee by praying about prayer, examining it, and reflecting on how the Holy Spirit is inviting the directee to pray. The following materials may give you a clearer picture of some of the topics that arise in these conversations.

Before we talk about prayer, however, it may be helpful to read the following prayers slowly as if you were praying and notice which of them seem to invite you to authentic prayer and which do not.

Prayers from Scripture

Lord, I believe; help thou mine unbelief.

Mark 9:24 KJV

God be merciful to me a sinner.

Luke 18:13 KJV

Father,
hallowed be your name,
your kingdom come.
Give us each day our daily bread.
Forgive us our sins,
    for we also forgive everyone who sins against us.
And lead us not into temptation.

Luke 11:2–4

For this reason I kneel before the Father, from whom his whole family in heaven and on earth derives its name. I pray that out of his glorious riches he may strengthen you with power through his Spirit in your inner being, so that Christ may dwell in your hearts through faith. And I pray that you, being rooted and established in love, may have power, together with all the saints, to grasp how wide and long and high and deep is the love of Christ, and to know this love that surpasses knowledge—that you may be filled to the measure of all the fullness of God. Now to him who is able to do immeasurably more than all we ask or imagine, according to his power that is at work within us, to him be glory in the church and in Christ Jesus throughout all generations, for ever and ever! Amen.

Ephesians 3:14–21

Prayers from Christian Tradition

Most merciful God,
We confess that we have sinned against you
in thought, word, and deed,
by what we have done,
and by what we have left undone.
We have not loved you with our whole heart:
we have not loved our neighbors as ourselves.
We are truly sorry and we humbly repent.
For the sake of your Son Jesus Christ,
have mercy on us and forgive us:
that we may delight in your will,
and walk in your ways
to the glory of your Name. Amen.

"A Confession of Sin,"
The Book of Common Prayer[4]

Our Father who art in heaven hallowed be Thy name. Thy kingdom come, thy will be done on earth as it is in heaven. Give us this day our daily bread and forgive us our trespasses as we forgive those who trespass against us. Lead us not into temptation, but deliver us from evil for thine is the kingdom and the power and the glory forever. Amen.

"The Lord's Prayer,"
The Book of Common Prayer[5]

I pray for Thy Spirit to enter me and fill me completely.
I pray for Thy kingdom to come in earth as it is in heaven.
I pray for my will to become completely and utterly Thy will.
I pray for my actual needs to be met by the right supply, in the right way and
    at the right time.
I pray for the right persons to come into my life, at the right time and in the
    right way.
I pray for the right ideas to come to me in perfect sequence and in perfect order
in the right time and in the right way.
I pray for my deepest soul's sincere desire to be fulfilled in the right time and
in the right way.

Glenn Clark[6]

Eternal One.
  Silence
    From whom my words come:
  Questioner
    From whom my questions arise:
  Lover
    Of whom all my loves are hints:
  Disturber
    In whom alone I find my rest:
  Mystery
    In whose depths I find healing and myself:
  Enfold me now in your presence
  Restore to me your peace
  Renew me through your power
  And ground me in your grace. Amen.

Ted Loder[7]

Take, O Lord, and receive my entire liberty, my memory, my understanding,
and my whole will. All that I am, all that I have, Thou has given me, and I will
give it back again to Thee to be disposed of according to Thy good pleasure.
Give me only Thy love and Thy grace: with Thee I am rich enough, nor do I ask
ought besides.

Ignatius of Loyola[8]

My heart I give thee, Lord, willingly and forever.

John Calvin[9]

The Nature of Prayer

Prayer is both an attitude and a behavior. In prayer we open ourselves
to God's love, because we desire to be God's companions who hear,
respond to, and are transformed by God. We give words to our expres-

sions directed toward the Holy One, who is God. We often pray the Lord's Prayer, our own words, or the prayers of others. Sometimes the flow of words slows down or diminishes in prayer, moving us toward attentive, expectant listening. Anything that enables us to speak honestly and listen to the Spirit of God facilitates prayer.

In our prayer we respond to God's initiatives by revealing ourselves, reflecting on our lives, and seeking to be aware of God's presence and guidance. This communicating love relationship develops as we awaken more fully to appreciate and open our lives to God.

Prayer is truly dependent on God's grace. Unless the Spirit enables us to recognize God's active presence with us, we have no sense of communion or prayerfulness. Prayer may then feel hollow, empty, and foolish. We can direct ourselves toward God, try to be open, and wait, but we cannot dictate whether we will have a sense of deep connection with God. God invites us to pray, so we can safely assume that God intends to communicate with us, but we do not control when, how, or what God will say. When we do have a sense of communing with God, we recognize that prayer is a gift.

How to Pray

We may begin praying according to methods or practices suggested by our church or ways that seem right because of specific characteristics of our relationship with God, or we may simply pray without thinking about how we do it. Some people study Scripture to learn how to pray. They pay particular attention to Jesus' prayers and hope to be influenced by his practices. They may regularly pray the prayer Christ taught the disciples and other prayers recorded in Scripture. We get ideas about prayer from our own and others' experiences and from the teaching of the church and material written about prayer. Our prayer is influenced by what we think prayer is and what we believe are appropriate topics and practices of prayer.

When prayer flows spontaneously, we may not think much about it because it seems so effortless. We feel as if we are communicating, open to, and aligned with God. Many people seem to pray most authentically when they are miserable or delighted. At these moments we may be surprised to discover we are praying because we cannot remember that we had any clear intention of beginning to pray. The events of a moment, a sight, or a feeling have taken us into prayer. It seems as if our real self has just spoken up. Something has broken through our usual ways of being and we sense release and relief. Until we have experiences that feel genuinely connected with what we truly care about, we may not even recognize some facades we have been maintaining with God, others, and ourselves.

Many prayers arise when we recognize that our expectations about life are not being met. Most of us do not need much encouragement to pray when we are in physical or emotional pain unless we have given up on God and prayer. If we have turned away from God, we are less apt to pray and more likely to try to cope through the support of loving human relationships, intellectualizing rationalizations, or by withdrawing and trying to make it through life's challenges on our own. Many people, however, who never pray otherwise, do so in the midst of crisis.

Our prayer seems direct, true, and effective when we are carried away or captured by prayer at the ends of the emotional continuum. But whether we remain in a place of agony or joy or move toward what feels like a more stable place in the middle, we have a lot to learn if we hope to develop as praying people.

Intentionality and discipline are necessary if we desire a prayer life. If there is such a thing as a prayer life, it more than likely parallels ordinary life. Ordinary life needs some repeating patterns to give it structure but also variety and interruptions that prevent stagnation. When we establish a structure for our prayer, we can focus energy into prayer itself rather than decisions about whether and how to pray.

Transitions in Prayer

Take a few minutes to write down all the kinds of prayer that come to mind. There are countless varieties of prayer.[10] It is clear that God calls people to different kinds of prayer at different times.

One way to think about prayer is to look at prayer itself rather than anything outside of it. How are we praying? What seems good about our prayer and what does not? One reason we struggle with prayer is because prayer changes. If we do not pay attention to it and nurture it, prayer diminishes or even disappears. If we attend to it, we and our prayers develop in interesting ways, as shown in the following conversation.

Directee: I've been thinking a lot about sickness and God lately.

Director: That sounds like a big topic.

Directee: Too big for me, but sometimes things are just there so I begin to pray about them. My friend has been struggling with cancer for three years. I know lots of people do, but this seems so unfair to me. [Silence. Directee seems to be considering what to say.] My friend has faithfully persevered for so many years against incredible odds that it just doesn't seem right.

Her entire family emigrated one by one to the United States from a difficult situation—dictatorship, surveillance, little freedom, imprisonment. They left at great personal cost, and the transition has been difficult. After many years, their lives were assuming some sense of normalcy. They were beginning to enjoy a new life . . . and then this.

Director: So what is this doing to your prayer?

Directee: I've prayed for them and with them—for the right resources at the right time, for response to treatments, for healing. I've prayed with them, by myself, and with others. You know, now that you ask, lately it feels as though my prayer energy has been directed more toward them than toward God. I'm not sure I can explain exactly what I mean, but it feels like I open more strongly to them than I do to God.

Director: Say more.

Directee: At times when I pray about them or for them, it feels as though I'm going through the motions rather than truly connecting with God. At other times it's not like that. I have a clear sense that I am praying how and what is called for from me—whether or not the words are just right. Now I'm wondering if the reason I feel like I'm talking to myself instead of God at times is that my anxiety in the situation has been so strong that my prayer really has been a way of talking to myself.

Director: I suppose everyone feels that way sometimes. But I hear you saying that you think you're noticing some insights that have meaning for you about this particular prayer.

Directee: These thoughts are pretty sketchy still, and I know that feelings cannot be the final word on the effectiveness of prayer. God seems to have answered some of what I thought were my least spiritual or maybe even careless prayers in remarkable ways. But this instance with my friend feels different. When I become aware of being involved in prayer that feels empty, I'd like to try just stopping whatever and however I'm praying and invite God. If I'm with someone else, that might mean telling them about my sense and asking if we could be quiet for a few minutes. I could give myself a little time to ask God what is going on, to ask how to pray, whom to pray for, what to pray about. It's easy for me to have so many ideas about how to pray in this situation. I know there are many things I would hope someone would pray about for me if I were in a cancer battle. The sense that nothing is happening might mean that God is desiring a different sort of prayer. You know, I could be praying for inner peace, and the Spirit might be encouraging prayer for stopping the nausea from the treatments. It could be almost anything. What I'm saying is that I'm feeling called to *listen* more, to listen more for God's heart and pray whatever seems right at the time.

Director: I'll be interested to hear what happens when you experiment with this.

Directee: I guess I can get kind of frantic inside, like I think I'm supposed to be able to do something because I want so badly for the situation to be different. Looks like I'm being stretched. It can be as hard to trust God for someone else's journey as it is for my own. I'd like to be a help along the way rather than getting in the way—my friend's way or God's way.

We often become more intentional about prayer when we sense some kind of authentic connectedness with God, or long for such a relationship. Then we may start to pray by talking with God about things of importance to us. We speak about what we want, hope for, or fear. If we continue in prayer, our concerns about ourselves lead to an awareness of other people's needs, and we include them in our prayer. Our commitment to intercessory prayer grows. The content, attitudes, and qualities of our prayer are affected when we see that God offers forgiveness, lovingkindness, compassion, mercy, guidance, and empowering presence—so much more than we thought was possible, for others as well as ourselves. The unique qualities of being in a close, deepening relationship with God begin to transform our prayer.

Our prayer grows toward God's heart and desires. Even when we pray about other people and their needs and hopes, we listen for what God is inviting us to pray about and how. We grow in willingness to let God choose which particular people we are to pray for. We may struggle with the issue of prayer lists if we have been even a little bit proud of our faithfulness to pray consistently for many people by using a list. It may be difficult for us to consider that God might be asking us to reevaluate our practice or let go of a list entirely—at least for a season—to trust that the Holy Spirit will guide our prayer.

We are wise to question our motivations and be observant in matters such as this, lest we lose our commitment to pray for others or become legalistic. As we learn what God intends, we learn to surrender to the Holy Spirit's loving guidance.

When we choose to pay attention to our relationship with God or sense the Holy Spirit is attempting to awaken or deepen our spiritual life, our prayer comes to life in new ways. Such prayer is often very worded at the beginning. We may write long prayer lists and faithfully attend to them. We pray about many things we have not realized or thought about before. We engage in discussion with God about almost everything.

When I was passing through a troubled season of life, I felt drawn to pray about my entire life up to that point. I drove to the house and schools where I had grown up, parked the car nearby, and prayed about the events and experiences of each place. It seemed like I was telling God my life story. I knew that God already knew everything about me, and yet as I prayed, I seemed to open myself to be more vulnerable with God. It was my way of telling God how much I longed for God to be a part of my every thought and breath, every action and relationship. This kind of worded prayer seemed to spring from God's love in me, my love for God, and my hopes for God's presence and life in the world. I prayed about and for family members, friends, and whatever else God brought to my attention.

At some point highly verbal prayer ceases to be as satisfying as it once was. At such times we can feel a little ashamed by our diminishing sense of commitment and interest and may feel so deficient that we do not attempt to talk to anyone about it. Prayer may seem boring, as though we are just talking to ourselves. We may have no idea what to do next and feel confused. We may stop praying or dutifully continue on in practices that seem empty. Feeling as though we are at an impasse can awaken us to look more closely at how, why, and what we pray. Let's listen to a directee describing what this is like.

Directee:	I thought God and I had this great love relationship going strong. It seemed like God was with me all the time. I'd chatter happily away and had the sense that God was listening and responding. Now it's like a telephone line went dead. I feel like I am talking to myself. "Hello, hello—anybody there? No answer."
Director:	So what do you make of it?
Directee:	I really don't know what to think. First, I sent out a search party looking for sin—mine.
Director:	Yes?
Directee:	I recognized some of my usual tendencies: not trusting God to take care of me, anxiousness, and other things like that. But nothing seemed to stir in me like it does when I know the Holy Spirit is showing me something.

Director: What is happening in your life?

Directee: It's busy. But it seems to be going okay. I've been taking time for prayer just about every morning before I'm out the door. Family life is full. You know how it is. We are involved in a lot of activities, but we've been able to make time to work on the Habitat for Humanity house our church is sponsoring.

Director: Your life sounds amazingly balanced.

Directee: I'd have said the same. Even if it only lasts for a short while, it is a nice relief. But that is part of the mystery. I've had my prayer go dead before—more than once. One of those times I saw that I was truly overly involved with good stuff—God stuff even. But I had forgotten I was a mere mortal. I was overloaded and anxious and became more like a machine than a person. My main goal was getting things done. Many good things get pushed into the background when I do that. My relationships—with people and with God—get shortchanged. When I would finally get around to taking time for God it was like I was trying to say, "Now it's your turn; we have to be quick." When I slowed down and made decent time and space for prayer, the prayer and sense of relationship gradually returned.

    Then there's the opposite side. I've experienced that too. You know the old cliché about being so heavenly minded you are no earthly good. Prayer time, Bible study, retreats, journaling—I got so immersed in me, my, mine, myself. It was like an obsession. In the beginning it seemed good for my relationship with God, but then it felt like the door closed between us. I cannot remember where the wake-up call came from, but it did. I started looking around, and the Spirit invited me away from myself as center toward God and toward hearing God's heart for others.

Director: So what is it this time?

Directee: I don't know. I've looked at everything I can think of.

Director: From what I'm hearing, it does sound like you have been exploring lots of possibilities. What does God say?

Directee: God?

Director: What does your prayer look like? What is going on?

Directee: Nothing. Like I said.

Director: What does nothing look like?

Directee:	When I set aside time for prayer, I begin by offering myself to God by writing in my journal. I take out my prayer list and begin to pray for the people on it. That's when I know I'm missing something. It feels like I'm talking to myself.
Director:	Is that a change for you?
Directee:	Is it ever!
Director:	I wonder. From what you have described it seems like your prayer up until now has contained a lot of words, lots of talking.
Directee:	Yes.
Director:	Does God ever get a real chance to communicate with you?
Directee:	I think so. But now that you mention it, I guess I do pretty much fill the time with my words.
Director:	Perhaps God is inviting you to listen more—to pray in a more meditative way in which you invite God to speak to you and you allow God to set the prayer topics.
Directee:	How would I do that?
Director:	Praying with Scripture would be a good place to begin. Between now and the next time we see each other, I'd like you to read this page about praying with Scripture and experiment with some of the suggestions for prayer. Prepare yourself to listen to God by getting quiet and then using a passage of Scripture as the beginning place for your prayer. Read the passage slowly, one word or phrase at a time. You may stop and read the same word or phrase a number of times. Then allow quiet space. Read slowly and reflectively. Notice how you respond to God. Move back and forth between reading and quiet waiting. Just let it develop as it does. There are several suggested passages you might want to work with.
Directee:	What about my prayer list?
Director:	Maybe you could put it aside when you are praying with Scripture. If you sense God inviting you to use the list afterwards, do so. If not, just ask God if there is some need that God invites you to pray about. If not, then gently offer God your list and see what happens.
Directee:	That sounds different, but I am willing to try your suggestions.

From this conversation, we can see there are many possibilities to explore when our prayer changes. It would be nice if we could discover or create a list of reasons why prayer disappears. In a very general way, we can. We can consider various sorts of attitudes, behaviors, and life situations that might be influencing our prayer. We can consider whether we are displeasing God or have been diverted from what God intends. We can reflect on whether we have been enjoying God for ourselves, using prayer primarily for our pleasure rather than as a means of allowing and inviting God to call us to reach beyond ourselves. Prayer dries up when it is only for ourselves rather than for God, when we turn in on ourselves for ourselves.

Sometimes we have the opposite problem. We can become exhausted when we pray, serve, expend time and energy, and do many things but forget that we need ongoing replenishment in order to pray and function effectively. We need to make time for longer, intentional times of prayer, an extended time of retreat in quiet solitude, or recreation, rest, and play. Sometimes it helps to read about obstacles to prayer and recognize ourselves and our difficulties through someone else's experience and wisdom.[11]

When we read about the lives and practices of Christians from many eras, denominations, and cultures, we see patterns in the growth of prayer. These patterns reflect a gradual development from prayer that seems self-initiated to prayer that seems more clearly invited and guided by God. Of course, any prayer is in response to God's initiatives, even when we are not aware of it, because true prayer is not possible without Divine involvement. But we can speak only from the human side of the relationship.

There are many ways to speak about the ways prayer changes. Teresa of Avila wrote in 1525 that the spiritual life is like a garden in which His Majesty (the Lord) uproots the weeds and sets out good plants. Prayer is the water for the garden. Teresa wrote:

> It seems to me that the garden can be watered in four ways: by taking the water from a well which costs us great labour, or by a water-wheel and buckets, when the water is drawn by windlass; or by a stream or brook, which waters the ground much better for it saturates it more thoroughly and there is less need to water it often, so that the gardener's labour is much less; or by heavy rain, when the Lord waters it with no labour of ours, a way incomparably better than any of those which have been described.[12]

Teresa describes how beginning and continuing in prayer involves work, and how prayer changes and moves toward meditation, listening to God, and contemplation. She says that God guides the soul that persists in prayer, and she describes hindrances that pray-ers encounter as they develop and deepen in loving communion with God.[13]

In the early stages of learning to pray, we may not recognize God's initiatives as frequently or as distinctly as we will later. Long-time prayers write and speak about the gradual transitions in their prayer. They describe how God softens their own desires to be in charge. God seems to entrust us with enough glimpses of the fruit of divinely directed prayer that we become more willing to proceed in this way. As we become more settled and centered in God, the Holy Spirit increases our ability to recognize and follow.

Any hindrance to authentic prayer is an opportunity for us to learn from God. The best place to begin when prayer disappears is to ask God what this change means and then persist in our asking, searching, and listening until God guides us. This process may take days, weeks, or months. Sometimes what seems to us like authentic prayer disappears because God wants to get our attention to teach us something new. We seldom look for anything different when our prayer remains good as it is. We are satisfied. Dissatisfaction can motivate us to explore.

Some people first come to spiritual direction because of difficulties in prayer. The Holy Spirit often leads us through a series of small steps before we get to the heart of things. It can be helpful to discuss our perceptions, interpretations, and responses with someone. As we have said earlier, speaking with another person about our prayer can be helpful, but when we do this within the context of a prayer relationship such as spiritual direction, we listen for more than another person's insights. Both of us ask God about the prayer of the directee. We are in prayer and speaking about prayer at the same time.

Meditative Prayer

Some people who discover that their verbal prayer seems less gratifying are being drawn by God toward meditation. Perhaps this is the case with the directee mentioned above. Only time and prayer will tell. Meditation is a kind of prayer that involves fewer words and encourages us to take a listening stance with God.

If we feel as though the Spirit is drawing us toward this type of prayer, we can experiment with it. We can read a Scripture passage in the way suggested to the directee—slowly with space for silence. In this way we can stay with a passage of Scripture in order to listen to the Holy Spirit and divert our attention from our usual interests. We may respond by praying about whatever arises through the passage and alternate reading with quiet waiting and worded prayer, noticing what the Spirit stirs in us.[14]

Scripture encourages us to meditate on God and on God's precepts, Word, and wonders.

> Within your temple, O God,
>   we meditate on your unfailing love.

Psalm 48:9

> Blessed are those
>   who do not walk in the counsel of the wicked
> or stand in the way of sinners
>   or sit in the seat of mockers.
> But their delight is in the law of the LORD,
>   and on his law they meditate day and night.

Psalm 1:1–2 NIV ILE

> I will remember the deeds of the LORD;
>   yes, I will remember your miracles of long ago.
> I will meditate on all your works
>   and consider all your mighty deeds.

Psalm 77:11–12

> Let me understand the teaching of your precepts;
>   then I will meditate on your wonders.

Psalm 119:27

> My eyes stay open through the watches of the night,
>   that I may meditate on your promises.

Psalm 119:148

When we meditate, we dwell on something. We remain with a passage of Scripture or with an idea about God, or we pay attention to God's works in the created world.[15]

Lectio divina, divine reading, is a type of meditation with a long Christian history. It provides a particular pattern for people to follow and begins with Scripture as a way to listen to God. *Lectio divina* contains four parts: *lectio,* reading; *meditatio,* meditation; *oratio,* prayer; and *contemplatio,* contemplation. *Lectio* means reading Scripture with the desire to be addressed by God. During this step, we invite the Spirit of God to show us whatever we need to see. During *meditatio,* we go deeper. We may visualize a scriptural scene or explore a word or a phrase. This step may include intellectual questioning, pondering, or study. It is a time for integration. During *oratio,* the third stage, we pray, responding to what we have been reading and reflecting on. The prayer may be short or a back and forth conversation with God. If the prayer opens us to new ideas, we may want to read or reflect further. *Contemplatio,* the fourth part of *lectio divina,* involves resting in loving silence with God. True contemplation is a gift that we can prepare ourselves to receive. Reading and praying with Scripture opens the way to attentive listening with God.

A twelfth-century Carthusian monk described *lectio divina* this way:

> Reading seeks for the sweetness of a blessed life,
> meditation perceives it,
> prayer asks for it
> contemplation tastes it.
>
> Reading, as it were, puts food whole into the mouth,
> meditation chews it and breaks it up,
> prayer extracts its flavor,
> contemplation is the sweetness itself which gladdens and refreshes.[16]

When we participate in verbal prayer or reading that leads to meditative prayer as an ongoing practice, we begin to slow down inside in ways that enable us to see differently. The action of slowing down influences ordinary life as well as prayer. When my husband and I were in Washington, D.C., at cherry blossom time, we enjoyed driving past magnificent trees heavy with flowers. But it seemed like another world opened when we walked along the path at the edge of the tidal basin. A canopy of blossoms brushed against our hair and shoulders. We were immersed in pale pink flowers, fragrant softness, the shape of branches, patterns of petals and leaves in shadow and sunlight, and shining reflections. Soon we found ourselves walking in silence except for the sound of a few bees. When we slowed down to the pace of walking and experienced our surroundings up close, these acts changed our perspective. Meditation invites us to pause and look more closely at interior and exterior details we do not notice at a greater distance and speed. It enlarges our recognition of the Holy Spirit's presence and encourages appreciation and worship.

The act of slowing down influences what we see about God and ourselves. Often when we attempt to quiet down we become aware of clamoring thoughts and wonder if we will ever become peaceful. Sometimes, this inner turbulence is what we need to bring to God in prayer, and at other times the Spirit invites us simply to ignore our own racket by turning to God through Scripture or creation and focusing on prayer. Meditative prayer possesses healing qualities that take effect gradually from the inside out. Little by little we open ourselves more freely to God and cooperate more fully with the Holy Spirit as we settle into deepening trust. It is as though we are discovering our true home where we enjoy satisfying companionship with God.

As we experience the fruits of prayer arising out of what may have seemed like wasted moments and hours, our desire to set aside a time and place to be available to God becomes a priority. We want to enjoy God's companionship, and our trust grows. Then, the prayer from our set times seems to overflow, spilling over into ordinary life. Although it is still important to set aside specific times for prayer, we realize that all the moments of ordinary living are also attended by God's loving presence, and we learn to listen and pray in the midst of life.

At some point, however, meditative prayer can also seem less alive. When we try to prepare ourselves to listen to God by using Scripture, devotional reading, or another means, we feel hindered rather than assisted in our loving attentiveness with God. Perhaps it feels as though Scripture is getting in the way. This does not mean we no longer need to read and think about Scripture; it merely indicates that our prayer may be changing.

Again, we should ask God what is happening and look closely at ourselves and our prayer. This may be a short or extended process depending on the source of our difficulties. One of the things we explore is whether God is inviting us to another kind of prayer. We should not always assume, however, that every difficulty with prayer is a call to a different kind of prayer. Our prayer gets blocked and freed many times by great and small challenges, and we grow through the process of paying attention to God in and through these situations.

If we do sense God is calling us to something new or unfamiliar, we may resist feeling vulnerable. We may sense both yes and no in our hearts as we consider continuing with God. We may wonder where God is leading. Other times, changes in our prayer take place over a long period of time. This development can unfold so gradually that we do not perceive it. All of a sudden, we may recognize we are praying in a different way.

Contemplative Prayer

When meditative prayer disappears, the Spirit may be drawing us toward contemplative prayer—prayer that has been described as a loving gaze at God, or resting in God's love, or prayer of the heart. This type of prayer often involves no words or fewer words. The experience of contemplative prayer is like tender, mutual love. It is more about our relationship with God and appreciating our relationship than about anything particular we might do. It is not that activity becomes unimportant, however, for as our desire for God increases, so do our longings and intentions to be involved in the activities to which God draws us. The basis for action is love—God's love for us and for the world. Prompted by God's indwelling love, many people become involved in activities they would not have dreamed of choosing, but they also become convinced that the relationship itself is what gives them life and feels like home. Any activity is secondary.

There has not been much teaching or discussion about contemplation among Protestants as a whole until quite recently. However, many fine resources are available for us to read and reflect on if we think God might be inviting us to contemplation. The following quotations speak about contemplation.

> It is only little by little that the soul becomes accustomed to look at and to love God Himself by a simple view of faith for a notable period of time, much as the artist contemplates his masterpiece, the details and elements of which he had previously studied. It seems indeed that here there takes place an ordinary psychological process which evidently presupposes a live faith, and even the hidden action of the Holy Ghost, but not a special intervention of God.[17]

> God produces in the soul an ineffable love and it is through this love that we understand by means of intuition. *Someone* fastens our gaze on God.[18]

> The mystery of contemplation (and it is a mystery) is the presence of the risen Lord and His action on and in the soul.[19]

> Contemplation is the experience of one's heart being touched by the Spirit of God who is Love. It is about one's heart being so taken by this God that it waits in silence, with a loving attentiveness to this One who is Love. Nothing else matters. All our techniques and formulas are forgotten as we are being healed and restored by this transforming Love. The contemplative comes from this central experience out to love and serve others.[20]

Little by little, we can dispose ourselves toward contemplative prayer by intending and learning how to be more available to God in the midst of everything, but we cannot work or think our way into such prayer. True contemplation is a gift. Happily, God seems to give glimpses of contemplative awareness and enjoyment to everyone.

Praying for others in a contemplative style might be described as intentionally offering oneself to God for others. But in contemplative prayer we open ourselves to God for the purpose of loving God rather than to ask for anything from God. Nevertheless, as we open our hearts to God in this way, we come as we are with all persons and situations that are a part of our lives. Contemplative pray-ers offer themselves and their concerns to God within the context of attentive love. Their prayer becomes a kind of willingness to be a channel of God's love for others rather than a way of asking. But they also offer themselves to God for particular intentions, desires, or needs and ask what their part is in them.

If we persist in prayer, we will learn more about verbal, meditative, and contemplative ways. But prayer does not develop in a strictly linear fashion. We may feel at home with one type of prayer but also explore other ways of prayer. We can move back and forth as the Spirit invites and our desires and needs influence us.

Prayer in Tongues

Some people wonder how prayer in tongues fits into this scheme. Prayer in tongues may be present in verbal, meditative, or contemplative prayer. I have known people who initially prayed in tongues with many words and much obvious intercession, others who used tongues in a meditative way, and still others who describe a prayer of adoration—singing to God in tongues, which becomes or leads to contemplation. I do not know but suspect that whatever type of prayer God is nurturing in people at the time they receive the gift of tongues will be evident in both their native language and in tongues.

At times we are afraid of the gifts of the Holy Spirit, and at other times we welcome them. Our background strongly influences our reaction. If we are drawn to learn more about the gifts of the Spirit and about prayer in tongues, it is good to begin by reading Scripture passages pertaining to these matters and to ask God what is right for us. Reading about contemporary Christians who practice the gifts of the Spirit can also be informative. Sometimes it is most helpful to talk to a person face-to-face and ask questions. Finding the right person to speak to about prayer in tongues becomes itself a matter of prayer. At times the Spirit invites directees to this kind of exploration and prayer.

Spiritual Direction and Prayer

As we develop, our prayer flows more and more out of the Holy Spirit's promptings. We pay closer attention to what is going on in our relationship with God. We may notice that our commitment to pray regularly is stronger. We may still struggle with finding time for prayer, but our desire to pray in spite of busy, cluttered, daily living continues to grow. Through persisting in prayer and speaking with a spiritual director, the limitations of our knowledge and awareness become clearer. More and more we realize that authentic prayer is dependent on God's guidance—and that will always be true.

The priority we give to prayer, the amount of time we spend in prayer, the frequency of our prayer, the topics we pray about, and our attitudes and agendas all wax and wane, grow and change. The American Way of independent accomplishment could cause us to behave as if getting to the end, praying contemplatively, is somehow best. But the Spirit often encourages us simply to enjoy being with God exactly where we are today.

We want to notice the kind of prayer the Spirit seems to be inviting and participate wholeheartedly. Spiritual direction can help us during times of transition in our prayer, but it can also help us stay put when the Spirit invites us to remain where God is blessing us through an established method of prayer. Through spiritual direction, many people discover that the best way to figure out what is called for in prayer is to ask God.

Things That Can Influence Prayer

In chapter 3, "Who Comes to Spiritual Direction?" we discussed some aspects of human uniqueness that shape who we are and influence when, if, and how we decide to participate in spiritual direction. I wrote briefly about genetic legacies of physical and familial traits, individual histories, and the characteristics of particular life stages. The list of factors that affect our prayer is endless, but three aspects affect everyone: how we picture faith, our individual personality, and where we are in the journey of faith.

Scripture includes a variety of ways of looking at faith. We probably identify more strongly with some than others. Do we think of ourselves as being on a faith journey? This picture of faith comes from Exodus and contains glimpses of wandering and grace, being directly guided by God, and progressing toward the Promised Land. Or do we see ourselves in a race as described by Paul in Hebrews 12:1 in which we put aside whatever hinders our progress? Or do we believe we are primarily called to be branches abiding in the vine as described in John 15, recognizing we are totally dependent on God for life and fruitfulness? Do we think of ourselves as part of a community brought forth by one Spirit but in which each member possesses diverse gifts in prayer, practice, and service (1 Cor. 12:14–31)? Is our relationship with God a hidden mystery as described in 1 Corinthians 2:6–16: "No eye has seen, no ear has heard, no mind has conceived what God has prepared for those who love him" (v. 9)? Or does Matthew 25:37–40, which speaks about feeding the hungry and visiting those in prison, describe what a life of faith means to you?

All of these and other scriptural pictures are helpful in understanding faith. But even though all represent truthful aspects, it is difficult, if not impossible, to live out all of them simultaneously. What seems most important for our developing relationship with God is different at different times in our lives. For several years one picture may be our primary way of picturing faith, and then later a different one or some combination of scriptural descriptions may seem more meaningful. The ways we think about faith shape what we think prayer is, who God is and what God is like, and how we believe we are called to live in relationship with God.

As we mentioned in chapter 10, "Experiencing God," individuality is a second influence. How might our personality influence our prayer and our perception of our experience with God? Does it make any difference at all? Some say that particular inclinations regarding prayer, such as preferring to pray alone rather than with others or choosing to praise God more than ask God for assistance, correspond with certain personality characteristics. Others are not so sure, because grace is not limited. Whether we choose to describe individual personality in terms of categories or lean toward no classification system, it is clear that what is life-giving for some is deadening for others. It is important to know who we are, what our relationship with God is like, and how our individuality influences what is helpful in prayer and what is not. When we know something about ourselves and about prayer and the life of faith, such knowledge can help us avoid being overly troubled by difficulties and to trust our prayer and relationship with God. When we do not know ourselves or are uninformed about the characteristics of prayer and faith, we can easily blame ourselves, God, or circumstances when our prayer disappears or becomes laborious or when our sense of God vanishes.

The life of faith has often been described as a journey because it is clear that we are going somewhere and that what is appropriate changes as we move along. A number of theorists have observed that faith seems to develop in identifiable, sequential stages. They believe people understand, reflect on, and practice faith in ways that are dependent on where they are in the faith journey. But our faith-related development is not the same as our chronological life journey. For instance, someone could be middle aged but only beginning to pay attention to an intentional relationship with God.

All development theories in regard to faith describe a similar unfolding pattern. A rough approximation of the stages involved include:

1. an awakening to God's love and a commitment to God
2. study and learning about God
3. questioning
4. receiving and giving—reaching out to serve God and others
5. going deeper with God
6. a radical outlaw stage, during which we decide or decide again whether to surrender completely to God
7. acknowledgment of the mysteries of good and evil present in the world and an ability to say, "Nevertheless, I trust in God," in addition to more Christlike compassion toward others and love for God

While these stages describe the faith journey of some Christians, they do not resonate with everyone. There are many interesting ways to describe maturation in faith. Some are more compatible with our experience than others.[21]

Pictures of faith, personality, and faith development are interesting lenses through which to view God, ourselves, and our spiritual practices. Sometimes, however, this information clutters our prayer. Interesting, extraneous information can divert us from what might help most. Often, what we really long for is a deeper awareness of God's love and present participation with us, rather than insightful ways to look more closely at ourselves. But even if this is the case, we can ask God whether it would enhance our relationship and prayer to learn more about any of these things.

A Special Consideration: Healing Prayer during Spiritual Direction Sessions

In a general sense, spiritual direction might be considered a healing relationship because within it obstacles and resistances to grace are often diffused. However, specific prayers for healing may also become part of spiritual direction. Some directors believe that prayer for healing is dependent on a particular kind of giftedness and call in the pray-er. Others speak more about the healing presence of Christ, of the Holy Spirit, and seek to hear when God is asking them to pray for healing. Some directors may not feel called or equipped to pray for any or certain kinds of healing and may refer directees to others.

No matter what we think about these matters, sometimes the Holy Spirit places the focus on healing, which may call for distinct kinds of prayer during direction sessions. There may be things going on that directees are not ready to speak about or do not know how to pray about. When directors listen to God and to directees, the Holy Spirit may reveal the prayer that needs to be prayed. When directors pray, they may not understand the significance of the prayer—they simply pray aloud according to what seems right. When directees hear the prayer, they may experience the Spirit's healing touch. They may feel an interior release, a resolution, a healing of old emotional wounds, or even a physical change, and they know it was from God.

Directors keep a careful, prayerful watch for any tendencies they may have to manipulate directees by their prayer. Directors seek to have an open, willing heart to respond to what the Spirit is inviting. When the prayer is completed, one or both persons may be aware that this specific prayer was uniquely appropriate for the directee for the present circumstances. When directors, in response to the Holy Spirit, pray in this way, prayer almost seems to have a life of its own. Both director and directee may be surprised by the content of the prayer and by the healing that follows.

At other times, the kind of healing prayer that seems right becomes clear through the direction conversation. Then the director and directee discuss possibilities for shared prayer and discern the Spirit's leading together. On occasion this may include prayers for emotional, physical, spiritual, or relational healing. Such prayers usually reflect an awareness that God has allowed certain matters to surface in the conversation and that the directee is seeking Christ's touch. Directees often address old wounds that could hinder their receptivity and responsiveness to God and to other people.

Directors should not automatically decide to pray for healing when needs arise but seek the guidance of the Holy Spirit. Directors may or may not be invited by God to pray for healing. Perhaps this is a matter that the directee and God need time to sort through and bring fully into view in solitude. Perhaps the prayer of the directee is most essential, or maybe the prayer needs to take place in a group or in a church.

It is important for directors to wait through any impulses they have to fix things and listen for what God intends. Quite often our particular troubles are used wonderfully by God. Directors frequently feel called not to pray immediately for healing but to walk alongside directees, pray with them in the midst of whatever is transpiring or revealed, and trust God to direct the process.

Of course, either or both persons can pray for healing. Sometimes directees need to be the ones who pray aloud in a direction session about their desire for healing. Or they may choose to pray alone or with someone else at another time. When prayer for healing seems right, it may not be clear exactly what kind of healing is called for. We may only sense the Lord's desire to bring about a deeper wholeness of some sort. Directors need to listen carefully to the Holy Spirit and directees, communicate clearly, and give directees freedom to choose an appropriate way to pray. Otherwise, directees can feel the director is intruding. Directors should ask God to guide their prayer so that it does not become a way of manipulating or influencing directees or communicating directors' agendas.

It is important to pay attention to what the Spirit is inviting in regard to physical aspects of healing prayer. Sometimes it is appropriate to anoint a person on the forehead with oil and/or lay hands on a person's head or shoulders during prayer. We may choose to sit, stand, or kneel. Some directors and directees share communion as a way of recognizing God's love expressed through Christ's life, death, and resurrection and as the source for human healing.

Directors should pray about the prayer methods that might be used. What is the Holy Spirit inviting? How are we called to cooperate with God? What might just be our own idea? The temptation to fix situations and people and the desire to be fixed show up with regularity and need to be noticed and offered to God. We are not called to fix ourselves or others but to be deeply connected to God in Christ, who invites us to be whole.

Both directors and directees are influenced by particular Christian traditions and their own prayer histories, hopes, and expectations as they explore possible ways of prayer. Sometimes our willing openness to pray however the Spirit invites takes one or both of us into new territory. The outcomes of prayer for healing, which are often different from what we expect, become evidence of God's presence, care, and creativity with us.

Although prayer for healing may include some uncomfortable moments, by the time we finish we often experience a sense of completion accompanied by our recognition that we have prayed what God intended. We may sense that God has heard our prayer—whether or not we have been able to articulate it, understand it, or pray in the "right way." The prayer has communicated our willingness and desire for God to touch our lives in healing ways, and we are aware of the present peacefulness of the Holy Spirit and that we have done our part.

After a prayer for healing, we may see evidence of change in a short amount of time, or it may appear gradually in the following days and weeks. Whether or not change seems to ensue, we need to continue talking, praying, and asking the Lord for guidance. All the while, we desire to remember that our primary intention is to be God's and to love, follow, and serve God. When prayer enables us to more fully realize God's love for us, whether or not we receive the particular healing we thought we were praying for, we experience grace.[22]

During spiritual direction conversations, directors and directees pay significant attention to prayer and where it leads. We have noticed that many things influence prayer from within and without. Some of these draw us to look at ourselves or our prayer; others encourage us to take the focus off ourselves and place it on God. At times we get sidetracked on our journey of prayer even when we deeply desire to hear and respond to the Spirit. Sometimes we become so narrowly focused by looking intently at ourselves that we miss seeing the largeness of God and God's intentions. At other times we are so outwardly focused in our prayer that we miss things in our own heart that need to be opened to God's light and life. It helps to back up a little and look at our prayer through the loving detachment of spiritual direction.

Reflections

One helpful way to explore what God is inviting in our prayer is to pray about prayer. The following questions are a place to begin that process.

1. What are your prayer practices and how have you chosen these particular ways of prayer? (You may wish to write a prayer autobiography.)
2. How do your prayer practices include or pay attention to your body, mind, emotions, will, imagination, and memories?
3. Where do you sense an aliveness in prayer?
4. What do you notice about how prayer seems to influence you? others? your life circumstances?
5. What do you think the Holy Spirit might be inviting in your prayer? What makes you think this is God's desire?
6. What are your desires related to your prayer?
7. Look over what you have written in response to questions 1–6, then complete the following sentences.
   I learned . . .
   I relearned . . .
   I am surprised that . . .
   I have always known . . .
   Take time to bring what you have noticed into your prayer.
8. Explore your prayer life by finishing the following sentences.
   The last time I took time for prayer was . . .
   The place I find most helpful for prayer is . . .
   The time I find best for prayer is . . .
   A method of prayer that seems good for me now is . . .
   I use Scripture in prayer by . . .
   Sometimes during prayer I . . .
   When I pray, God . . .
   I talk about my prayer with . . .
   My life influences my prayer by . . .
   My prayer influences my life by . . .
   I pray with . . .
   A way that God touches me in prayer for which I am grateful is . . .
   My favorite name for God is . . .
   When I pray I sometimes feel . . .
   I find out what God wants by . . .
   My prayer leads me to . . .
   Going to church influences my prayer by . . .
   My prayer influences my relationship with my church by . . .

Life in general influences my prayer by . . .

What I want to say to God now is . . .

What I would like to have happen in my prayer life is . . .

Look over what you have written. Circle the number of any sentence that the Holy Spirit seems to be nudging you to pay closer attention to through prayer and reflection. Your responses to these sentences may have pointed you toward some other things you would like to write about in relation to your prayer. Write down a few words or phrases that will help you recall what seemed important so that you can return to these insights for prayer and journaling at a later time.

9. Things I notice about my prayer:

Things I wish someone had told me about prayer:

Look over what you have written. Which two or three items seem most important to you?

13 | Discernment

> I must learn to pay attention to the movements of my heart, to reflect on them wisely and carefully with the help of others, and to test them over time. In this process I must learn two equally difficult and seemingly incompatible attitudes: to trust myself and my reactions and to recognize how easily I delude myself. Discernment requires that I believe that God will show himself in my experience and that I yet be wary of mindless credulity toward that same experience.
>
> William Barry[1]

> Do not be conformed to this world, but be transformed by the renewing of your minds, so that you may discern what is the will of God—what is good and acceptable and perfect.
>
> Romans 12:2 NRSV

Is this what the Spirit of God is saying to me? Or is it something else? How do I decide? Finding answers to questions about God's presence, desires, and intentions is often called discernment.

Discernment involves discriminating among numerous ideas and feelings and identifying what is from God. To do so we need to be awake to the Holy Spirit and aware of what is happening, to perceive great and subtle differences between God's initiatives and our responses.

Our ability to discern is influenced by our willingness to observe. When we look closely at our lives, we see that we pay conscious attention to only a part of an endless stream of stimuli that bombards us. Some of us tend to notice outward objects, relationships, and experiences more readily than interior experiences. Others pay attention to interior matters first. We cannot pay equal attention to all information that comes our way. Much more is going on at any given moment than we can take into conscious account or become involved with. Of the things we do notice, some remain in the background while others draw our energy and attention for moments or hours. Still others, such as significant human relationships, keep us involved for years.

There is nothing particularly new or startling about this information, but it can help us recognize how much attention we give to various things—what we notice in passing, what we focus on intently, and what we ignore. When we begin to observe our own thoughts and behaviors and monitor more of our experience, as we often do in spiritual direction, we may be surprised by how oblivious we have been to much available information.

When we look more intentionally at our lives, we may also see that some things that pass through our hearts and minds do not arise from exclusively human sources. Although we easily identify many thoughts and attitudes as our own, others have qualities of deeper compassion or grace than we have come to expect from ourselves. At the opposite end of the spectrum, we may become aware of a kind of mean-spiritedness that seems to be something other than just our own orneriness. At times we know clearly that these kinds of responses are not ours alone. They seem to point toward other sources. It can be encouraging to recognize the Holy Spirit's nudging and unsettling to suspect some unfriendly or even evil source that seems to be trying to distract or divert us from recognizing or responding in the best possible way. We want to understand and recognize the true sources of our attitudes, opinions, and behaviors. Practicing discernment can help.

Whether we are looking for God's communication to us through external data such as biblical writings or internal data such as observing our prayer and reflecting on it, any analysis of our relationship with God takes place within the cluttered, noisy environment of all that passes through our minds. Sometimes looking for God's presence, grace, and words amid a barrage of stimulation from within and without seems like an overwhelming task.

As we grow more accustomed to seeing what marches through our minds, we notice that we are unaware of so much (some of it blessedly so) that we could easily miss what the Spirit is saying. At the same time, we may also realize that we have acted many times in response to the Holy Spirit's direct promptings and invitations. As we continue to practice discernment, we can become more trusting about our ability to hear the leading of the Spirit.

First, however, we need to consider two areas of discernment: (1) discernment about spiritual experiences—whether or not they are from God, and (2) discernment practices.

Discernment and Experiences of and with God

"Do not come any closer," God said. "Take off your sandals, for the place where you are standing is holy ground." Then he said, "I am the God of your father, the God of Abraham, the God of Isaac and the God of Jacob."

Exodus 3:5–6

All this I have spoken while still with you. But the Counselor, the Holy Spirit, whom the Father will send in my name, will teach you all things and will remind you of everything I have said to you. Peace I leave with you; my peace I give you. I do not give to you as the world gives. Do not let your hearts be troubled and do not be afraid.

John 14:25–27

Although it is unlikely that you have seen God in a burning bush, you probably have had some sense of an encounter with God. Think about an experience when you "knew that you knew that you knew" that you were encountering God. If you have had many such experiences, pray and ask God which one to pay attention to now. It should be a time when you felt alive to God and open to hear the Holy Spirit. It may be a recent experience or a distant one. Pause right now and take a few minutes to think about which one you would like to consider. Then, quiet yourself and ask the Holy Spirit to show you aspects of your relationship with God and some of its qualities based on the experience you have chosen. After a time of prayerful attention to your experience, answer the following questions:

1. How would you describe this experience with God?
2. How did you feel?
3. What seemed good? Was any part of it scary? What was that like?
4. How would you describe the qualities, characteristics, "flavors" of the time you have chosen? What was God like? What were you like?
5. What seemed to be the short- and long-term results of this experience?
6. What questions did the experience raise?

Looking at our own history with God is one way to help identify the genuineness of subsequent experiences. When we appreciate, verify, and act on a sense of God, such an occasion can become a standard with which to compare ongoing encounters with God. But we should also ask ourselves questions about where the experience came from, what was going on in our minds at the time, and how it was related to our prayer. We need to notice how a particular experience influenced our attitudes and daily living and how it colored our ongoing relationship with God. How are we responding to other people, and how would we describe the graces or changes that seem to flow out of our experience?

If a person's experience is an authentic experience of God, it may bear defining earmarks. It could, in the long run, bring a more meaningful integration to someone's life, bear good fruit for that person and others, and decrease self-preoccupation.[2]

However, immediate response to encounters with God may not look like that at all. We may feel overwhelmed and confused and even unsure about whether we should call the experience positive. We may be aware of love that is beyond anything we could have imagined. Our usual sense of self or personal boundaries may seem momentarily nonexistent, which can be disconcerting. Then we can be drawn into self-preoccupation, self-protectiveness, and analysis. We may be in a state of awe at the sense of God's holiness or feel whole in ways we have never experienced before. Or we may feel so unworthy of being in communion with this Holy One, who is God, that we want to hide. There may be long periods of time—days, months, even years—when we simply do not know why God is approaching us in particular ways or is seemingly absent from us. In either case, we need to pay attention to our experience through prayer, searching Scripture, solitude, and journaling. We may also want to speak with a spiritual director or other trusted person about our experience.

Even when encounters with God open new vistas that surprise or over-whelm us, they also seem to evoke a deep yearning for more of God. We are created to be in an ultimate love relationship with God—nothing else can satisfy our hearts.

When we consider our experiences, we can learn about our "spiritual fingerprints." We can recognize how God has created us and become less hindered by our history and culture.

When we have an experience with God that is different from anything we have experienced previously, we may ask questions. The following direction conversation is an example of this:

Director: How was your trip to Israel?

Directee: Interesting, amazing, puzzling, exhausting, and lots more. You may remember that I was wondering where I would be touched by God on this trip. I was so interested in what it would feel like to be in the land where Jesus lived. I kept asking myself where I would meet him. What would touch me? What would be important? I think I was looking at myself so much it's a wonder that God could get near me. Will it be the Garden of Gethsemane? Or maybe Bethany? The Mary and Martha stories have always been special for me. Or would it be on the road to Emmaus? I had seem-ingly endless ideas about the possibilities.

Director: And?

Directee: And once again God fooled me. I should have expected it.
               I felt absolutely nothing of significance at any of the places
               where I thought I would. It was informative and interest-
               ing but no music. Hello, hello, where are you, God? No
               answer. No answer until the day we stopped at the West-
               ern Wall, the Wailing Wall. Many Jewish people go to pray
               there—men on one side, women on the other. You see peo-
               ple writing on tiny pieces of paper and stuffing their notes
               into the cracks in the wall—as if God would read their mes-
               sages. It seemed a little odd, but then I decided that I'd write
               the prayer I'd been praying all day, go to the women's side,
               and tuck my prayer into the wall.

               As I got closer I noticed that many women had their
               hands raised over their heads and that they placed their
               hands on the wall when they prayed. So I decided I would
               do that too. I am not quite sure why, but I did. Almost
               instantaneously I began to weep in deep sobs. It swept over
               me and through me, and I prayed—really prayed. I prayed
               whatever came to me. When the tears subsided, I noticed
               that another woman from our group was next to me. She
               was also weeping. We looked at each other in silence. We
               stayed a little longer and then went slowly back to the group.

Director: What happened then?

Directee: It was really good to have someone to talk to because we
               had both been touched by God and did not know quite what
               to say or what to make of it.

Director: What made you think it was God rather than just some kind
               of an emotional response to the crowds and heat, the for-
               eignness or fatigue?

Directee: The tears seemed to come out of a very deep place, deeper
               than my own soul. I prayed about the experience and asked
               God about it. It seemed like I had been given a glimpse of
               God's heart in that place, weeping over Israel. That would
               fit logically as well as experientially. It was something I
               will never forget and was not at all what I would have
               expected.

Director: Does this say anything to you about your relationship with
               God or about the future?

Directee: Mostly it feels like it is important for me not to try to fence
               in God—to invite and reach out to God, who is beyond my
               comprehension and categories, and to be willing for the

> Holy Spirit to show me whatever God intends. At times I behave as if I think I am the one in charge of my spiritual life. It is clear that this is not the case, and I pray to be available to hear God as God wishes to be to me.

Genuine experiences with God often leave trailing questions and a glimpse of God, who is more than the God we have understood.

Discernment Practices

As we reflect on our discernment practices, we can discover how we actually arrive at decisions and actions. What do we say we do to discern what God intends for us? What do we actually do when we're trying to see and hear God's invitations and guidance? Sometimes we are surprised to see that what we think or say we do is not what we have actually done. This is not necessarily bad or good, but it is informative.

Most of us have some familiar, favorite practices of discernment that we use almost automatically on a regular basis. These might include particular ways of reading Scripture, seeking out trusted people for counsel, or taking a quiet retreat day. Because these practices have been satisfactory, we may not have stopped to explore whether they are appropriate in all instances or what God thinks about the methods. We may or may not be used to praying about how we are to pursue discernment when great or small opportunities arrive, but it is quite likely that the Spirit could invite us to recognize God's word through a variety of different people, contexts, and experiences as we continue on the journey of faith. A continuing prayer might include, "Spirit of God, how are you inviting me to discern?"

Christians have used a wide variety of discernment practices, and all of them are centered on a prayerful openness to God. Such practices include, among others, reading Scripture, teaching, worship, prayer, fasting, consultation with other people, our own sense of God, silence, solitude, and the Lord's Supper. Anything that can awaken us to what influences us and detach us from self-interest so that we are free to hear and follow God can aid discernment.

Discernment can become an underlying way of life, a *habit* of turning to God and listening no matter what is transpiring. In this sense it becomes almost inseparable from the life of faith, and therefore, is difficult to examine in isolation. But there is also the *practice* of discernment, which denotes a specific activity people engage in when they are seeking to discern what God intends.

When our discernment practices consistently help us discover God's ways for us, we have no need to explore others. However, sometimes we are unable to come to a satisfying resolution when we diligently seek to recognize the Spirit's guidance by means that have been fruitful in the past. Then we may question whether we have been relying too heavily on one particular method of discernment and perhaps unwittingly begun to trust in the method rather than in God. Every opportunity to learn how to be more discerning calls attention to our radical dependence on the Spirit of God. We frequently find ourselves in need of reminders that we are in an unfolding relationship with God, a relationship that cannot be reduced to routines.

Elements of Discernment

Although there is no one way to approach discernment and we intentionally seek what God intends regarding particular occasions for discernment, common elements usually appear somewhere in the process:

intentionally inviting the Spirit of God to speak to us

asking for the grace to recognize and accurately interpret the Spirit's intentions

framing the discernment (What is the focus of this discernment process? What are we seeking?)

using Scripture, prayer, and other means of gathering and evaluating information

continuing to pray throughout the discernment process

arriving at a provisional resolution

testing the resolution

moving forward based on our decision and noticing what transpires

Because of life circumstances and our preferred approaches, these steps may appear in various orders. For instance, the focus of discernment may become apparent before we intentionally ask God to guide us. Or we may have considered a question and even arrived at a provisional resolution before we decide it would be wise to enter a process of discernment. Sometimes we receive information from various sources before we understand that a question of importance for us is embedded in the data. Often, discernment does not begin as an ordered process. The need for discernment arises out of the natural flow of life and its challenges. At some point, we recognize that we desire God's perspective and guidance and enter a process of discernment.

Factors That Can Influence Discernment

The need for discernment never ends. Some situations that call for discernment such as deciding on a life partner or career path seem more crucial than others, and these major choices will influence large portions of our lives. But it is often beyond our ability to determine which decisions will turn out to be most significant in the long run.

At times when we are faced with choices, our responses are direct, straightforward, and immediate. It is clear what is called for. In fact, we may be startled by how easily we made a decision. Everything is over and done almost before we thought about a process of discernment. This level of clarity is a sacred gift.

When we encounter situations in which we must weigh two good possibilities, both possessing benefits and drawbacks, we often wish we had more help in figuring out exactly what God has in mind. Then, we long for a more focused recognition of what God intends.

In ambiguous circumstances we become more keenly aware of factors that could compromise our freedom to recognize and follow God. Whatever we fear or desire has the potential to divert us. We are challenged to identify and name our fears and desires and to ask to recognize the Spirit's leadings. Jesus' struggle with his own and his Father's desires in the Garden of Gethsemane is an example of such a dilemma. We, too, often find ourselves in situations in which we must choose between God's way and our personal preferences.

We can assist the discernment process by paying attention to whatever nurtures trust in God's love and trustworthiness and by being aware of our own fears and desires. We want to identify what influences us and bring our observations into prayer.

At times we have a tendency to hide important information from ourselves. The following factors point toward aspects of willingness that affect discernment. Reading about these characteristics may bring other things to mind that are significant to our freedom to discern—our freedom to hear and follow God.

Willingness to trust in God's goodness and generosity. God loves us. God wants us to take the way that is best not only for God's sake but also for our sake. We may ask God to remind and reassure us that we are not setting out alone on an impossible task. (Some of our fears may include wondering if the Spirit will be present or if God cares or will give us guidance we can understand.) We may need assurance from the Holy Spirit that our decision will not be destructive for others or ourselves. We can pray for grace to recognize God's presence in the midst of everything that arises through the discernment process.

Willingness to follow God's way no matter what the cost. It is important to be straightforward when we describe our level of commitment
to hear and follow God. At times we may want to hear God's perspective
but are uncertain about what we will do with what the Holy Spirit shows
us. We want to be open about our reasons for hesitating. Sometimes we
need to ask God to soften our attitudes even when we are not sure we
want to be more willing.

Willingness to be authentic. God invites us to be genuine—to be and
say what we really think, feel, believe, desire, and fear—no matter what
that reveals about us. For instance, I would like to be patient. Revealing
what I think and feel often uncovers radical impatience with myself, others, and God. When I am honest, God brings some qualities into the open
that I would prefer to ignore.

Willingness to notice our own sense of well-being. Our decision-mak-
ing ability is strongly influenced by hunger, anger, loneliness, illness, or
fatigue. When we are experiencing such conditions, it is wise to remain
with decisions we have made previously until we can consider new
options from a less dominating viewpoint.

Willingness to notice and pray about our preferences. We need to identify our opinions and preferences and think about which desires and/or
fears may be influencing our judgment.

Willingness not to rely on any one method of discernment. We need to
ask God which discernment method is appropriate for a particular situation (going on a retreat, asking others for counsel, writing lists of possible options, etc.). What is the Spirit inviting us to learn through a specific opportunity or the process itself? The answer may not be the only
significant outcome to our question. The process itself can deepen our
trust in God.

Willingness to be open to information regardless of the source. Resolution of a discernment question may come from what we consider an
unlikely source. A child or an adult who does not have much information about a given discernment issue may suggest the best possible
response. The Spirit invites us to remain open to God's guidance through
various sources.

Willingness to be active or passive. We may be eager to seek all perti-
nent information, but sometimes God asks us to wait rather than become
actively involved. We need to pray for God to reveal what is our part and
what belongs to others. What belongs to everyone and needs to be shared?
What belongs to God? How are we to pray? to act?

Willingness to confront. As we seek to discern God's heart and mind,
we may need to address unpleasant, uncomfortable, and unwanted information—repeatedly. We need to continue this process until God's way
becomes clear.

Willingness to accept an answer of wait. It may be difficult to hear "wait" when we think the time is ripe for yes or no, or when we feel pressure because of financial concerns, work circumstances, or relationships.

Willingness to take whatever time is required for us to be clear about a course of action. If we are faced with a deadline, that fact becomes a part of our prayer. Sometimes it is necessary for us to move ahead with whatever seems best and trust that the Spirit will show us differently if something else is intended.

Willingness for Scripture to be the authority. Any resolution we consider needs to be compatible with Scripture, and therefore, something God could be intending.

Willingness to continue to pray. In discernment we need to continue praying no matter how we feel or what we think. We may withdraw momentarily if we become uncomfortable or concerned, but our underlying attitude needs to be, "Even if I run, God, please help me come back. I will come back to you even when I do not feel like it. I will continue to communicate authentically." Sometimes we need time alone before we are able to turn to God.

Willingness to understand the process that will be used in group discernment. In a group each person needs to choose whether to participate in a particular discernment process. Each person must make the decision freely without being manipulated.

Working our way through a list such as the one above may stimulate a wide range of thoughts and feelings. We gather a great deal of information through such a process. But rather than judge ourselves or others for any particular thoughts or feelings, it is important to take what we have learned into our prayer. We are not trying to force ourselves or anyone else to change. We want to be attuned to our real opinions and responses and invite God to participate with us as we are. Openness with God enables us to recognize, release, and resolve many things that could compromise our ability to hear the Spirit and influence our courage to say yes to God.

Ignatius of Loyola wrote about five additional areas we need to cultivate to prepare ourselves to hear God's voice. These five aspects are as relevant today as they were in the sixteenth century when he first wrote about them. They include:

1. *Interior freedom*—We must cultivate inner freedom so we will not be swayed by desires for riches, honor, and self-sufficiency. Lack of interior freedom causes us to order our lives around ourselves rather than God. Self-centered orientations inhibit the possibility of true discernment.

2. *Knowledge*—Knowledge of ourselves and our deepest desires and acknowledging our personal history of grace and temptation provide an essential background to present discernment opportunities. Knowledge through education helps us think critically, recognize complexities, and understand structures and systems. Particular kinds of knowledge pertain to what God calls us to be and do.

3. *Imagination*—The process of discernment can come alive when we are rested and refreshed because we are able to imagine new possibilities. When we cannot imagine things being different from what they are, we are truly at an impasse.

4. *Patience*—It is difficult to wait for God and difficult to wait with integrity for our own process of development. We may be tempted to settle for what is at hand or force an alternative rather than wait when life as we have known it begins to unravel or we are in transition.

5. *Courage to act*—Even when God's intentions seem clear, others may find it difficult to accept and support our decision. We need to test confirmation of the discernment by noticing its fruits. What happens as we begin to act? It is important to continue to pray. The God who calls us also goes with us.[3]

Many Christians have participated in the *Spiritual Exercises of St. Ignatius.* These exercises include daily Scripture reading, prayer, and journal writing, with the intention of learning more about godly discernment. Ignatius wrote about three "times" of discernment. First, when we know that we know that we know—which we take to prayer to ask God to confirm. Second, when we pay attention to feelings when we are weighing options. Ignatius tells us to bring our options to prayer and notice the patterns of consolation and desolation. Consolation is when we feel energized, hopeful, and alive with godly contentment. (Sometimes when we are in painful, dark places we are also in consolation because we sense we are going toward rather than away from God.) Desolation is when we feel our energy is sapped or that we are being drawn away from God or godliness. It is important to listen to our feelings and bring them to our prayer. Third, when we pay focused attention to reasoning, or reflect on the logical ramifications of possible decisions. Sometimes it is helpful for a person to consider what they would tell someone who came to them with the identical situation or from the vantage point of their deathbed. "What will I wish I had done?"

If we come to a resolution through noticing our feelings in prayer, Ignatius recommends that we test our response by rationally examining the logical aspects of the situation and asking God to confirm what we have discerned. If we come to a resolution through reason, we should take our decision into prayer and notice our feeling responses. When we arrive at a clear discernment with logical and emotional congruence, we cease weighing options and notice we are at peace.

Participating in the processes of discernment has many benefits beyond determining what God intends for a particular situation. When we become intentional about discernment, we may discover surprising aspects of our relationship with God and become more attuned to our own heart's desires.

Discernment and the Body of Christ

Discernment often depends on gifts that we do not have. We need one another's insights, resources, and prayer. Scripture describes the church as the body of Christ—a group of separate individuals functioning in cooperation with Jesus as the head. It is not possible for any one part of the human body or any one person in the community of faith to know or do everything that is needed, even for ourselves. We are created to be interdependent in loving, listening to, worshiping, and serving God. Christians assist one another in prayer, worship, and service. We encourage each other through one-to-one and small and large group relationships. We pray and reflect together to discern how God is present and inviting. Some groups such as the Quakers have established methods by which a group of people supports an individual seeking discernment. These discernment groups are called Clearness Committees. The five or six people on a Clearness Committee ask questions but do not give answers.[4]

It can be helpful, and at times absolutely essential, to talk to someone about our ways of discernment as well as about what we believe God is saying to us. Many people participate in spiritual direction for this purpose. In direction conversations we describe, discuss, and pray about discernment opportunities, possibilities, and choices.

Topics for Discernment

All spiritual direction meetings contain aspects of discernment because these conversations are dedicated to distinguishing the Spirit's voice from all others. Topics that directees often consider include their attitudes and choices, lifestyle considerations, decisions that need to be made, and areas in which they trust God and respond freely to the Spirit's invitations and areas in which they sense resistance to the Spirit's promptings. The truth of the matter is that anything that raises questions about what God intends can become a subject for discernment. That touches everything—decisions, relationships, where we live and with whom, which interests we will pursue and in what way, and how we will love and live in relationship to God. A quick summary of discernment questions might be, What does God intend and invite related to questions such as Who am I? Whom should I be with? What should I do? Where should I go? What does it all mean? How is the Spirit inviting me to love and serve God now?

One topic that seems to surface rather frequently in direction meetings is discernment about church affiliation and involvement. We may feel out of step with others when we experience a call to deepen our relationship with God. We may become puzzled, frustrated, angry, or disappointed that other church members are not gripped by a similar sense of calling, vision, and desire for God. A spiritual direction friendship provides a safe, confidential place to explore what God is saying to us about our church and other spiritual group affiliations.

Sometimes we believe the Spirit of God invites us to move out of the group in which we worship and serve. This kind of discernment is best approached cautiously and with attention to our mixture of motivations for considering such a move. We hope and expect that Christ wants us to belong to a group in which we can live out of our God-given potential and freedom, be ourselves, learn whatever God intends, and share the life and grace of God with others. God may call us to stay where we are, move to another church of the same denomination, or join a church of a different denomination. Sometimes, however, even when we think we are ready to move, God clearly directs us to remain.

Recognizing Discernment

Guidance that comes from the Spirit of God is marked by several identifying characteristics. Some are straightforward; others are more difficult to assess. Asking whether a proposed action is in harmony with the teachings, person, and behavior of Christ is a central question. Will our actions, if we follow through with our decisions, reflect Christ or not? Will they reflect the principles that guided Christ's life?

A second primary avenue for inquiry is related to Scripture. How does the proposed activity align with scriptural teaching? What fruit of the Spirit—love, joy, peace, patience, kindness, goodness, faithfulness, gentleness, and self-control—might be developed or embodied in the alternatives we are considering? We should examine possible choices through the lenses of Scripture and our relationship with Christ, asking for grace to be attuned to God.

As we have already said, however, many times we are faced with two worthy options, two ways of behaving that are both compatible with the life of Christ and Scripture. After we look at both of these models, we may still be confused. Mentally trying on options in an attitude of prayer may help us notice how the possibilities might fit with what and how God has already communicated with us. We assume that we have decided in one way and notice all the thoughts and feelings that arise in response. We ask God to show us how a particular decision would settle into our lives. We notice whether we feel energized and excited or if considering a possibility seems to sap our energy. We can also notice what happens to our prayer and sense of relationship with God in the light of possible choices. Is our prayer alive and moving, or does it seem to be foundering? We give ourselves a day or two to think, pray, and reflect on each of the possible options in this way.

Observing what follows in our hearts and in outward circumstances is also important. When the Spirit of God is guiding us in a particular way, the outward conditions will align with our inward sense of God's direction. When circumstances do not reflect what we anticipated, either the timing is not appropriate or we are misunderstanding the Spirit's guidance. Until the time is right and the way God is taking us is open, we waste energy trying to force circumstances.

Discernment and Peace

According to Christian discernment traditions, when we recognize and assent to God's leading, we will become peaceful, settled, and quiet. We will no longer continue to weigh options or feel confused. We will have peace in our heart.

Yet we know that the presence of peace is not a sufficient sign by itself that we are going in God's direction. People who are deliberately going away from God may experience counterfeit peace at least for a while. If someone feels at peace after choosing values and actions that are opposed to scriptural principles and Christlike responses, it is a signal to continue the process of discernment and ask questions such as, "Why do I feel at peace about this when it is clearly contrary to Scripture?"

Discernment is a complex process that must be contextualized within our own history of grace and temptation. Discernment about what God desires does not follow a formula. It flows out of a relationship and personal history with God. We can observe this even in the life of Jesus. Luke 4 describes Jesus' encounter with Satan in the wilderness after Jesus had fasted for forty days. Satan tempted Jesus to (1) turn stones into bread, (2) receive the splendor and authority of all kingdoms by worshiping Satan, and (3) throw himself off the highest point of the temple because God would send angels to rescue him. Satan tempted Jesus to affirm that he was God's Son without waiting for God or God's intentions about addressing evil in the world. All three temptations included an appeal to Christ to carry out his mission in his own way. Yet Jesus answered Satan through words of Scripture, pointing toward God and God's ways.

The same core temptation—to live out his life and mission in his own way rather than God's—was present in Jesus' struggle in the Garden of Gethsemane. Jesus had agreed with and embraced God's path long before the night in the garden and had told his disciples he would be crucified. When he set his face toward Jerusalem, he knew he was moving toward death (Matt. 26:1–2). In the Garden of Gethsemane, he confronted the grief and desperation of realizing that if he said yes to God at this moment, his death was very close.

From Scripture we know that Jesus understood that this was his destiny, that this was what he was meant to do. His relationship with his Abba and his pattern of seeking to do only what his Father desired was the foundation of his life (John 8:28–29). Jesus had a profound trust and willingness related to his heavenly Father that transcended any formulas or rules about discernment.

Jesus followed through on what he had discerned by allowing the grim process of mockery and crucifixion to be carried out. He suffered emotionally and physically as any person would who experienced crucifixion, and he also carried the additional weight of the world's participation in evil.

So what about peace? Shalom? In the Old Testament the word *shalom*—peace—means well-being, fulfillment, completeness, and contentment. It indicates a sense of inner harmony, stability, and serenity, but it is much more than that. God is the source of shalom, the source of true peace, the initiator of divinely wrought wholeness. Jesus lived in and alongside the fullness of God, in communion with his Father, as an ongoing way of life, not just as a by-product of discernment questions. Jesus was filled with the reality of the peace of God.

Jesus spoke to his disciples about peace and blessed them with peace. He said, "Peace I leave with you; my peace I give you. I do not give to you as the world gives. Do not let your hearts be troubled and do not be afraid" (John 14:27). Paul wrote about the peace of God in his letter to the Philippians, saying, "Do not be anxious about anything, but in everything, by prayer and petition, with thanksgiving, present your requests to God. And the peace of God, which transcends all understanding, will guard your hearts and your minds in Christ Jesus" (Phil. 4:6–7).

But Jesus did not sound peaceful when he cried out on the cross, saying, "My God, my God, why have you forsaken me?" (Matt. 27:46). These words arose out of desolation, agony, and Christ's participation in the brokenness of humanity. Some scholars have said that Jesus was a man of Scripture and that he was praying aloud using the first words of Psalm 22. No one knows if his prayer continued silently through the words of this psalm, which moves from desolation to consolation. There are many unanswered questions. God, who is always present, was present with and in Jesus through the entire agonizing process, whether or not Jesus was able to recognize divine presence. And God is present with us when we can and cannot recognize God. Perhaps looking at the experience of contemporary Christians can assist us in our considerations of Jesus.

Many people who choose to participate in and rely on discernment prayer as a basis for life choices do the following:

bring all that is in their own hearts into the open, holding nothing back from God

ask to see

struggle and do battle with themselves and with God

believe they hear God's desires

willingly choose what God shows them—even in the midst of personal grief and at times against what seems to be the necessary choice

When they do these things, they come to a deep inner congruence that includes agreement of thoughts and feelings. Or, even if they are unable to come to any rational understanding of what is called for, they come to a sense of the rightness of what they believe God is inviting and feel at peace about acting on their sense of God's invitations.

What they describe sounds like shalom—the fullness of God dwelling in them. There is a kind of interior stability. They experience a quality of heart that has been given by the Spirit of God and received by them. But their willing agreement is essential.

We may experience a sense of tenderness after we have assented to what we believe is of God. The struggle for a conclusion is over and whatever difficulties may arise when we move ahead have not yet appeared. We may discover that we are touched by joy—an impossible to define quality that flows like freshwater through the soul and makes any sacrifice or surrender of ours seem small. It is God, and it feels so good that we are willing to consider many things we might never otherwise explore. Whatever we agree to because of God leads to good. It is undeniably "right." We may know that something seems right but not know why. Much remains outside our view, but we know God is present and affirming.

When we experience the reality of God's peace, it is not erased by circumstances, even if they are difficult. The peace of God can remain intact underneath confusing surface thoughts, feelings, and physical pain. When we turn to God in prayer, allowing ourselves to be gently detached from whatever captures our energy or troubles us, we may be surprised to discover that sustaining peace is present.

At times people say they have a sense of peaceful clarity, resolution, or wholeness that is all-embracing. They may attempt to describe this peace by using words such as *sublime* or *transcendent*, but they are likely to give up searching for words that communicate what they feel, because it is beyond words. They say that when they realized what the Holy Spirit desired and they assented, they were carried by God and buoyed by a sense of unspeakable peace. Circumstances that would normally make them concerned seemed inconsequential or absent. Everything in their own hearts seemed to be exactly where it needed to be.

A deep interior peace or a peace that is beyond words is sometimes an aspect of confirmation when we have chosen well. Knowing contemporary persons who have experienced peace in the midst of tragic and chaotic circumstances causes me to believe that Jesus had this experience of peace also. The unbearably awful miseries of crucifixion and the wholeness of God, including the peace of God, stood alongside each other and were present at the same time.

The Mystery of Discernment

Sometimes when discernment is clear we have a sense of what we are to do, when we are to do it, and we have the energy to do it. At least it is clear what we are called by God to do *now*. The Holy Spirit may then ask us to take the next small step with no information regarding how long something will take or what succeeding steps will be.

At other times, even after we have done everything that seems called for to discern what God intends, we would be hard-pressed to say that we know very much. It may seem as though the Spirit of God is more interested in our willingness not to know and our willingness to trust God without reservation, live with ambiguity, and continue in faith and love. Unfolding discernment is dependent on our obedient response and actions related to what we believe God is saying to us. The Spirit may draw us to pray for and about situations for a long time. Many things remain hidden in the mysteries of God.

Discernment is a complex topic to which we have only opened the door, and we need to remember that God comes to us uniquely, individually, and personally. Yet, there are recognizable components of discernment. No matter what method we use or what particular questions we bring into our prayer, the discernment process involves God's love and our willing responsiveness, surrender, and relinquishment of our perspectives in favor of God's.[5] When we discern God's initiatives, we look for (1) congruence with Christlike attitudes and behaviors, (2) alignment with scriptural teaching and values, (3) congruence with our personal history and present relationship with God, (4) the fruit of the Spirit evidenced in us through varied relationships and circumstances, (5) the way being open for what we believe God invites, and (6) a sense of core stability that is peaceful.

Most of all, true discernment is related to attitudes of the heart—attitudes of love and desire for God and God's ways. Open listening, a willingness to trust in God, and an awareness of our dependency on grace are foundational to recognizing the Spirit's promptings. If you are drawn to explore discernment more thoroughly, you might want to begin with the references in the bibliography.

Reflections

1. What experiences have you had with discernment?
2. If you were to divide your discernment history into chapters, what titles would you use? How has the process, your awareness of it, and the particular methods changed?
3. From where do you seek information?
4. How are prayer and Scripture a part of your discernment processes?
5. Are other people part of the process? Who? What weight do you give to the ideas and opinions of others in comparison with your own best sense of what is called for?
6. How do you decide whether a particular resource is credible?
7. What are your favorite methods of discernment?
8. What unhelpful ways of discernment have you tried?
9. Have you misinterpreted what God was saying to you? What were the consequences of that? When and how did you reenter a discernment process? What made you aware of grace, freedom, and restoration?
10. What questions do you have about discernment? Are there areas related to discernment in which you think the Spirit is inviting you to grow? to explore?
11. Whom could you talk with about discernment processes and questions?

14 | Christian Disciplines

> The whole authentic history of spiritual discipline in the Church and in all deep religious traditions is to aid human digestion of the Holy, so that we do not 1) reject divine nourishment 2) throw it up by not allowing room inside for it 3) mistake "artificial flavors" for the real thing 4) use its strength for building an ego empire.
>
> Tilden Edwards[1]

> "Are you tired? Worn out? Burned out on religion? Come to me. Get away with me and you'll recover your life. I'll show you how to take a real rest. Walk with me and work with me—watch how I do it. Learn the unforced rhythms of grace. I won't lay anything heavy or ill-fitting on you. Keep company with me and you'll learn to live freely and lightly." . . .
>   "Here's what I want you to do: Find a quiet, secluded place so you won't be tempted to role-play before God. Just be there as simply and honestly as you can manage. The focus will shift from you to God, and you will begin to sense his grace."
>
> Matthew 11:28–30; 6:6 *The Message*

We come full circle in this chapter by once again identifying spiritual direction as a Christian discipline and looking more closely at disciplines in general and asking God to guide us as we continue in faith. We have already said that spiritual direction is one among many Christian disciplines, but it is often the discipline that encourages people to choose and practice others and provides a context in which to explore and notice the benefits of these ongoing habits. I invite you to observe how what you have learned about spiritual direction influences your understanding and appreciation of the Holy Spirit's invitations through all Christian disciplines.

Describing Christian Disciplines

A Christian discipline is any practice that helps us listen to and follow God. It is something we do to make ourselves available to hear and respond to the Spirit of God more intentionally and wholeheartedly. We attempt to focus more attention on God and less on other things that crowd into our hearts, minds, and lives by setting aside time and space just for God. The practices themselves have no particular power or goodness, but we hope that the Holy Spirit will use them to enable us to see God, culture, our families, and ourselves from God's perspective and help us to be awake and attentive to God.

Rueben Job, a Methodist bishop, pastor, writer, and retreat leader, talks about the role of disciplines in his story about living in a sod house on the plains of North Dakota.

> I grew up on a farm in North Dakota. I was born in the twenties and lived through the dust bowl years. If I close my eyes I can still see fence rows covered with dry earth, blown like snow into wavy drifts four feet tall. The sight of grass hoppers like dark clouds shutting out the sun being blown across the sky by the hot and dry wind is a memory I shall never forget.
>
> And yet, our farmstead was like a little oasis in the midst of the desolation and destruction of the dust bowl. There was only one reason for this. We had a deep well that never ran dry. Summer and winter, this deep well supplied a continuous stream of life giving water so that the garden, trees, animals and our little family received nurture and sustenance enough to survive even this great national tragedy. Spiritual disciplines help us to sink those wells into the life giving source that comes to us only from God.
>
> While the wind was often fierce on that prairie farm, there were other times when it was just a whisper. The huge windmill on a forty foot tower in the middle of the farmstead was silent and no fresh water was being lifted from deep within the earth. On some of these calm days my father would climb that tall tower, reach up and turn the giant eight foot wheel into the wind. Then he would pull on the edge of the wheel until it started to turn. Facing into the wind and once started, the windmill would pump water with just a gentle breeze rustling the leaves of the nearby trees.
>
> Spiritual disciplines help us to turn into the wind, to turn toward God and to be shaped and powered by God's Spirit. Spiritual disciplines can be that turning of the wheel, that help we need to bring to our awareness God's presence in all of creation and specifically in the entirety of our lives.[2]

The potential fruits of participating in spiritual disciplines assist us in our pursuit of the great commandment—our quest to love the Lord our God with all our heart, mind, soul, and strength, and our neighbor as ourselves (Matt. 22:37–38). They enhance our intention and ability to listen to and follow God. (See chapter 16, "Potential Benefits of Spiritual Direction.")

Christian disciplines include both individual and corporate pursuits such as the familiar practices of worship, Bible study, and prayer. But Christians also participate in practices such as fasting, service, living simply, and appreciating God in the beauties of the created world, to name a few.[3] Disciplines such as silence and solitude provide opportunities for uninterrupted attentiveness to God. When these activities become part of a habitual, repeating life pattern, they are identified as disciplines. They are practiced at regular intervals with intentionality and a way of being involved. Any wholesome activity we regularly engage in with the primary intention of listening to and following God could be called a Christian discipline.

A friend told a story about a piano concert given by Rudolf Serkin at the Boston Orchestra Hall. Boston audiences are often considered sophisticated, cultured, and perhaps even jaded because they have heard much of the splendor the musical world has to offer. It is a challenge to play in the presence of such an audience. On that spring night no one could have guessed what awaited them. Rudolf Serkin did not know either. The concert ended with Serkin playing Beethoven's Appassionata Sonata. He had played it many times before, but on this night he played beyond mere human skills. After the last note faded, the crowd leapt to their feet in applause, but that was not enough. They climbed onto their chairs and cheered—cheered, clapped, shouted, whistled, and danced—for the Holy Spirit had come. Only God can grant such moments. And what did Rudolf Serkin have to do with it? He practiced the piano eight hours a day—every day. When the Spirit came, the vessel was ready.[4]

This story speaks to us about the role of personal discipline in developing our readiness for the Spirit's arrival. It isn't just about our work; it's also about having a true understanding of the gifts God has given us, and then working in accordance with that understanding. Dallas Willard, in his book *The Spirit of the Disciplines,* points out how Jesus, the unique Son of God, lived a life of preparation, mostly hidden from the public eye. Scripture describes Jesus' commitment to prayer and seclusion and attentiveness to his relationship with the First Person of the Trinity as well as his openness to the Third Person of the Trinity. Willard's book challenges the erroneous hope that we can live a Christlike life without being involved in the rhythm of the same sorts of disciplines Jesus practiced.[5]

These stories of turning the windmill and playing the piano show us how we can align ourselves with the work of the Spirit. They awaken our hopes that the Spirit will visit us with grace and surprise. Disciplines open the way to life—God's life in us and in the world.

Disciplines Are for the Whole Person

Disciplines influence every part of human personhood. They are incarnational. They are not merely spiritual, as if we could separate the material and nonmaterial aspects of our humanity. Christian disciplines involve the body, intellect, emotions, will, imagination, and memories.

Body

Although we may be used to paying attention to some of our thoughts and feelings, which can alter attitudes and behavior, many of us pay scant attention to the physical factors involved in Christian disciplines. In fact, we often simply try to ignore our bodies, thinking we can proceed as we like without taking them into account. And even if we do notice that our bodies are responding to something either through pleasure or complaint, we seldom stop to inquire how God might be using these sensations to teach us something. Whether we attend to them or not, however, our bodies are part of the practice of disciplines, contribute to our ease or struggle with various disciplines, and influence their effectiveness.

Bodily condition, position, and comfort come into play. For instance, the positions we select for prayer contribute to our attitudes, subjects that arise, language, quality of our speech and attentiveness to God, and our ability to remain in prayer until we choose to move on (hopefully taking prayer with us but changing our activity). We experience physical sensations related to whether we are hungry, satisfied, or too full and whether we are fatigued or well rested, all of which influence our attentiveness and awareness in any discipline.[6]

Our bodies respond so directly and clearly that they can be an important source of information when we are willing to notice rather than ignore or suppress their cues. We may not consciously think our bodies play a part in spiritual discernment, but the tightening and relaxing of muscles often give us clues about our withdrawal or receptivity toward what God is inviting in the same way we respond to human encounters.

As an example, we may notice that we frequently feel physically hurried or pressured when we try to set aside time to spend with God. Through prayer we can explore what this sense of rushing is about, whether it is related to an overcrowded schedule, avoidance of time alone with God, or something else. At other times we observe that we enjoy a kind of holy leisure and experience a physical settledness even in the midst of a busy schedule. We discover that we are willing to spend whatever amount of time is needed to be with God in meaningful relationship. This, too, may be a source of insight.

Sometimes body responses let us know we are avoiding something or pushing ourselves into situations or experiences that are not right for us. The location of tense muscles or pain in the head, neck, shoulders, back, or stomach gives us clues about our lives. As we notice our body's complaints, we may recognize hidden objections of our minds and hearts and bring them into our prayer. We can also pray about our bodily responses and ask God what they imply.

Some people find that physical activity helps them become quiet so they are free to speak and listen to the Holy Spirit. Walking, jogging, skating, swimming, or any other kind of even, repetitive motion assists their prayer. These people say that when they begin to move, they turn their thoughts toward God and talk about ideas, feelings, questions, and cares—letting whatever is inside flow out to God.

Swimming is like that for me. I often go to the pool after teaching a class, and when I get into the water, I start talking to God about what went well and what did not. It becomes a time of debriefing—letting whatever thoughts arise flow to God. As I continue swimming laps, I release myself and my concerns to God. Then my prayer becomes simpler, sometimes settling into a phrase or a word or two such as "thank you" or "I love you."

Moving rather than sitting still in prayer enables some people to settle into a quiet awareness of God's present love and feel more able to be themselves with God. Out of this place of trust they notice their prayer extending to situations and people beyond their own immediate concerns. They may sense they are interceding with a love or compassion that is more far-reaching than they know themselves to be. They may feel they are praying *with* God as well as *to* God.

A well-known contemporary Christian, Richard Foster, describes how shooting baskets, a very physical activity, became for him a part of a spiritual discipline.

> One summer I went outside each evening about 10 PM to the little basketball court we had set up in our driveway. Alone, I would shoot baskets, all the time inviting God to do a spiritual inventory on the day. Many things would surface to memory. Sin was there to be sure: an angry word, a missed courtesy, a failed opportunity to encourage someone. But there was also the good: a small obedience, a quiet prayer that seemed to do so much, a word fitly spoken. It was for one summer only, and I have never tried to repeat the experience, but it was one way of experiencing examen of consciousness.[7]

As some people participate in physical activity, they experience a release of restlessness so they are better able to pay attention to prayer even while they are exercising. Others discover that after exercising they are more able to give quality attention to prayer.

In contrast, many people choose physical stillness as a way of declaring their desire to let go of their own activities, mental and physical, and be available to God. They select a place and decide to remain there for a period of time during which they pray, write in a journal, study the Bible, or engage in other disciplines. They, too, notice their own clamorings when they begin. It seems as though their body is the only thing that is still, but then in the stillness they become conscious of the racings and wanderings of their minds and feelings, and they slowly let them go as they turn their thoughts and attention toward God. They choose a position that is comfortable yet keeps them alert.

Waiting in stillness is modeled by those who practice centering prayer, a method of prayer that involves repeating "Jesus Christ, Son of God, have mercy upon me a sinner," or words of their own choosing such as, "I love you, Lord." Centering prayer is one of the ways that some people find God uses to draw them toward contemplative prayer. Others find that praying with Scripture, *lectio divina*, invites them to contemplation (see chapter 12, "Prayer"). In either case, the words become a way of expressing our love for God and are secondary to our sense of being touched by God's loving presence.[8]

None of us can make anything happen as far as God is concerned, but we can present ourselves to God, open ourselves, and invite the Spirit of God to help us pray. Physical stillness can help us get off our merry-go-round of inner and outer activity and move beyond our self-centered preoccupation.

Intellect

Our minds are a splendid gift from God that we can use for God and with God. At times we become aware that God invites us to study diligently and intentionally. We may know what we are to study, where, and with whom, and that our cooperation with the Holy Spirit will involve intellectual effort and challenge. At other times it seems God causes us to pay closer attention to the limits of human intellect. In fact, we may discover that the Spirit of God is encouraging us to be willing *not to know*, to trust God and grow in our appreciation of mystery, otherness, and unknowability. We may feel called to expand our trust in God rather than in our own ability to understand when we cannot know something even through rigorous research or study. The underlying question we ask is, "How is God inviting us to use intellect in our practice of particular Christian disciplines for a specific length of time?"

Emotions

We also experience the Spirit's prompting through emotions. At times God calls us to pay attention to feelings that we may not have dared to name even to ourselves, or to feelings we cannot name because we cannot find a name for them. Then, it can appear that God is inviting us to express ourselves and ask God not only to listen to our feelings but to help us with them—to clarify our recognition of what they are and where they come from and to draw us toward healthy, godly feelings. We may also experience moments during which we recognize that no matter how good we feel about a particular situation, God is calling us to walk away from it, to ignore our strong feelings and to behave in a way God chooses. So, again, in Christian disciplines our attention is focused on God. Rather than focusing on our emotions, we ask ourselves what the Spirit is inviting us to feel and how God is calling us to attend to those feelings. Should we express them, act on them, or just let them be and wait and watch God?

Some ways of prayer, Scripture reading, and other disciplines evoke powerful feelings and stir emotional responses along a wide continuum. God uses these awakenings and our awareness of them to teach us when we bring them into prayer. At times we may shy away from looking squarely at emotions because we are embarrassed by the roller-coaster qualities of our feelings—one moment calm and the next miserable. We may think we are unspiritual and foolish to vascillate so widely and may fear that our careening feelings are indicators of shallowness. But there is a lot to be gained if we stay with God and prayer in the midst of emotional variations. When we are willing, God will reveal many things to us about ourselves, others, life situations, and God's faithful love through the lens of feelings taken into prayer. We have nothing to fear when we open any and every feeling to God—no matter how extreme or unacceptable it seems.

We may discover great comfort in praying with the psalms when we wonder how we should express our feelings to God. The psalms include a wide range of human emotions. Meditating on a psalm that expresses feelings we consider unacceptable can help us learn more about the extent of God's care.[9]

Will

Many feelings help us recognize our will because they swirl around our desires and fears, preferences and things we avoid. Will is the center of willingness/willfulness—the place of both momentary and labored questions about our relationship with God. Are we willing to notice our will and its processes? Are we receptive to or resisting God? We may prefer to push recognition of our willingness and willfulness away because we fear what we might see. We may question whether it is wise to trust God to reveal unrecognized aspects of ourselves and wonder if we will be overwhelmed by seeing more about our willingness and willfulness than we can tolerate.

Through practicing Christian disciplines, we become better acquainted with our willingness and willfulness, and we get a clearer view of the boundary between the two. This boundary is sometimes firm and sometimes soft—in places we are willing, in others we are a little willing, and in still others we resist God. Some parts of the boundary may stand for years, while others stand only momentarily. When we become aware of the particulars of our willingness and willfulness, we recognize countless opportunities in our responses to God. Our recognition of these aspects of ourselves opens new possibilities for prayer and reflection in an ongoing way.

Imagination

Imagination, too, can draw us toward or away from God and godliness. As we practice Christian disciplines, we can exercise and develop our imagination in godly ways.

Some practices of Christian disciplines invite a person to use imagination intentionally. For instance, one way to use Scripture as a basis for prayer and meditation is to read a passage and then think and pray about what it would have been like to be in the story. What was the scene like? The setting? Who was there? Was it warm or cool? Was there a breeze? What did we see, hear, taste, touch, smell? How did we feel? We can ask the Spirit of God to show us a particular event or how we would have responded had we been present. Readers read the passage silently or aloud a number of times, immersing themselves in it, praying, listening for God, and responding to whatever they notice. This way of reading Scripture is one example of an appropriate use of the imagination in disciplines—offering our imagination to God and inviting the Holy Spirit to speak to us through it.

Memories

Memories influence our practice of disciplines. Sometimes memories nourish our disciplines and prayer and lead us toward God. When we remember times God nurtured us in the past, we become more trusting that God is present for whatever is needed now. This helps us engage in prayer and other disciplines with hope. At other times, however, when we recall unpleasant experiences, they pull us away from God. It is often easy to follow a thought and forget about the discipline. We may tend to revisit unresolved experiences, hoping to put them to rest in a satisfying way. There is a difference, however, between recycling memories and bringing them consciously into prayer. We need to bring memories into the foreground where we can open them to God's presence and healing.

Our body, intellect, emotions, will, imagination, and memories are six aspects that are always present and that influence our ability to listen to God. We do not want to make any of these aspects the center of our practice of disciplines, but God can use all of them to bring insight and renewal. At different times one or another of these aspects may be emphasized through a particular discipline. We need to pray about and discern when each should be attended to peripherally and when the Spirit of God is inviting us to greater care and intentional prayer about these matters.

Ways to Facilitate the Practice of Christian Disciplines

Establishing a rule, setting aside a place, writing in a spiritual journal, and participating in spiritual direction are four practices people often use to help them discern which other disciplines God is inviting them to choose for a particular length of time.

Setting a Rule—Listening for a Way

Setting a rule or listening for a way simply means we reflect on, pray about, and consider the Holy Spirit's promptings regarding disciplines. Questions such as what, when, where, how, and with whom become an intentional part of our prayer. Sometimes it seems as though it would be easier to choose a few disciplines on our own and combine them in a way we know we can manage. When we decide on our disciplines through a process of prayer and reflection, however, we are more likely to choose disciplines that engage and interest us and avoid getting involved in a routine for its own sake. Participating in God-invited disciplines sets a tone and expectation from the beginning that disciplines are about being with and listening to God. This kind of planning embodies our desires to depend on the Holy Spirit.

Once we have ideas about which disciplines God is leading us to, we make a provisional plan. We decide what methods we will use to practice the disciplines, how much time will be involved and at what interval, when we will take part, where, and for what purposes. These details also become part of our prayer. A rule or plan usually contains a number of disciplines. Some of them may be practiced daily. Others may be practiced a few times a week, weekly, monthly, or a few times a year. The plan may include individual, small group, and large group disciplines.

Having a rule or plan can be helpful or harmful. If we adopt a plan as a way of taking control of ourselves and our spiritual development, it can be injurious. It is easy to lose sight of grace and get caught up in spiritual good works and ideas about our holiness rather than God's. We can get sidetracked. When we are light-handed and openhearted in the creation of a rule, however, inviting the Spirit of God to guide us in shaping it, we are more likely to choose disciplines that are helpful and freeing rather than inhibiting. If we are willing to let our plan grow and change as we continue to listen to God, the process can be part of the Spirit's work in our lives rather than exclusively our own.

There is no typical rule or plan, but the following disciplines appear frequently: Bible reading, personal prayer, silence and solitude, a yearly retreat, solitary walks, group prayer, group worship, participation in the Lord's Supper, spiritual reading including classic and contemporary authors, spiritual direction, world awareness, stewardship, family disciplines, appropriate eating and sleeping habits, exercise, and abstinence from certain things. Some people include what they consider minimum disciplines, practices they will not put aside even during busy times. They also plan for disciplines they can practice when pressures are less or they feel called by God to set aside more time and space with God. A good rule is not something we *do* nearly as much as something that describes who we desire and intend *to be*. A rule should include practices that support our desire to be intentional about nourishing our Divine/human love relationship.

Even though we allow for ongoing flexibility, one of the gifts of having a plan is that we do not have to waste time and energy making decisions on a daily basis. The disciplines we choose for a regular, patterned practice usually reflect many aspects of our relationship with God. We have set our course through prayer, reflection, and genuine examination of our heart's desire, seeking the Holy Spirit's guidance about how we can make ourselves available in the midst of normal experiences and pressures of life to know God's love and provision—to be God's people.

Noticing what other people practice can help us consider possible options. I am grateful to a writer friend whom I have observed living by a growing rule for more than twenty-five years. As she writes, travels, and speaks, her routine usually includes morning and evening Scripture reading and prayer, time spent writing in a journal, and quiet solitude before bed. She also frequently participates in communion, and she worships and teaches in a welcoming church community. She has learned that this is what is necessary for her to listen to and enjoy God and be happily engaged in life. My observations of her have encouraged me to identify and practice what nourishes God's life in mine.

Setting Aside a Place

The complexity of our lives and persistence of self-interest often pull us away from spiritual disciplines. Having a set place to go to for prayer, meditation, Scripture reading, journal writing, and other disciplines is a concrete way to lessen this pull. It also helps us focus in the same way that going to a carrel in the library helps us focus on study. Going to the place we have set aside for the practice of a discipline helps us make the transition from daily life to intentional spiritual practices.

Sometimes the place we choose yields clues regarding how serious we are about spending time with God, and sometimes our choice reveals other kinds of information. Do we go to our prayer chair or corner or remain at our desk? Either place can indicate an attitude of intentionality or urgency, or the place we choose can suggest that we are doing something in an offhand way or are becoming overly controlled by a routine rather than seeking relationship. One place is not automatically better than another, but it can be helpful to notice what motivates us to choose one place over another. No place is magic, and God is not limited to meeting us in any one place. In fact, many people who have pursued spiritual disciplines have noticed that they prepared the altar and the fire struck somewhere else. Even if we often do not feel particularly spiritual while we are engaging in disciplines, we will more than likely notice the fruit of our practice in the midst of daily life.

Keeping a Spiritual Journal

Some people find that writing in a journal about their relationship with God nurtures their prayer and their ability to recognize God's present activity in their life and remember God's involvement with them in the past. Such a journal may contain many different kinds of entries: portions of Scripture; personal responses to a passage of Scripture or an event, including questions and insights; sorrows, joys, and neutral observations; and descriptions of what God seems to be urging them to notice. Some people like to write letters to God. Others write out prayers, or they write about their prayer—how they pray, what they are praying about, the qualities of their prayer. They write about the ebb and flow of communication, confusion, and love in their experience with God.

The purpose of a journal is to record snapshots of how we are perceiving and interpreting what is happening in our relationship with God. It can be helpful to have our faith-story written down so that we can read and remember experiences that have shaped our understanding and practice. Reading about situations in which we opened our hearts to the Spirit or times when God helped us through difficulties can help us place our hope in God for the present and the future. Our thoughts, feelings, prayers, and behaviors can be strongly influenced by revisiting some foundational and ongoing moments with God.

Journals are as unique and individual as the people who write them. Some people write in different styles to denote variations in content—one way for Scripture, another for their responses, a third for questions, another for quotations. Many people divide their journal into sections for Scripture, questions, prayer lists, or other categories that suit them. There is no wrong or right way to keep a journal. Any method that supports a person's open communication and attentiveness with God and that does not merely recount daily activities is appropriate.

In order for a journal to be an effective tool for spiritual development, it must be private. Many of the things we need to express and reveal to the Spirit of God are the things we do not want to discuss with anyone else, at least not at the level where our truest heart, attitudes, hopes, and fears reside. It is important to discuss the necessity for privacy with those who share the same living quarters. Even so, some people feel more comfortable writing in a kind of code about certain subjects. Many excellent resources are available for those who are interested in exploring the discipline of keeping a spiritual journal.[10]

Many people who keep a journal find that the practice assists them as they participate in spiritual direction. They prepare for direction appointments by reading what they have written since their last meeting. Then they pray about which things to discuss with their director.

Participating in Spiritual Direction

Spiritual direction is a discipline that naturally connects with other spiritual practices. Direction meetings provide an opportunity to discuss and review with another praying person the disciplines we practice. Directees may discuss particular disciplines they believe the Holy Spirit is inviting them to pursue and describe their responses, speaking about areas in which they follow easily and with clear benefit and where they sense some kind of resistance. They may discuss whether they have outgrown a practice or ask questions when their practices seem unsatisfying or inappropriate. They attempt to discover why they have become disinterested or bored, or why they never seem to find time to do what they have decided to do. They may inquire about whether the Spirit may be drawing them to something different or to the same discipline practiced in a different way. Through prayer, reflection, and conversation with God and a spiritual director, we may decide to adjust our practices from time to time so that they continue to reflect and nurture the heart of our relationship with God.

Direction meetings do more than just provide an opportunity to discuss which disciplines we should participate in and in what way. Spiritual direction contributes to our ability to be more discerning about what God intends in the whole of life. Daily life and our practice of disciplines, including spiritual direction, interweave in interesting ways. Because of our practice of disciplines, we notice and reflect on many things that could have escaped our notice. This influences our prayer and behavior, which in turn influences our practice of disciplines. It becomes a kind of circular process with both life and our reflective practices as part of the cycle. We listen for God in spiritual disciplines and in the midst of life and consider what we notice in the prayerful context of spiritual direction conversations.

Is This Really a Christian Discipline?

At times we may behave as if disciplines should work the same way for everyone and assume that something is wrong if they do not. But that does not coincide with what we know about the varieties of human personalities or what we know about God, who created us as unique, one-of-a-kind individuals.

No matter who we are or which Christian disciplines we believe the Holy Spirit invites us to pursue, however, we all hope for certain benefits. What qualities make a discipline a useful one—one that helps us pay attention to God? When we pray and think about this question, we may identify some factors that seem essential and others that seem less central. The list that follows may help you as you ask God for insight about disciplines and your own practice.

When engaging in a Christian discipline, we may notice the following benefits:

We become settled and focused on God. We quiet down, let go of the clatter and clamor, and focus our attention on the One who has created and called us, loves us, has redeemed us, and participates with us in life.

We open ourselves to God. As we do so, we become more trusting rather than defensive, we are ready and able to listen rather than always needing to speak, and we are present, attentive, and vulnerable with God.

We experience an increasing awareness of God. We recognize the unique qualities of God, our Divine/human love relationship, and godly values. We begin to understand what God is like and what God intends, and we develop other aspects of knowing God and letting ourselves be known by God.

We experience an increasing willingness to be limited human beings in relationship with Divine completeness. We let go of our willful take-charge attitude that says, "I can do it myself." We develop an attitude that enables us to depend on God more fully.[11]

We surrender to God. Disciplines help us choose God's ways and prefer God over ourselves. When we are even a little bit honest, we glimpse how often and how much we like our own way and prefer to be in control. Sometimes it feels as though God invites us to oppose ourselves for God's sake, to let go so we can see God's faith-

fulness and sufficiency. Disciplines remind us of the joyous outcomes of surrender to God, even when the surrender itself may not
seem pleasant.

We believe in God's love for us. Spiritual disciplines help us recognize
and connect with Divine love. If we feel condemned when we participate in a discipline, something is wrong, and we need to invite
the Holy Spirit to show us what is called for. But while we should
question this type of self-denigration, sometimes the Spirit of God
confronts us with areas that need attention. In these cases, God's
love is refining us even though it does not always feel good, especially when God separates us from ungodly attitudes and practices
that we have grown to like. Still, we need to remember that God is
calling us to live as new creations, which is a deep act of love. God
loves us and desires our freedom and wholeness.

We are renewed by God. Through spiritual disciplines, God cleanses,
clears, and refreshes our hearts, perceptions, attitudes, and actions.
God draws us away from self-centeredness and removes the accu-
mulations of life that can blur our love and perceptions.

We become free to hear God. Spiritual disciplines bring greater objectivity and provide space to see, appreciate, and discern. We grow
in our ability to listen, interact, question, wait, respond, and act.
We are less often pushed around by our own desires and fears.
Our freedom expands to explore what God desires. We grow in
freedom to hear, care about, and respond to whatever the Spirit
brings.

We continue to move along. We are not likely to stay at an impasse for
long because the ongoing practice of spiritual disciplines helps us
recognize what hinders us. The Spirit of God may show us what
needs to be done, or God may move us by grace or call us to make
specific changes in attitudes or actions. As we respond with obedient actions, God propels us out of resentful or self-pitying attitudes, out of an attitude of hopelessness or crippling self-centeredness, or out of any one of an endless number of attitudes that
can sidetrack us. (Even though the above is true, there are also seasons in the Christian life when no matter what disciplines we practice or how we endeavor to seek God, it seems as though God does
not respond. Nothing seems to help us move along. We feel isolated
and alone. These experiences have been called a dark night of the
soul. The darkness refers to the fact that God's activity is hidden
from us. During such seasons, it can be helpful to have a spiritual
director who walks alongside us, prays with and for us, and waits
with us.)

We recognize fruit. As we participate in disciplines that are right for us, we notice that the fruit of the Spirit of Galatians 5:22–23—love, joy, peace, patience, kindness, goodness, faithfulness, gentleness, and self-control—seems to appear more often in our thoughts, prayers, words, and behaviors. We are not always the best judge of our growth in these areas, but every now and then the Spirit gives us a glimpse of positive changes that we know could only come from God.

We experience increasing satisfaction and an increasing desire for God. We may discover a deeper satisfaction and joy with God and almost in the same breath say we are much thirstier for God than ever before. We are more fully satisfied and yet also powerfully drawn to return to experience more and more of living in relationship with God.

Some of the above qualities need to be present if something is to be considered a Christian discipline. It can be helpful to think about one of the disciplines you practice in the light of each of the characteristics described. When doing such an analysis, a gentle, nonjudgmental attitude can help you discern whether God is directing you to a more effective way.

Even the best plans have a way of becoming merely part of a routine after a while. When our practices become deadening or listless, we need to make this a matter for intentional prayer. It may seem as though our practices come between us and God rather than encouraging us to listen and respond to the Spirit. Periodically, we all need to be reawakened by God. Sometimes when the Spirit calls us to a face-to-face relationship, we are startled because we had not realized we had drifted. God challenges our ways of avoiding authenticity. This is not true for just some of us but for all. We are dependent on God and grace, which is both humbling and a relief. When we are honest, we acknowledge that we cannot do much except be willing to listen to and try to cooperate with the Holy Spirit. God will do the rest.

Exploring Unfamiliar Disciplines

At times we may sense the Holy Spirit is inviting us to learn more about a Christian discipline that we know by name but not by knowledge or experience. We may be curious or feel drawn to read about a particular discipline. What does Scripture say? How have other Christians participated in it, and how have they described their motivations, actions, and sense of God's involvement? We may want to talk to people who are already involved in this discipline or discuss it with trusted friends who are willing to explore with us.

God prompts us to learn about disciplines for many reasons, and they may not be clear to us at the beginning of our study. Sometimes the Spirit calls us just to learn more about a discipline. At other times God leads us to become involved in some way. Whatever God intends, however, will eventually be made clear if we proceed one step at a time and remain in conversation with God.

As we explore a discipline, we want to pay attention to our motivations. Is God calling us to a discipline, or are we interested because of what others are doing or curious because of something we have read or heard? We can be attracted by spiritual fads, and an unfamiliar discipline can seem glamorous or "more Christian." We need to ask God to show us the roots of our interest as well as what we might think about ourselves if we practiced this new discipline and if it is likely to draw us to Christ. Disciplines that are God's idea usually lead to servant-like attitudes and actions.

Trying on a discipline either mentally or in actual practice for a short period of time is a helpful way to listen for confirmation of our sense of God's leading. When we do this, we will usually get a sense of whether the discipline will help us be open and responsive to God or not. A yes or no answer is a gift of grace, and through this process we learn more about how God is with us. We learn more about discerning God's intentions and desires for us. We learn that when the Spirit says no it is because God has a different yes. Learning how God is with us means learning about the uniqueness of our relationship with God—what it is, what it feels like, and how we decide something is of God.

After we have spent time learning about a discipline and practicing it regularly for a period of time, it may seem as though we are ready to integrate it into our life. Then the new discipline may recede a bit, take its place within the context of other disciplines, and receive a more ordinary amount of time and emphasis. At this time, we may feel free to develop the newly learned discipline in our own way. Perhaps we shift our intensive study to another area.

Sometimes new disciplines or new ways of being involved in familiar disciplines replace old ones. At other times we may incorporate new practices into our pattern of life. In either case, before we decide what our practice will be for the next month or months or year, we want to consider our personality and background, how we describe faith and the characteristics of our relationship with God, and in what way we are sensing the Spirit's participation and call.

Deepening through Christian Disciplines

By participating in Christian disciplines, we live out our desire and intention to cooperate with the Holy Spirit. As we do so, we are encouraged, instructed, healed, challenged, loved, renewed, and beckoned to God and godly living.

While it is true that God is in every when and where and that many other things besides disciplines contribute to our deepening relationship with God, we discover that it makes a meaningful difference in everyday life when we set aside time, space, and ourselves to be more fully present with and attentive and responsive to God. Disciplines are like faithful companions on the way. The benefit we seek and desire most is deepening companionship with God. We come away from other pursuits to listen for the still, small voice that is our best friend, our beloved Savior, the Holy One, our Creator, God.

Reflections

1. What is your history with spiritual disciplines? Which ones have you used? How have they changed over time? How does that influence your interest in them now?
2. Design a spiritual rule. What could help your life blossom at this time? What could assist you to be yourself as God has created you and called you to fullness of life? What practices seem as though they would be life-giving, and what practices seem as though they would be deadening, boring, or exhausting?

PART 3

Possible Complications and Benefits of Spiritual Direction

Possess your soul in patience

Own it. Hold your heart the way
you'd hold a live bird—your two hands
laced to latch it in, feeling
its feathery trembling, its fledgling
warmth, its faint anxieties
of protest, its heart stutter
against the palm of one hand, a fidget
in the pull of early light.

Possess it, restless, in
the finger cage of patience, Enfold
this promise with a blue sheen
on its neck, its wings a tremor
of small feathered bones
until morning widens like
a window, and God opens
your fingers and whispers, *Fly!*

Luci Shaw[1]

Common Areas of Difficulty | 15

Most of our conflicts and difficulties come from trying to deal with the spiritual and practical aspects of our life separately instead of realizing them as parts of one whole. If our practical life is centered on our own interests, cluttered up by possessions, distracted by ambitions, passions, wants and worries, beset by a sense of our own rights and importance, or anxieties for our own future, or longings for our own success, we need not expect that our spiritual life will be a contrast to all this. The soul's house is not built on such a convenient plan: there are few soundproof partitions in it. Only when the conviction—not merely the idea—that the demand of the Spirit, however inconvenient, comes first and IS first, rules the whole of it, will those objectionable noises die down which have a way of penetrating into the nicely furnished oratory, and drowning all the quieter voices by their din.

Evelyn Underhill[1]

For I am convinced that neither death nor life, neither angels nor demons, neither the present nor the future, nor any powers, neither height nor depth, nor anything else in all creation, will be able to separate us from the love of God that is in Christ Jesus our Lord.

Romans 8:38–39

We do not know what obstacles might threaten to hinder our resolution and desires when we set out to follow God. But we do know that we will meet difficulties. We may ask at times if the journey is worth it or question more than once whether our commitment to God is sufficient to draw us to particular courses of action. Whenever we willingly set our hearts on deepening our faith by being more fully attentive and responsive to God, it seems that other voices object. Some of them come from inside ourselves and are rooted in a preference for having our own way. Others speak through family, friends, and culture, and some are from spiritual sources.

Sometimes we see our resistance to any discipline—prayer, Bible study, worship, or service. At other times, although we have good intentions and make ourselves available to listen to God, we run into problems. Circumstances develop differently than we anticipated. In spiritual direction these hindrances show up as anything that distracts us from pursuing our desire to hear the Holy Spirit. We discover that spiritual direction, like any other Christian discipline, does not always go smoothly.

We do not want to go looking for problems, but thinking about potential difficulties may help us identify and confront them early on so we can avoid the consequences of larger problems. Early recognition may also draw us to pray specifically for grace and assistance.

Problems in spiritual direction seem to fall into two categories: (1) those that are related to disturbances in the direction relationship, and (2) those that pertain primarily to the directee's relationship with God. Either kind of problem, however, influences the other.

Of course, we cannot anticipate every possible difficulty or guess which ones we will encounter. We hope to trust God rather than become overly involved in thinking about troubling expectations. We need to affirm our dependency on God and trust the Holy Spirit's ability and desire to alert us when needed and guide us even as we consider potential concerns. We need to remind ourselves that some things may become a nuisance or distraction but that nothing can truly interfere with God's love for us (see Rom. 8:38–39). It is important to keep these thoughts in mind as we examine areas of potential difficulties in spiritual direction relationships.

Finding the Right Distance

We are dependent in childhood, learn independence in adolescence, and continue to grow toward interdependence in adulthood. Part of the challenge in spiritual direction is discovering the appropriate level of interdependence between two adults who are listening to the Holy Spirit on behalf of one of them.

Qualities of dependence, independence, and interdependence ebb and flow in relationships. The amount of closeness and dependency we feel is related to our sense of how things are going, including our recognition of the Spirit's presence, what God seems to be bringing to our attention, our anxiety level, and the condition of our prayer. There is a healthy and helpful range along which we alternately move closer to and farther away from each other. We can be diverted from paying attention to God rather than supported in our faith if we become either too dependent on or independent from our director.

Willful Independence

We may not pay sufficient attention to our director's sense of God, discernment, or loving counsel if we remain too independent. We may not allow ourselves to be vulnerable enough to listen or learn and may hold on to our own way so fiercely that we are not free to interact meaningfully. When we are too independent, we may not pray about what we have heard from our director or dismiss it without due consideration. Of course, our ultimate relationship is with God, not another person, but presumably we have entered spiritual direction because we believe the Spirit of God is inviting us to spiritual companionship. When we do not listen to our director, it may hinder our ability to hear and follow God.

Unhealthy Dependency

Unhealthy dependency is at the opposite end of the continuum from willful independence. Yet it is just as detrimental to our relationship with God, because when we are overly dependent on a spiritual director, we are less likely to depend on God. The probability that we will become overly dependent on a director is influenced by numerous variables such as (1) our background, (2) our age, (3) our level of satisfaction with other relationships that are important to us (family members, friends, church members, and coworkers), (4) whether we are passing through a crisis, (5) our usual style of interaction with mentors, pastors, authority figures, and friends, (6) our level of commitment to being responsible for ourselves, (7) the particular invitations of the Holy Spirit that are encouraging us to seek spiritual companionship, and (8) our willingness to notice and address imbalances within relationships.

In some ways it is perfectly all right to depend on a spiritual director. Every time we participate in spiritual direction, because of the nature of our conversation and intention to be open to the Holy Spirit, we knowingly place ourselves in a vulnerable, somewhat dependent position. We are trusting the director to be willing to hear God with us. At times a director may seem to be so available to the Spirit on our behalf that we want to hold on to that person because doing so makes us feel more secure. Our realization that God has touched us through another person may draw us to return to that person whenever we are seeking God.

Some of this is healthy and expected; it is why we have arranged to meet together. Exclusivity, however, can create problems. We do not want to behave as if this relationship provides the only person, place, or way that God uses to speak to us, as if all that matters happens when we are with our director. We need to ask whether we are growing more dependent on our director than on the Holy Spirit if we notice that we are pursuing our own spiritual life less and less outside of direction conversations. If that is the case, the intimacy of our relationship with God could be jeopardized rather than encouraged. We also need to pay attention to whether we are substituting our director for God or copying our director's journey.

Substituting the Director for God

Sometimes we may be tempted to hold on to a director's perceptions when we encounter ideas or experiences that seem threatening. We may respond by taking less responsibility to pray, think things through carefully, and discern and decide things for ourselves. Our strong desire to have a guide in unknown territory may blur our recognition of just how tightly we are clinging to another person. Hanging on is understandable for short periods of time, but it is not what we or God intend for the long term. We desire to be directly available to the Holy Spirit, and we do not want our deepest intentions sidetracked when we are feeling vulnerable, fragile, or uncertain.

If we think we may be developing an unhealthy dependency, becoming more intentional about our continuing conversation with the Lord, our prayer, Scripture reading, worship, and everyday choices may help us gain some perspective. Returning to or choosing appropriate spiritual disciplines may help us notice where the Spirit is inviting adjustments. At the same time, we should remember that it is easy to shift our dependency from a spiritual director to ourselves, instead of turning from our director to God.

At times the Spirit may show us how we got into difficulty and point out ways to avoid becoming diverted again in the same way, but we can miss learning all that we might from our side trips by becoming overly analytical and self-critical. Criticizing ourselves may cause us to withdraw from the prayerful objectivity and openness through which the Holy Spirit moves with greater freedom. We want to remain available to God and ask for grace to grow in our trust in God in all circumstances. When we follow a path that is clearly counter to God's desires for us— either intentionally because we have closed ourselves to God, or unintentionally because the busyness of our life has made us oblivious to our actions—we can experience a deep love and appreciation for grace and for God when we reawaken to God's search for us.

Copying the Spiritual Director's Journey

We choose someone as our spiritual director because God invites us, but we also may be drawn by a person's prayer or service, volunteer work, teaching ability, committee work, hospitality, speaking ability, or the way that person seems to trust God during troubling times. We may be aware of many challenges someone has faced and wonder whether he or she could help us with our own struggles. Perhaps something in a person's public or private life leads us to believe he or she is a friend of God.

The qualities that beckon us toward a particular person may be related to specific graces or godly habits or attributes we would like to have. It is natural to be drawn to such a person for spiritual direction, but we need to remember that the Spirit does not call us to emulate another person's relationship with God.

Evidence that we have been diverted from listening to the Spirit and have begun copying our director's spiritual journey may be subtle or blatant. When a director's life appears to be blessed, we may be inclined to conduct our relationship with God in the same way the director does. We may have some expectations that if we respond as that person does, God will bless us in similar ways. We may notice that we feel proud to be known as the directee of someone we consider important, learned, or a person of unusual faith. We may speak frequently about our director and his or her practices, prayer, and life rather than about our own relationship with the Lord. Sometimes family members or close friends tell us we are starting to sound just like our director.

If we regularly hear ourselves saying, "My director says . . . ," it may be a gentle reminder to look at our relationships—human and divine. If we realize that we are organizing our time like our director does, choosing the same spiritual disciplines, using the same prayer methods, going to the same church when we did not before, or reading the same books, we need to examine our own prayer, motivations, and relationship with God.

At times God does take people along parallel pathways, and the Spirit may show us others who are living examples of specific behaviors to which God is leading us. But unless the Holy Spirit is calling us to follow closely in another's footsteps, the distinctive flavor of our relationship with God can become blurred. Further, some of what we admire in another person may be different from what the Spirit is inviting in us.

When we recognize that we have been copying our director's spiritual journey, it is time to turn to God in prayer and ask to see our own individuality and what God intends for us. We ask to recognize and appreciate human similarities and differences and for freedom to be and become all God desires.

Interdependency

There is a healthy range of interdependency in which both persons continue to maintain their separate identities and also have a sense of a shared life in Christ.

Sometimes it is comforting to lean on a director's prayer when we are struggling to be patient during a time of spiritual dryness or when we are learning new ways of listening to and following God. When it seems the Holy Spirit is inviting us toward unfamiliar ideas, experiences, or actions, we may depend on our director for support and companionship. Or we may want the assurance of our director's prayerful presence when we are not sure whether we can remain in God's loving closeness or endure God's seeming absence. Times of spiritual dryness may seem like an invitation to trust God, to lean on God more than ever, which may cause us to feel less dependent on another person and rely more on God. At times, conversation with a spiritual director provides no more than an affirming background.

The changing pattern of closeness and distance between director and directee usually carries information about our relationship with God, which then becomes part of our prayer. Most direction pairs find an appropriate, satisfying interdependence that characterizes their time together. Still, discovering the right distance is an ongoing, ever changing dimension of spiritual direction.

Answering questions such as the following can provide information that helps directors and directees as they seek to discern appropriate levels of interdependence.

- How do you honestly feel about your director or directee and your conversations?
- Do you seem to welcome him or her and the opportunity to listen and speak about spiritual life, or do you feel self-protective?
- Are you praying for your director or directee? How? Does the Holy Spirit seem to be inviting this prayer, or does it feel like something you do primarily because you think you ought to?
- What is your sense of your director's or directee's relationship with God?
- What do you do with information arising from direction meetings?
- When you are together, what clues arise about your acceptance of each other, of God in each other, and your interdependence?
- Are you usually early, on time, or late for direction appointments?
- How does your body respond when you think about going to a direction appointment, relaxed or tense? What does this say to you?
- How would you describe your sense of being open or closed to God, to your own heart, and to your director or directee during spiritual direction conversations? What seems to cause you to close down or become defensive?

After answering these questions, we need to spend time in prayer, asking God for clear discernment as to whether a spiritual direction relationship is leaning toward dependency or willful independence. If we are concerned about the direction relationship, we may want to discuss our sense of imbalance with our director. If we feel confused or concerned about our freedom to be objective with our director, we may want to talk with a third person.

Diminishing Freedom

We need to explore whether we experience increasing freedom with God or seem inhibited in our recognition of and responsiveness to the Holy Spirit as a result of participating in spiritual direction. If we are in an unhealthy spiritual direction relationship, it can actually diminish our freedom to listen to the Spirit and live authentically. Like any other crippling human relationship, it can work against us rather than for us.

We need to observe whether we are consistently feeling less loving, trusting, or responsive to God, less generous of spirit, or less willing to offer our gifts to God and others. This may indicate a negative influence on our freedom to hear and follow God.

But our immediate sense that our freedom has been compromised is not always trustworthy. We can experience a diminished sense of freedom after exposing areas of vulnerability. We may become fearful of consequences we imagine could result from our discussion of certain matters. After some time has passed, however, we may realize we do not need to fear, that God is still with us, and that our director will maintain confidentiality and continue to pray on our behalf. Then we may pray and reflect on what has taken place and allow ourselves to let go of whatever unnecessary self-protection has arisen.

Because our natural assumption is that we will experience freedom in a direction relationship, we need to ask God to alert us when spiritual direction is inhibiting our freedom to hear and follow God.

Distracting Aspects of Sexuality

Distracting aspects of sexuality seem to appear in a number of ways. We will discuss two of them. The first is related to not recognizing linkages between sexuality, spirituality, and our whole selves. The second is related to sexual attraction between directors and directees.

For various reasons, we may simply try to ignore or at least dampen our sexual awareness. But if growth related to our sexual thoughts, feelings, and behaviors is what God is inviting, we are hindering that progress by not paying attention. Sometimes God is encouraging us to settle more fully into being a man or a woman. At times religious subcultures encourage us to behave as if we are asexual beings, but God created us male and female and said that creation was good. The Holy Spirit may be inviting us to enjoy and appreciate all that it means to be a man or a woman (sexuality, sex, and gender).

At other times it is important to confront and resolve some of our sexual and gender concerns in order to live in more satisfying ways in day-to-day human relationships and in our relationship with God. For instance, if a woman who feels strongly called to ministry feels prohibited from following that call in particular ways solely because she is female, she needs to address these concerns (gender). Or if a man notices that his thoughts seem to drift toward sex in settings in which other things are of primary importance, this may be a clue that he needs to pay closer attention to what sex and sexuality mean to him. God might be encouraging him to identify his sexual ideas, needs, and desires and bring them into his prayer. If we pay attention to sex and sexuality in appropriate ways, they are less likely to interfere when other matters need to be central.

Sexuality can become a diversion from listening to the Spirit when a directee or director notices he or she is sexually attracted to the other. Sexual attraction may appear in various forms: recognizing compatibility, physical desire, or a desire to express with our whole selves—spirit, mind, and body—the love we feel with and for another person. When such attraction becomes evident, it is important to begin and continue praying for protection, guidance, and courage to do what is pleasing to God.

Careful discernment is required in deciding whether to discuss sexual attractions that occur within a direction relationship. Such a discussion can awaken more interest than it puts to rest. On the other hand, occasionally there are times when the Spirit invites such conversation. Whether the sexual stirrings come from God, ourselves, or spiritual influences that want to divert our attention from God, when they are brought into the open at God's invitation, they can be used by the Spirit to increase our dependency on God. However, if it becomes apparent that a direction pair is becoming diverted from listening to God by sexual attraction, we may rightly conclude it is time to end the relationship.

Sometimes the Spirit calls us to wait, pray, and do nothing when we feel sexually attracted. God may ask us to wait through these feelings without speaking about them in direction meetings. Such feelings often dissipate when we do not dwell on them, discuss them, or act on them. But we may be called by God to provide some means outside the direction relationship for accountability as well as continue in our prayer about these matters. Sexual feelings do not immediately signal that a direction relationship should end. However, this is always delicate ground because we can easily fool ourselves by assessing the situation inaccurately, especially at times when our relational intimacy needs are not being met in appropriate ways.

Evil has often challenged people who intend to love and serve God by drawing them toward inappropriate sexual behavior. Being aware of this can help us decide to pay attention to our sexual interests, questions, and stirrings honestly with ourselves and God rather than attempting to ignore them.

Thinking Spiritual Direction Is *the* Way

Some directees become so enthusiastic about how God has been present and loving, guiding and influencing them through spiritual direction that they think all Christians should be in direction relationships. It is easy to get excited about whatever practices or experiences the Spirit uses to deepen our sense of God's love for us and increase our responsiveness to God. Spiritual direction, however, like any Christian discipline, is not right for everyone or at all times.

Sometimes the Spirit invites us to be and feel more alone. In fact, we may feel quite lonesome but recognize that for the time being the Spirit is calling us to this experience. Of course, it is wise to pay attention to and pray about our motivations, because it is easy to think we do not need others, which is an illusion. The Spirit just may not be calling us to a spiritual direction companionship at the present time. When we do sense the Spirit is inviting us to a helping relationship, we need to discern which kind: counseling, mentoring, discipling, spiritual direction, or something else.

It can be damaging even to imply that everyone interested in cultivating an intimate relationship with God should see a spiritual director. The best help directees can give others who are questioning whether spiritual direction is appropriate is to model the way of spiritual direction by praying and listening to the Holy Spirit with the others as they speak about their relationship with God. In such cases, directees behave like directors. When we see ourselves in the role of director, we are likely to realize that prescribing direction for others contradicts the underlying desire of spiritual direction—to encourage someone to discover what *God* intends.

Thinking *We* Are the Primary Cause of Spiritual Growth

Growth in faith is a gift—a gift of God. As Paul says in 1 Corinthians 3:6, "I planted the seed, Apollos watered it, but God made it grow." No matter what we or others do to encourage development, true transformation comes from God. But we may get the idea that our involvement in spiritual direction is responsible for our inner transformations and the changes in our life because we are doing more than we ever have to pay attention to God in an ongoing way.

It is unsettling to catch glimpses of self-righteousness in ourselves. We may deny what we see and be embarrassed by our self-centered thoughts, or we may not recognize them. God is not the source of our interpretation when we are feeling holier than others. Self-inflating attitudes place barriers between God and us, interfere in our relationships with others, and interrupt the flow of the Holy Spirit's anointing in and through us. When we recognize such attitudes in ourselves, opening them to God in prayer, writing in a journal, or speaking with a spiritual director can lessen their hold.

Lacking a Sense of Humor, a Lightness about Ourselves

People who embark intentionally on a path that they hope leads to spiritual growth usually do so through serious self-examination. They want to explore who God is, how they are called to be related to God, and the meaning of human life—their life in particular. This searching reflects important, foundational values and choices.

It is possible, however, to become paralyzed by believing we are in charge of this journey. Some people feel they are responsible for their own growth in these matters or for the growth of those involved with them in spiritual direction. They become weighed down with responsibilities that are not within their control. Such an attitude is different from desiring to share the genuine overflow of the Spirit's life in us that draws others to God.

Sometimes we need to laugh at ourselves, with ourselves, and with others, and even to laugh at our unrealistic sense of responsibility. Laughter helps us let go of ideas of self-importance and frees us to be God's creation instead of our own. When we abide in God, we find it easier to rest. Then there is space for laughter, lightness, and joy, which are evidences of our growing freedom to trust in God's generosity, grace, and care.

Awareness of Vulnerability

The nature of life, God, and spiritual direction guarantee that we will not be fully in control. We cannot predict what topics will arise for discussion or what actions the Spirit will invite us to. We may have thought of ourselves as a good Christian, or at least as good as others. In spiritual direction, however, attentiveness to the Spirit's leading is the agenda rather than comparison with others. We will experience shocks to our self-esteem, self-perception, and awareness of how closely we have been listening to and cooperating with the Spirit. I have been surprised numerous times by discovering I have not been praying at all about something I say is important, or at least not in the way I describe the details of a situation. This information surfaces when my director asks, "How does that seem in your prayer?" We may feel wounded by new awareness and even feel as though we are being abused by God, or we may be startled by the profound completeness of God's love for us. What the Spirit reveals or asks of us is not necessarily difficult, but it is often different than expected. The Holy Spirit's ideas of purity and availability to God and others extend beyond our own.

We may speak rather easily about many things in spiritual direction that we have never shared with anyone. Going beyond our usual boundaries in this way may make us feel more vulnerable than we intended. Direction may include conversations about topics we have not discussed with a spouse, family members, or close friends. Sometimes this seems wonderful, freeing, and exciting, and sometimes we want to withdraw and run, to hide for at least a short time while we catch our breath.

Although we may experience dry seasons in our prayer, Scripture reading, and church fellowships, and our relationship with God may seem to be going nowhere, we will also experience seasons in which we are deeply appreciative and know that God is blessing us. There will also be moments when we are just plain scared—wary of how dependent we are becoming on the Lord, questioning whether we have ventured too far along the road of self-surrender and prayer, and frightened because we sense the presence of Jesus, God, or the Holy Spirit more intensely than we imagined possible. We may wonder how to "be" with God or worry about what the Spirit is asking of us.

Some directees leave direction when they recognize how threatened they feel and how truly vulnerable they are. They discover they do not want as much information, accountability, or even as much love from God as they thought they did. When directees bring their fear and vulnerability into prayer and direction conversations, however, they often find that the Holy Spirit increases their ability to respond to and accept all that the Spirit reveals. Recognizing they have been stretched, intentionally praying about it, and asking the Lord for help can open the way to deepening relationship with God. Many graces that do not thrive in other contexts develop when we are aware of our limitations and run to God.

Problematic Direction Relationships

Direction relationships do not always work out well in spite of our prayer and best efforts. When a relationship does not flourish, it is easy for a directee to wonder if someone is to blame: the directee, the director, God, or something evil. We could spend a great deal of time and energy on such questions, but it is more important to bring our disappointment or anger into prayer and ask to hear what the Spirit is saying to us through this situation.

Sometimes when our direction expectations are not met, we consider the outcome only a nuisance; other times we feel devastated. For a time, our director becomes one of the lenses through which we see and appreciate God more fully, so when we are disappointed or angry with our director, we may feel that God has hurt us. When we are questioning the faithfulness of God because of a derailed direction relationship, we need the support of praying, caring friends who will walk alongside us without attempting to explain away our concerns or immediately seek to make everything all right. It may take time before we are willing or able to trust another director, or even God, again.

Sometimes direction relationships do not function effectively because the people involved are mismatched. They may be so different from each other that they do not have enough shared perceptions to make meaningful connections and insights possible. Words mean different things to different people depending on background, education, and experiences. It may require too much work for some direction pairs or groups to be open and vulnerable to the Holy Spirit and each other. On the other hand, some difficult relationships bear abundant fruit and are invited by God. Differences alone, therefore, do not provide a sufficient reason to end a direction relationship unless the Spirit guides us to do so.

Some relationships do not begin successfully; others deteriorate after a promising start. No matter when a spiritual direction companionship flounders, however, both persons share responsibility for the quality and conduct of the relationship and for continuing to pray. Neither party gains by suffering in silence. When evidence surfaces that a director and directee are mismatched, they need to pray together and individually, discuss their concerns together, and decide on appropriate action.

Discerning spiritual direction and authentic prayer may be drowned out by disturbances in a direction relationship. Paying attention as soon as possible to a struggling relationship may shorten the days of difficulty and assist both people to address and care for each other and themselves and refocus on God.

A Reason to Hope

I have described a few of the areas that may cause concern for directors and directees. In reality, our list of difficulties could be as lengthy and as varied as any list we might create of hindrances possible in human relationships. It is easy to get discouraged by these possibilities, and at times we do. But we need to remember that we are not depending on ourselves alone, nor on our good intentions, wisdom, or skill. Spiritual direction friendships are dependent on the Holy Spirit from start to finish, and therein lies our hope.

Reflections

Thinking and praying about possible distractions and problem areas can elicit helpful information.

1. Dependence, independence, interdependence—how do these words describe your present relationships? When you get out of balance, are you more likely to become overly dependent or independent?
2. What seems to blur your ability or willingness to listen to the Spirit?
3. When have you desired to model your behavior after someone else's? How did that turn out?
4. How is your sexuality a gift? What do you notice about your comfort level related to your own and others' sexuality? How do sexuality and spirituality relate to each other in your experience?
5. Some people do what everyone else is doing, others do the opposite, and still others settle in the middle ground. Regarding Christian practices, where do you usually find yourself, with the group or alone?
6. How willing are you to provide for what you need in your relationship with the Lord? What helps you to make space for yourself in this way?
7. What is your experience with mismatched relationships? Do you usually stay in the relationship, get out quickly, or stay longer than you should?
8. How might you be naturally inclined to respond to a mismatched spiritual direction relationship?

16 | Potential Benefits of Spiritual Direction

Scripturally speaking, the spiritual life is simply the increasing vitality and sway of God's Spirit in us. It is a magnificent choreography of the Holy Spirit in the human spirit, moving us toward communion with both Creator and creation. The spiritual life is thus grounded in relationship. It has to do with God's way of relating to us, and our way of responding to God.

In Christian experience, the work of the Holy Spirit is to conform us to the image of Christ:

Now the Lord is the Spirit, and where the Spirit of the Lord is, there is freedom. And all of us, with unveiled faces, seeing the glory of the Lord as though reflected in a mirror, are being transformed into the same image from one degree of glory to another; for this comes from the Lord, the Spirit (2 Cor. 3:17–18).

Marjorie J. Thompson[1]

But stay constantly with a godly [person] whom you know to be a keeper of the commandments, whose soul is in accord with your soul, and who will sorrow with you if you fail.

And establish the counsel of your own heart, for no one is more faithful to you than it is. For a [person's] soul sometimes keeps them better informed than seven watchmen sitting high on a watchtower.

And besides all this, pray to the Most High that he may direct your way in truth.

Ecclesiasticus 37:12–15 RSV

Participating in spiritual direction or any other Christian discipline will not automatically make us persons who listen to and follow God. Only God can do that through the Holy Spirit's invitations and our willing collaboration. We do hope to be awake and attuned to God through spiritual direction, but that is quite different from suggesting that spiritual direction will guarantee our continuing desire to hear and follow God. The effects of any spiritual discipline we pursue depend on grace and our willing cooperation with God. Our hope is in God, not in spiritual direction.

We enter spiritual direction because we wish to live in growing intimacy with God, recognize the Spirit of God, and be attentive to God's desires and values. We hope God will use the process of spiritual direction to deepen our love—to love God with all our heart, mind, and strength and our neighbors as ourselves (Matt. 22:37–38; Mark 12:30–31; Luke 10:27).

We cannot predict what will develop through spiritual direction, but distinct qualities seem to be enhanced as people tend their hearts in a prayer-centered environment. Although spiritual direction does not create godly attributes, it often helps people discern God's presence and activity. It also encourages and supports their continuing desire to listen and respond to the Holy Spirit. Many directees also notice a development of their awareness, appreciation, and trust, and that they seem to respond more frequently out of their connection to God, Scripture, and prayer.

As you read the following sections, remind yourself occasionally that even though intimacy with God does bring about change and that spiritual direction provides many benefits, it is the loving Divine/human intimacy itself that is of greatest importance—learning to dwell in and live out of God's love.

Increasing Awareness

After participating in spiritual direction for a while, we may be surprised at how often we notice God's presence. Perhaps we thought of ourselves as praying people before, but through direction we begin to observe many things that had not appeared in our prayer until now. More of life finds its way into conscious prayer, and more choices are rooted in prayer. We see and hear different things than we used to. The light of growing sensitivity brings everything into clearer view. The still, small voice of the Holy Spirit becomes easier to hear and separate from other voices. It is like background music that has now become the foreground melody.

Of Discomfort

Our growing awareness helps us recognize when and why we become uncomfortable, anxious, or unsettled. We see that self-concern is dominant in many of our perceptions and interpretations and that we often want things to be different for our own sake and give little or no thought to what might be better for others or pleasing to God. The Holy Spirit enables us to identify and respond to feelings and ideas that are stirred when we are confronted with scriptural principles and values. We grow in our willingness to be uncomfortable for God's sake in order that we might become more like Christ, more attuned to the true self God has created and called us to be, and receptive to grace, which is essential if we wish to live based on our communion with God. Sometimes we will feel ashamed at what we notice and wish it were not so, but we learn little by little to run to the Lord rather than away from him when we are troubled by what we see, especially in ourselves. We may never be completely comfortable when the Spirit illuminates our perceptions, but life-restoring grace touches us through both discomfort and comfort and nourishes our longings to be awake to God.

Of Comfort

Through spiritual direction we may become more aware of the comforting, sustaining love and presence of God. We are more likely to pray for a sense of God's comforting nearness and to pray for and receive a sense of peace that is not destroyed by outward circumstances or accounted for by rational explanation. God reassures us. Julian of Norwich's often quoted affirmation, "All shall be well, and all shall be well, and all manner of things shall be well," reminds us of God's loving intention to bring good out of all things.[2] Having another person alongside to pray, listen, and discern can help us recognize the Holy Spirit's comforting, strengthening presence.

Of Our Closeness to God

We may feel closer to God because we see evidence of our trust of and eagerness, desire, and love for God through our conversations with a spiritual director. When we are closer to God, however, we also notice that we often set our minds and hearts on having our own way. Our deepening sense of closeness to God makes us consciously aware of our choices for and against the promptings of the Spirit.

Of Humanity and Divinity

As we participate in spiritual direction, we often let go of our need to pretend we are perfect as our flawed humanity and God's generous love and continuing care are revealed. As long as we perceive or present ourselves as perfect, we are not available to be liberated by God. When we acknowledge our limitations, however, illusions about personal perfection are less likely to color our thoughts and behavior. Our needs and efforts to "fix" ourselves and others diminishes, because it is strikingly evident that God's love for human beings does not depend on anything we do or do not do. We experience greater freedom to celebrate our humanness as God's gift to us rather than hide or harrass ourselves. It is an enormous relief to be God's persons, to accept God as God, and to be truly human as God intends—desiring and living in relationship with God. Spiritual direction can help us acknowledge, accept, and love God, ourselves, and others.

Of God's Invitations

God's invitations become more obvious when we listen intentionally in spiritual direction. God is always inviting us through large and small experiences, thoughts, feelings, and prayers to love God and to enjoy God's love for us. Every moment contains offerings of Divine love that invite us to be in communion with God. Sometimes we sense the Spirit beckoning us to ask that Christ be more fully formed in us, or drawing us to be God's person in the world through a specific opportunity, or to trust God more. It is not that the Holy Spirit addresses us more often when we participate in spiritual direction, but when we do so, we may be more awake to God's ever present aliveness.

Of Willingness and Willfulness

As we have said all along, willingness is the opposite of willfulness and involves following God's unfolding self-revelation rather than living independently. As we participate in spiritual direction, we grow in willingness—willingness to listen to the Spirit, willingness to surrender our ways in favor of God's ways, and willingness to wait when we are unsure what God is saying. We are often impatient and in a hurry. Spiritual direction can help us develop patience and remain willingly available to God, continuing in what we already know, until the Spirit reveals God's desires. Willingness is part of trusting God. At times it feels as though we are sitting when we would prefer to be doing something—anything. Willingness may seem a little easier when we are aware that we are moving, responding to the Spirit of God rather than waiting. But this is not always the case, because sometimes the Spirit calls us to step outside our previous familiar experiences and to follow God in new ways. The companionship of spiritual direction can help us identify the ebb and flow of willingness and willfulness in our lives and bring it into our prayer.

Of Truth

It becomes easier to recognize truth when we pay attention to information in a prayerful context that encourages discernment. Speaking to a spiritual director about our experience with God and our perceptions of life in general helps us remember and consider how God is with us. We notice what becomes important to us and how we respond. Little by little, we grow in our ability to discern what is true among everything that appears. We learn to distinguish messages sent by God as we listen more closely to the Holy Spirit. We see that spiritual direction facilitates our ability to recognize what is true.

Of Spiritual Challenges

As we develop spiritually through participation in spiritual direction, we notice that God's desires for us do not go unchallenged. Sometimes it feels as though we are encountering something other or more than our own resistance or stubbornness. We may recognize that we are side-tracked or at an impasse but are unable to identify what hinders us. It is good to have a spiritual companion to talk to when we are trying to distinguish among possible causes of our confusion: ourselves, others, circumstances, God, or something evil. Our awareness of spiritual challenges may be sharpened as the Holy Spirit calls us away from self-centeredness toward Christlikeness. Through spiritual direction we can learn to rely more on God's assistance and ask the Holy Spirit what to do rather than plunging ahead independently to confront questionable spiritual experiences or our resistance to God. Through spiritual direction we may become more attuned to recognize spiritual confusion, learn to turn quickly to God, and grow in our understanding of how to cooperate with the Holy Spirit.

The Benefits of Awareness

God uses spiritual direction to develop our awareness, which in turn affects our ability to recognize God in ourselves, others, and the world, to notice God's invitations, and to be deliberate about our responses. We can see so much more than we ordinarily do if we allow God to enlarge our view. We can see more than ever before in creation, creatures, people, systems, institutions, experiences, and our own lives.

This does not always make us happy. I can remember feeling angry and troubled listening to women tell their stories during an international denominational conference. I thought I was at the conference because of God's leading, and it was becoming decidedly unpleasant. I asked God if I really needed to hear the extent and depth of personal pain of women representing numerous nations and ethnic groups. Each afternoon five women told about their journeys through persecution, injustice, and closed doors and the way that God was present and became the one who comforted and guided them. I found myself asking how God could bear knowing everyone's sorrows. These experiences and questions, and the ways my prayer changed because of their influence, became topics I discussed with my spiritual director. I got a glimpse into God's heart and gained a greater awareness of possibilities for prayer and caring.

Numerous new insights and questions can be stirred up when we are willing to look more closely at what God brings across our path. Expanding vision ultimately fosters growing appreciation for God and for grace, which is present in the uniqueness, beauty, and power of what we have heretofore thought of as ordinary human life.

Appreciation

We are freer to appreciate God, others, ourselves, and life in general when we do not have to expend energy trying to control these things. Through spiritual direction, we focus our attention less on our own concerns and become more attuned to God's loving presence. We relax more, savor the gifts found in ordinary daily life, and discover deepening joy.

For God

Appreciation includes insights that overflow into love. When gratitude flourishes, God and God's abundant care become more apparent to us. We are more likely to take pleasure in and enjoy our lives in spite of human limitations and failures. Enjoyment replaces complaining, because we see more of God and God's present aliveness in the world.

As our appreciation for God grows, our horizons expand so that we give importance to all three persons of the Trinity—God the Father, Christ the Son, and the Holy Spirit—and their participation in creation, redemption, and ongoing life, rather than focusing our love on only one person of the Trinity. More of God's characteristics and attributes also come to our attention. We grow in appreciation for God's presence, guidance, and loving care for all.

For Others

Through spiritual direction, a vibrant, worldwide network of prayer and Christian community becomes more visible. It seems that when we are more open to the Spirit, God brings other people of faith across our path. We talk to them and learn from them. We begin to see that we are not alone. At times directors suggest that directees read about the lives and faith journeys of Christians from the past and the present. Such stories broaden their acquaintance with numerous expressions of Christian faith. Directees grow in respect for people of every culture, race, country, social class, and denomination and learn to cherish people who are different from themselves.

For Ourselves

As God's love for and attentiveness to humanity in general and us in particular become more obvious, our perceptions, interpretations, and

self-concept change. We may notice that we are expressing kinder attitudes toward ourselves. We recognize that we are not worthy of Divine
love but also sense God's love for us. We want to cooperate with the Holy
Spirit and have fewer illusions about our ability to be our truest selves
without God's help. Acceptance of ourselves as we are grows. We are more
able to appreciate who God has created us to be and how God is guiding
and enabling us to be that person. We are freer to be glad that God blesses
everyone. When we trust that the Spirit will lead us to the place and life
that are ours, we have less need to compete or compare ourselves with
others. We realize there is a place for everyone in the kingdom of God.

Our false humility and self-diminution also lessen. We are able to live
openly and are less hindered by our lack of perfection. We do not flaunt
our limitations but sense our growing acceptance of ourselves as limited beings who are loved perfectly by God. We are liberated to be both
appreciative and realistic about ourselves and to trust God. Because of
our awareness of God's love and the presence of the Holy Spirit, our center of attention shifts; we become less compulsive about looking at ourselves and more interested in others. Our awareness of God's love for all
becomes more important and occupies more of our attention than it did
previously.

For Life

The God-givenness of ordinary human life becomes more apparent,
and our appreciation for beauty, complexity, diversity, and mystery, for
every aspect of human bodies, minds, emotions, relationships, and the
created world grows. We see more of the distinctiveness of each moment,
day, taste, fragrance, work to do, friend, prayer, way of thinking, and
awareness of God. Inner slowing enables us to savor. Patterns and opportunities—past, present, and possible—are seen as gifts. Sometimes we
are even able to be grateful for grace that comes to us through difficulty,
to cherish grace in the midst of shattering experiences.

Appreciation for God as God, for ourselves as God's beloved, for God
in others and the world, for divine radiance in the beauties of creation,
and for the extraordinary ordinariness of life expands whenever we notice
God. Spiritual direction is one of the ways the Spirit of God draws people
to deepen in appreciation and to savor and celebrate life as given by God.

Trust

In chapter 4, "Spiritual Direction and Trust," we considered aspects
of our personal trust history that influence our willingness to trust God,
ourselves, and others and how that might affect our readiness to enter

spiritual direction. Once we are involved in spiritual direction, we speak about what challenges our trust and rejoice when we trust appropriately.

In the beginning of an intentional faith journey, it seems as though the Holy Spirit reveals enough of God so that we are able to trust God. Our trust expands as we experience Divine love, presence, and guidance. Little by little, we come to trust more fully that the Spirit of God is and will remain present and will show us whatever is needed.

God invites us to grow in trust through opportunities and challenges that become more complicated, less obvious, and closer to our hearts. We notice our tendencies to trust ourselves, others, expertise, money, time, individual and institutional power of various sorts, and many other things. Through spiritual direction we begin to see what we have been foundationally relying on and ask the Lord to lessen our dependency on all that is not God. As our trust deepens, God enables us to be less anxious about our inability to foresee outcomes. Our comfort and trust gradually become more invested in God rather than dominated by our perception and evaluation of our own foresight and abilities. Trust grows as we recognize repeatedly that God cares for us and for all that influences us even more than we care ourselves.

Our love for God grows, and we realize that we are hearing the Spirit and responding with trust. Our experiences with God and our recognition that God is near and involved deepens our capacity to trust God with more of what is important to us. This draws us to trust God in everything—nothing left over, nothing left out.

As our trust in God grows, we also seem to trust ourselves and our spiritual director more completely. We grow in our recognition that the Holy Spirit is at work in both of us and is using our spiritual direction friendship to nurture growing intimacy with God. Seeing this can make us less fearful and self-protective and help us trust and appreciate each other and the Spirit of God even more.

Spiritual Development

Many changes take place as we move along life's path and grow as companions of God. Living with an awareness of God's love encourages us on the journey. The Spirit prompts us, and we consider and adjust our behavior.

It may seem as though we move through transitions more rapidly or easily when we are taking part in spiritual direction. When we are at an impasse, describing hindrances and confusion in the context of a prayer-centered direction conversation assists us in noticing and responding to circumstances with more discernment. Part of our increasing sense of resolution also comes because we are paying closer attention to and praying about a wider range of our experiences, perceptions, and responses.

Sometimes, however, evidence of our cooperation with the Holy Spirit appears gradually. Change is exceedingly slow—so slow that we do not know it is taking place until we perceive it in retrospect, long after the fact. Other times we find ourselves in a place where we just have to wait. This, too, is part of growth. The Spirit of God relates to us differently at different times but never abandons us.

Life is always changing. Our values change. Our prayer changes. God's invitations to us change and so does how we understand, love, and follow God. At every stage of life there are possibilities for new friends, work, play, and prayer. Spiritual direction helps us identify areas we need to examine and where specific changes seem to be leading us—toward or away from God.

Sometimes change is difficult. We realize we no longer fit where we once were comfortable, and we have no clear idea where we belong. We may feel different, confused, and vulnerable. At the same time we can be startled to discover how much we enjoy the changes in spite of their uncomfortable aspects. It is deeply satisfying to cooperate with the Holy Spirit. At times we overflow with energy, delight, and a sense of newness. We enjoy God and life. We feel whole and settled and sense we are growing. We consider and ask about God's desires more frequently, which influences our responsiveness to others. Changes in behavior that come about through spiritual direction draw us to love God, others, and ourselves.

Responses

It is not helpful to compare the responses and actions of Christians who are in spiritual direction with those who are not. We hardly know what is in our own hearts, let alone what motivates others. Further, our natural and spiritual gifts and our personalities dispose us toward certain kinds of behavior. One person is naturally gentle or patient, another is not. We also have differing underlying limitations and temptations. Some of us are more troubled by fear, others by anger or anxiety.

God encourages us to develop in areas of both strength and weakness. While our willingness to hear and follow the Spirit shapes particular outcomes, evidence of godly actions also reflects the indwelling of God's Spirit and the intertwining of our life with God. With this in mind, and appreciating our dependency on grace and God, let's examine some responses that directors and directees have observed as they participated in spiritual direction.

Directees want more of God. Their attraction to God can appear in numerous ways: seeking time alone with God; love of prayer, Scripture, people, or service. Although directees often sense God's love for them in satisfying and fulfilling ways, they recognize they are eager to continue developing in their relationship with God.

Directees seek to pray always. This means they make themselves available to listen to God even in the midst of a busy life. Because of this, they may notice more quickly when they are out of balance and are more intentional about asking God to help them. Directees discover that prayer is extending and expanding into their entire life because they are more intentional about praying about everything. They set aside specific times for prayer but also discover that prayer infuses their day. They notice they are more conscious of God's presence and are often lovingly attentive to God.

Directees are encouraged by God's love, presence, and care. A deepening awareness of God and God's presence influences directees' feelings and responses not only to God but to the challenges of life. They perceive themselves as created and called by God to be a particular person living at a specific time in history. Their courage grows when they recognize that the Spirit of God is truly with them, encouraging and empowering them to be a unique person. This awareness overflows into life in general and specifically into the ways directees perceive and respond to institutional standards of spirituality. Having greater freedom means they are less anxious about what others think, because they are clearer about what God desires—authentic spirituality rather than humanly contrived spirituality. Sometimes directees become aware of artificial standards, rules, and constrictions that are not from God and are not scriptural. They discover that being in intimate relationship with God enables them to recognize healthy, Spirit-prompted perceptions and behaviors and live with greater freedom.

Directees say they feel more open and available—more open to themselves and to God. Through spiritual direction directees come to know themselves more fully and function out of an ever widening perspective. It is quite common to function out of a familiar portion of the self that has fairly clear boundaries. In direction they may discover little-appreciated, underused aspects of their personalities and capacities and also become better acquainted with their deficiencies and favorite ways of resisting God. Although they already recognize that they are less gifted in some areas and more able in others, they may be surprised when they discover new aspects of themselves. They grow in their ability to be open to God's participation in all dimensions of their lives, whether they perceive them as weak or strong. It does not feel quite as threatening as it once did to see how awkward they are in some areas, and it becomes easier to affirm their growing understanding of what it means to be a particular human person. This increasing freedom allows them to become more integrated and choose to love and serve God gratefully, as they are, rather than waiting for some distant day when they hope to achieve a sort of completeness.

Directees' inner lives and outer behaviors grow to reflect the heart and mind of Christ. They become less concerned about their status and desires, and they experience a growing compatibility between their stated values and their behavior. What they say is important to them is more often reflected in what they do.

Directees desire to choose their priorities and involvement in prayer, relationships, work, and play according to scriptural values, and they experience increasing freedom to do so. Directees grow in their willingness and ability to examine requests for involvement through prayerful discernment rather than immediately saying yes because there is a need, or immediately saying no because they are overextended. Their willingness to serve increases along with their awareness that God invites them to *particular* activities, not just to activity. They ask, "Lord, is this where you are leading?" It is no longer a question of whether they are willing to be God's people in the world. Rather, they question the specifics— when, where, how, and with whom. They desire to cooperate with the Holy Spirit and follow God's leading.

Directees grow in their desire and practice of being fully present for meaningful interaction and relationship. They become conscious of their own ways of being partially present and recognize characteristics of scatteredness in themselves such as trying to do or think about several things simultaneously. They help themselves by encouraging their willingness to be one person in a particular place doing one thing. Such behavior grows out of their relationship with God. Some directees turn to a simple inward prayer such as, "Now is enough, God is enough."[3] The characteristics of our relationship with God influence how we relate to others.

Directees' deepening dependency on God overflows into their relationships with other people. They are likely to be less dominated by their agendas and more willing and able to listen for and respond to God and others. They often have less need than they did to manage, control, or fix other people. They also find their attitudes softening, and they have more love, patience, and appreciation for others. They listen for God's initiatives toward others and encourage others to notice and enjoy God.

Directees become more interested in people who are on the margins of society because they begin to care more about what God cares about. Every source of human sorrow, degradation, and bondage is of interest to God including poverty, discrimination, abuse, unfair labor practices, war, and injustice of every sort.

Having a greater sense of God's love for all people influences directees to pray and to act. Directees notice life-numbing, destructive social conditions and bring them into their prayer. "God, what are you asking me to do here? Pray, write letters, demonstrate, counsel, volunteer time, give monetary donations, walk alongside a particular person or group of people?"

Personal intervention is not the first response. Possibilities for social action are always tested in prayer. The root of Christian social action is *God's* compassion, guidance, and empowerment. Spiritual direction helps directees sort out God's desires from other possibilities and receive energy and wisdom to participate in appropriate, meaningful action. Social action arising out of spiritual direction contexts embodies incarnational love. It is not rooted in strong people helping weak people, rich helping poor, or other categorizations that suggest some people are better than others. Rather, it is social action grounded in God's love for humanity.

Directees grow in love. They develop a greater capacity to notice, appreciate, and receive God's love. They grow in their desire to embody love and express love to God. Their interactions with people are more often characterized by God's love flowing through them.

A Last Word

No matter what particular awareness, appreciation, or actions are enhanced through spiritual direction, there is a deepening sense that the gifts of spiritual direction are just that, gifts—God's gifts, gifts to be savored, appreciated, celebrated, and offered to God. Listening for the Holy Spirit and speaking in the context of the soaking, surrounding prayer of spiritual direction conversations feed our souls and increase our desires to be embraced by God and to embrace our own lives as sacred gifts.

If you have persisted to the end of *Holy Invitations*, it is likely that you have considered your journey of faith, explored aspects of your relationship with God, and discovered new questions and hopes. As God invites and nourishes you, and as you continue to tend your soul, may you recognize again and again and again

Life's holy invitations
Love's generous grace

Reflections

Look back through the chapters of this book and consider how you responded to the questions at the end of each chapter. Then answer the following questions.

1. How are you and God getting along? How does God seem to be with you now?
2. What do you desire in your relationship with God?
3. What practices are you drawn to that could encourage and support your love relationship with God?
4. What hinders pursuit of your relationship with God?
5. What does the Spirit seem to be saying to you about spiritual direction? as a directee or a director? individual or group direction?
6. What next steps seem right for you?

> May the blessing of the Lord God Almighty,
> Maker of heaven and earth,
> Redeemer of humankind,
> Rest upon you,
> Dwell within you,
> Be the song of your heart,
> The word of your mouth,
> The strength of your life,
> Today and always.
> Amen.

Notes

Part 1: An Introduction to Spiritual Direction

1. Robert Frost, "Two Tramps in Mud Time," *Complete Poems of Robert Frost* (New York: Holt, Rinehart and Winston, 1958), 357–59.

Chapter 1: What Is Spiritual Direction?

1. Eugene Peterson, *Working the Angles: The Shape of Pastoral Integrity* (Grand Rapids: Eerdmans, 1987), 103–4.

2. Spiritual direction arises out of scriptural practices, was developed and deepened through the lives of the desert fathers and mothers, and is present in the practices of the church. For fuller treatments of the history of spiritual direction, see Tilden Edwards, *Spiritual Friend: Reclaiming the Gift of Spiritual Direction* (New York: Paulist Press, 1997), chapter 2, "Living Waters of the Past"; and Kenneth Leach, *Soul Friend: The Practice of Christian Spirituality* (San Francisco: Harper & Row, 1977), chapter 2, "Spiritual Direction in the Christian Tradition."

3. Gerald G. May, *Care of Mind, Care of Spirit: Psychiatric Dimensions of Spiritual Direction* (San Francisco: Harper & Row, 1982), 99. I have used Gerald May's description of pastoral care and the description of spiritual direction as a starting place. The mentoring and discipling dialogues are my own.

4. Formal education in spiritual direction usually includes instruction in the areas of Scripture, theology, human development, prayer and other Christian disciplines, the history of spirituality, and spiritual discernment. It also includes information about the spiritual life, the normal progressions that a person of prayer passes through, and similar issues of spiritual maturation. Awareness of and deepening of skills and inner sensibilities are included. Inner sensibility includes learning to recognize where nudgings come from—ourselves, God, or other spiritual sources. Accountability and supervision are aspects of the formal training of spiritual directors. No matter what academic studies are pursued, it is essential that a person's sense of the Spirit's calling and gifting them to offer spiritual direction remain of primary importance.

5. In some ways it is misleading to compare spiritual direction to these other kinds of relationships, because we may begin to view spiritual direction through formal relationship lenses. The heart of our desire is to be available to God rather than shaped by any human system.

6. Gerald G. May, "Varieties of Spiritual Companionship," *Shalem News* 22, no. 1 (winter 1998): 5. The article is available on the Shalem web site at www.shalem.org.

Chapter 2: The Heart of Spiritual Direction

1. William Barry and William Connolly, *The Practice of Spiritual Direction* (New York: Seabury Press, 1982), 8.

2. Shaun McCarty, "Basics in Spiritual Direction," in *Handbook of Spirituality for Ministers*, ed. Robert J. Wicks (New York: Paulist Press, 1995). A fine, concise introduction to spiritual direction.

Chapter 3: Who Comes to Spiritual Direction?

1. Gerald G. May, *Care of Mind, Care of Spirit: Psychiatric Dimensions of Spiritual Direction* (San Francisco: Harper & Row, 1982), 7–8.

2. Carolyn Gratton, *Guidelines for Spiritual Direction* (Denville, N.J.: Dimension Books, 1980). Carolyn Gratton's suggestions about why people enter spiritual direction became the beginning seeds for this list.

3. Many books have explored stages of adult development through varying perspectives. Some of the early works that are now classics include James W. Fowler, *Stages of Faith: The Psychology of Human Development and the Quest for Meaning* (San Francisco: Harper & Row, 1976); Daniel J. Levinson, *The Seasons of a Man's Life* (New York: Ballantine Books, 1978); Carole Gilligan, *In a Different Voice: Psychological Theory and Women's Development* (Cambridge: Harvard University Press, 1982); Mary Field Belenky, Blythe McVicker Clinchy, Nancy Rule Goldberger, and Jill Mattuck Tarule, *Women's Ways of Knowing: The Development of Self, Voice, and Mind* (New York: Basic Books, 1973); James and Evelyn Whitehead, *Christian Life Patterns: The Psychological Challenges and Religious Invitations of Adult Life* (Garden City, N.Y.: Doubleday, 1979); and more recently, James Fowler, *Faith Development and Pastoral Care* (Philadelphia: Fortress, 1987); and Elizabeth Liebert, *Changing Life Patterns: Adult Development in Spiritual Direction* (New York: Paulist Press, 1992).

Chapter 4: Spiritual Direction and Trust

1. C. S. Lewis, *The Four Loves* (New York: Harcourt, Brace and Company, 1960), 126–27.

Chapter 5: Preparing for Spiritual Direction

1. Dietrich Bonhoeffer, "Life Together," in *Writings on Spiritual Direction by Great Christian Masters*, ed. Jerome Neufelder and Mary C. Coelho (New York: Seabury Press, 1982), 86–87.

2. Howard Rice, *The Pastor as Spiritual Guide* (Nashville: The Upper Room, 1998), 63.

3. Gerald G. May, *Will and Spirit: A Contemplative Psychology* (San Francisco: Harper & Row, 1982), 5–6. "Willingness and willfulness cannot be explained in a few words, for they are very subtle qualities, often overlapping and very easily confused with each other. But we can begin by saying that willingness implies a surrendering of one's self-separateness, an entering-into, an immersion in the deepest processes of life itself. It is a realization that one already is a part of some ultimate cosmic process and it is a commitment to participation in that process. In contrast, willfulness is the setting of oneself apart from the fundamental essence of life in an attempt to master, direct, control, or otherwise manipulate existence. More simply, willingness is saying yes to the mystery of being alive in each moment. Willfulness is saying no, or perhaps more commonly, 'Yes, but.'"

4. Evelyn Underhill, *The Spiritual Life* (Wilton, Conn.: Morehouse Barlow, 1955), 95–97.

5. James B. Nelson, *Embodiment: An Approach to Sexuality and Christian Theology* (Minneapolis: Augsburg, 1978), 20.

Chapter 6: Selecting a Spiritual Director

1. Henri Nouwen, "Hearing God's Voice and Obeying: A Dialogue with Richard Foster and Henri Nouwen," *Leadership* (winter 1982): 7.

2. Lyle Dorsett and Marjorie Lamp Mead, *C. S. Lewis' Letters to Children* (New York: Touchstone, 1985), 52–53.

3. Edward C. Sellner, *Mentoring: The Ministry of Spiritual Kinship* (Notre Dame, Ind.: Ave Maria Press, 1990), chapter 2, "C. S. Lewis as Spiritual Mentor."

4. Spiritual Directors International, 1329 Seventh Avenue, San Francisco, CA 94122-2507; http://www.sdiworld.org.

5. Henri Nouwen, *Reaching Out* (New York: Doubleday, 1966), 98.

Chapter 7: Shaping the Spiritual Direction Relationship

1. Rose Mary Dougherty, School Sisters of Notre Dame, *Group Spiritual Direction: Community for Discernment* (New York: Paulist Press, 1995), 17.

2. A number of training centers and Spiritual Directors International have worked on developing a code of ethics for spiritual directors. Directors should think about appropriate guidelines, but it is essential that spiritual direction remain a ministry flowing out of the gifts of the Holy Spirit rather than become a "profession."

Chapter 8: Spiritual Direction Conversations

1. Gerald G. May, *Care of Mind, Care of Spirit* (San Francisco: Harper & Row, 1983), 14.

2. Richard J. Foster, *Celebration of Discipline: The Path to Spiritual Growth* (San Francisco: Harper & Row, 1978), 159–60.

3. Max Thurian, in *Writings on Spiritual Direction by Great Christian Masters*, ed. Jerome M. Neufelder and Mary C. Coelho (New York: Seabury Press, 1982), 96.

Chapter 9: Group Spiritual Direction

1. Rose Mary Dougherty, *Group Spiritual Direction: Community for Discernment* (New York: Paulist Press, 1995), 36.

2. See the bibliography for resources on group discernment.

3. Rose Mary Dougherty, *Group Spiritual Direction: Community for Discernment* is a foundational resource for anyone who is considering entering or organizing spiritual direction groups. An excellent video with the same title that demonstrates group spiritual direction is available from Paulist Press. See also Tilden Edwards, *Spiritual Friend* (New York: Paulist Press, 1997), for an excellent chapter on group spiritual direction.

4. The practice of group spiritual direction is not as common as one-to-one spiritual direction. Resources (including those listed here) that describe group direction in detail are few in number but are sufficient to inform and guide the practice of group spiritual direction.

5. Dougherty, *Group Spiritual Direction*, 48–55, describes in detail how each segment of time is used by the group.

6. Two models of group spiritual direction that are different from what we have described are (1) "one for all," in which a designated person directs the entire group, and (2) "all for one," in which one specific person is the directee for the full session and other group members act as director. The model we are talking about, with an insider or outside facilitator, is more like "everyone for one at a time."

Part 2: Subjects Frequently Considered in Spiritual Direction

1. George Herbert, *The Country Parson, The Temple*, ed. John N. Wall Jr. (New York: Paulist Press, 1981), 316.

Chapter 10: Experiencing God

1. Teresa of Avila, *Way of Perfection*, ed. E. Allison Peers (New York: Image Books, 1964).

2. Ann Ulanov, "Picturing God," in *A Guide to Prayer for All God's People*, ed. Rueben Job and Norman Sawchuck (Nashville: The Upper Room, 1990), 171.

3. David A. Seamands, "Healing Our Feelings about God: Why People Feel Bad about a God Who Is Good," *Good News* (March/April 1986): 88–93. Article excerpted from David A. Seamands, *Healing of Memories* (Wheaton: Victor, 1985).

4. Sherwood Wirt, ed., *The Confessions of Augustine in Modern English* (Grand Rapids: Zondervan, 1986).

5. George Fox in *Quaker Spirituality*, ed. Douglas V. Steere (New York: Paulist Press, 1984).

6. C. S. Lewis, *The Problem of Pain* (New York: Macmillan, 1966), 34–35.

7. Richard Foster, *Streams of Living Water: Celebrating the Great Traditions of Christian Faith* (San Francisco: Harper & Row, 1998).

Chapter 11: Scripture

1. Frederick Buechner, "A Room Called Remember," in *Disciplines for the Inner Life*, ed. Bob W. Benson and Michael W. Benson (Waco: Word, 1985), 95.

2. *The Spiritual Formation Bible: Growing in Intimacy with God through Scripture* (Grand Rapids: Zondervan, 1999) is a helpful tool for people who feel invited by God to explore different ways of reading and praying with Scripture.

3. The New Revised Standard translation of the Bible, 1990, uses inclusive language where the original Hebrew or Greek makes that an authentic choice. The New International Version Inclusive Language Edition (London: Hodder & Stoughton, 1996) uses inclusive language where the original Hebrew or Greek makes that an authentic choice.

4. The International Standard Bible Encyclopedia, vol. 1 (Grand Rapids: Eerdmans, 1979), 719.

5. Father George Niederauer, "The Spiritual Direction Relationship." Notes from a talk given to spiritual directors, Fuller Theological Seminary, 14 March 1980.

6. Tilden Edwards, *Spiritual Friend: Reclaiming the Gift of Spiritual Direction* (New York: Paulist Press, 1997), chapter 3, "Living Waters of the Past"; Kenneth Leech, *Soul Friend: The Practice of Christian Spirituality* (San Francisco: Harper & Row, 1977), chapter 2, "Spiritual Direction in the Christian Tradition."

7. Wilkie Au and Noreen Cannon, *Urgings of the Heart: A Spirituality of Integration* (New York: Paulist Press, 1995), 54–63, includes several exercises suggesting ways to pray with Scripture that open the reader to God in contemplation and healing.

Chapter 12: Prayer

1. Bill Hybels, *Too Busy Not to Pray: Slowing Down to Be with God* (Downers Grove, Ill.: InterVarsity Press, 1988), 7.

2. Ted Loder, "Calm Me into a Quietness," *Guerrillas of Grace: Prayers for the Battle* (Philadelphia: Innisfree Press, 1984), 21.

3. C. S. Lewis, *They Stand Together: The Letters of C. S. Lewis to Arthur Greeves*, ed. Walter Hooper (New York: Macmillan, 1979), 361.

4. "A Confession of Sin," *The Book of Common Prayer* (New York: Seabury Press, 1979), 116–17.

5. "The Lord's Prayer," *The Book of Common Prayer*, 336.

6. Glenn Clark, *I Will Lift Up Mine Eyes* (San Francisco: Harper & Row, 1937), 23–25.

7. Ted Loder, *Guerrillas of Grace: Prayers for the Battle* (Philadelphia: Innisfree Press, 1984), 5.

8. Ignatius of Loyola in *The Joy of Listening to God*, ed. Joyce Huggett (Downers Grove, Ill.: InterVarsity Press, 1986).

9. *Seal of John Calvin* in the Reformation Window, Westminster Presbyterian Church, Minneapolis.

10. Worship prayer (singing to God), natural prayer (arising out of circumstances), confessional prayer, prayer in response to reading Scripture or devotional writing, why? prayers, "yelling" at God, repetitions of prayers that were effective in the past, prayer in tongues, unceasing prayer, healing prayers. One person even wrote "competitive prayer" on their list to describe their discomfort with praying in groups. Richard Foster's excellent book on prayer, *Prayer: Finding the Heart's True Home* (San Francisco: HarperSanFrancisco, 1992), describes twenty-one different kinds of prayer.

11. Mary Coelho, "Removing Obstacles in Prayer," *Review for Religious* (March 1981): 182–91.

12. Teresa of Avila, *The Life of Teresa of Jesus*, trans. and ed. E. Allison Peers (New York: Image Books, 1960), 127–33.

13. A Discalced Carmelite Nun, *A Guide to the Stages of Prayer according to St. Teresa of Jesus and St. John of the Cross*, Imprimatur, Leo C. Byrne, D.D. Coadjutor Archbishop of St.Paul-Minneapolis (1971), is an excellent small book that clearly describes Teresa's teaching about prayer.

14. One method of praying with Scripture is to (1) prayerfully select a passage; (2) settle yourself comfortably where you will not be disturbed; (3) thank God for being present with you and offer the time and yourself to the Holy Spirit; (4) get in touch with the word of your life by expressing to God how it is with you as you begin (Are you anticipating? bored? tired? happy?); and (5) read the passage slowly. You may repeat a word or phrase. Notice where ideas or feelings begin to stir. Ask God what that is about. Read the passage again. Pray in whatever ways seem appropriate. Stay with the passage, alternately reading and listening, until nothing seems to be stirring in relationship to it. Then thank God and move on to another passage or depart. You may wish to write in a journal.

Thelma Hall, *Too Deep for Words: Rediscovering Lectio Divina with 500 Scripture Texts for Prayer* (New York: Paulist Press, 1988); David Rosage, *Speak Lord, Your Servant Is Listening* (Ann Arbor, Mich.: Servant Publications, 1987); Norvene Vest, *Gathered in the Word: Praying the Scripture for Small Groups* (Nashville: The Upper Room, 1996); Jim Wakefield, *Listening Prayer: A New Annotation and Introduction to the Spiritual Exercises of St. Ignatius* (1990) available from Our Saviour's Lutheran Church, 1040 C. Avenue, Lake Oswego, OR 97034; 503-635-4563. This book is an invitation to deepen our relationship with Christ through meditating on Scripture. This annotation was done especially for Protestants.

15. Learning to listen in prayer is often more difficult than learning to speak. There are fine resources, including the following titles, available to anyone who is interested in reading, exploring, and experimenting in their prayer. Walter Brueggemann, *Praying the Psalms* (Winona, Minn.: St. Mary's Press, 1986); William E. Hulme, *Celebrating God's Presence: A Guide to Christian Meditation* (Minneapolis: Augsburg, 1988); Benedict J. Groeschel, *Listening at Prayer* (New York: Paulist Press, 1983); Leanne Payne, *Listening Prayer: Learning to Hear God's Voice and Keep a Prayer Journal* (Grand Rapids: Baker, 1994); and William R. Callahan, *Noisy Contemplation: Prayer for Busy People with Deep Faith* (Hyattsville, Md.: Quixote Center, 1994).

16. Guigo II quoted in Vest, *Gathered in the Word*.

17. Adolphe Tanquerey, *The Spiritual Life*, trans. Herman Branderis, rev. ed. (Westminster, Md.: Newman Press, 1930), 646.

18. Guigo II quoted in Vest, *Gathered in the Word*, 33.

19. Ibid., 35.

20. Joann Nesser, "Love," *Laudem Gloriae* (winter 1998): 1.

21. Teresa of Avila, *Interior Castles*, trans. and ed. E. Allison Peers (New York: Doubleday, 1989); Janet O. Hagberg and Robert A. Guelich, *The Critical Journey: Stages in the Life of Faith* (Salem, Wis.: Sheffield Publishing Company, 1995); James W. Fowler and Sam Keen, *Life Maps: Conversations on the Journey of Faith* (Dallas: Word, 1985); and James W. Fowler, *Stages of Faith: The Psychology of Human Development and the Quest for Meaning* (San Francisco: Harper & Row, 1981). This book opened the faith stage conversation. Since its publication, many have responded favorably, negatively, and in clarifying ways.

22. The following books include excellent scriptural and experiential insights and practices regarding Christian prayer for healing. Francis MacNutt, *Healing* (New York: Doubleday, 1990); Leanne Payne, *The Healing Presence* (Grand Rapids: Baker, 1989); *Restoring the Christian Soul through Healing Prayer: Overcoming the Three Great Barriers to Personal and Spiritual Completion in Christ* (Grand Rapids: Baker, 1991).

Chapter 13: Discernment

1. William Barry, "Toward a Theology of Discernment," *The Way Supplement* 64 (spring 1989): 136.

2. Gerald G. May, "Authentic Spiritual Experience," *Shalem News* 12, no. 1 (February 1988): 5.

3. James Wakefield, *Listening Prayer: A New Annotation and Introduction to the Spiritual Exercises of St. Ignatius of Loyola* (1992), available from Our Saviour's Lutheran Church, 1040 C. Avenue, Lake Oswego, OR 97034; 503-635-4563. See also Wilkie Au, *By Way of the Heart: Toward a Holistic Christian Spirituality* (New York: Paulist Press, 1989), 76–78; and Phillip Boroughs, "Using Ignatian Discernment," *Review for Religious* 51, no. 3 (May/June 1992): 373–87.

4. Parker J. Palmer, "The Clearness Committee: A Way of Discernment," in *Communion, Community, Commonweal: Readings for Spiritual Leadership*, ed. John S. Mogabgab (Nashville: The Upper Room, 1995), 131–36; and Richard J. Foster, *Celebration of Discipline: The Path to Spiritual Growth* (San Francisco: Harper & Row, 1988), chapter 12, "The Discipline of Guidance" (an excellent discussion of group discernment).

5. In response to a questionnaire about their discernment practices, seminary students listed the following helpful means they had used at least once: (1) listened for and heard the "voice" of the Holy Spirit; (2) Scripture; (3) solitude, quiet space, meditation, contemplation; (4) other people—trusted friends, family members, occasionally people in authority, and children; (5) books—classical Christian works, biographies, literature, hymnals; (6) a process of prayer; (7) worship and worship communities including liturgies; (8) music—listening and singing, hymns, classical, choral, Gregorian chants, meditative; (9) gut instinct—intuition; (10) sermons; (11) present life experiences and circumstances; (12) past experiences; (13) logical consistency; (14) opportunities embodied in open and closed doors; (15) common thread, convergence, harmonization; (16) specifically asking for the grace/gift of discernment; (17) journaling; (18) verifications, confirmations; (19) fasting; (20) scholarly sources; (21) the role of persistent, recurring thoughts, the "lightbulb" experience; (22) bodily influences including exercise, walking, massage, and normal bodily responses such as tensing or relaxing while considering various options; (23) nature—God's created world, being in a naturally beautiful or stark place.

Chapter 14: Christian Disciplines

1. Tilden Edwards, *Spiritual Friend: Reclaiming the Gift of Spiritual Direction* (New York: Paulist Press, 1997).

2. Rueben Job told this story when we were teaching a professional development training workshop for Navy, Marine, and Coast Guard chaplains in 1997 with an ecumenical team. Used by his permission.

3. Disciplines that have been practiced by Christians to make themselves available to listen to God, to be touched and transformed by the Holy Spirit include: (1) Bible study; (2) prayer; (3) the Lord's Supper; (4) fellowship groups/accountability; (5) confession (purga-

tive way); (6) self-evaluation (illuminative way); (7) focus on life of Christ (unitive way); (8) devotional reading/Scripture reading; (9) silence; (10) meditation; (11) fasting/eating disciplines; (12) simplicity—vow of poverty; (13) submission—vow of obedience; (14) purity—vow of chastity; (15) worship; (16) service; (17) confession; (18) guidance; (19) celebration; (20) daily prayer covenant; (21) singing and praises; (22) memorization of Scripture; (23) listening to tapes; (24) daily witness; (25) proportionate financial stewardship; (26) ecological stewardship; (27) social justice; (28) visiting prisoners; (29) sacrificial acts of compassion; (30) family altar; (31) spousal prayers; (32) quiet days with God; (33) spiritual life retreats; (34) spiritual direction; (35) spiritual journaling; (36) affirmation; (37) soliloquy; (38) physical conditioning; (39) foot washing; (40) examen of consciousness; (41) spiritual pilgrimage; (42) setting a rule; (43) living in the present moment; (44) Sabbath; (45) prayer of the hours; (46) artistic practices—painting, dancing, theater, music group, mime, poetry; (47) spiritual reading—biographies, autobiographies, Christian classics (old and contemporary); (48) secrecy—keeping silent about things we do with/for God; (49) visiting awesome places—places of natural or humanly created beauty, devastation, or where significant events have taken place; (50) gardening; (51) work/daily routines/employment; (52) paying attention to dreams; (53) your additions.

4. Madeleine L'Engle, "The 10,000 Names of God," Staley Lecture, Bethel College, 1979.

5. Dallas Willard, *The Spirit of the Disciplines* (San Francisco: Harper & Row, 1988).

6. It can be helpful to experiment with different positions for prayer. You might start by lying on your face on the floor. Then move to a variety of kneeling, sitting, and standing positions. Experiment with how you hold your hands—together, facing up or down, or lifted above your head. Take sufficient time in each position to notice what you seem to pray about. Is there any position that seems as if it is for more *serious* prayer? What position seems routine or boring? Where do you seem to come to life and engage in authentic prayer? Take your time and ask the Holy Spirit to teach you about the influence of your body on your prayer.

7. Richard Foster, *Prayer: Finding the Heart's True Home* (San Francisco: HarperSanFrancisco, 1992), 34.

8. Thomas Keating, *Intimacy with God* (New York: Crossroads, 1994); Basil Pennington, *Centered Living: The Way of Centering Prayer* (New York: Image Books, 1988); William Volkman, *Basking in His Presence: A Call to the Prayer of Silence* (Glen Ellyn, Ill.: Union Life Ministries, 1994).

9. Walter Brueggemann, *Praying the Psalms* (Winona, Minn.: St. Mary's Press, 1983).

10. Ron Klug, *How to Keep a Spiritual Journal* (Minneapolis: Augsburg, 1993).

11. Gerald G. May, *Will and Spirit: A Contemplative Psychology* (San Franciso: Harper & Row, 1982), 5–6.

Part 3: Possible Complications and Benefits of Spiritual Direction

1. Luci Shaw, *Angles of Light* (Wheaton: Harold Shaw, 2000), 37.

Chapter 15: Common Areas of Difficulty

1. Evelyn Underhill, *The Spiritual Life* (Wilton, Conn.: Morehouse Barlow, 1955), 33–34.

Chapter 16: Potential Benefits of Spiritual Direction

1. Marjorie J. Thompson, *Soul Feast: An Invitation to the Christian Spiritual Life* (Louisville: Westminster/John Knox Press, 1995), 6.

2. Julian of Norwich, *Enfolded in Love: Daily Readings with Julian of Norwich*, ed. Members of the Julian Shrine (New York: Seabury Press, 1980), 15.

3. Tilden Edwards, Executive Director of Shalem Institute, Bethesda, Md., a suggested prayer during a Shalem Institute extension program in spiritual guidance, 1984.

Bibliography

Spiritual Direction

Barry, William A., and William J. Connolly. *The Practice of Spiritual Direction.* New York: Seabury Press, 1982. This book enables the reader to participate in spiritual direction conversations through the perspective of living relationships. It describes the goals, practices, and some of the resistances within spiritual direction friendships. Particularly suitable for people who feel called to be directors.

Cambell Johnson, Ben. *Speaking of God: Evangelism as Initial Spiritual Guidance.* Louisville: Westminster/John Knox Press, 1991. Assists us to hear God's leading as we walk alongside others who are exploring faith.

Chan, Simon. "The Art of Spiritual Direction." In *Spiritual Theology: A Systematic Study of the Christian Life.* Downers Grove, Ill.: InterVarsity Press, 1998.

Edwards, Tilden. *Spiritual Friend: Reclaiming the Gift of Spiritual Direction.* New York: Paulist Press, 1997. A foundational, contemporary treatment of a classic Christian discipline. Excellent resource for anyone considering entering spiritual direction.

———. *Tending the Soul: Companionship for the Deeper Spiritual Journey.* Mahwah, N.J.: Paulist Press, 2000. A basic text for directors and directees with a special emphasis on contemplative presence. Includes ways of nurturing the soul and of understanding spiritual experience.

Gratton, Carolyn. *The Art of Spiritual Guidance: A Contemporary Approach to Growing in the Spirit.* New York: Crossroads, 1992. Contains a wealth of resources, information, and guidelines for effective spiritual guidance. Helpful for directors.

Guenther, Margaret. *Holy Listening: The Art of Spiritual Direction.* New York: Cowley Publications, 1992. A gentle, basic introduction to spiritual direction for laypersons and ministers. In-depth aspects of spiritual direction are explained in ways that clarify differences between spiritual direction, counseling, and discipling relationships. Very reader-friendly.

Jones, Alan W. *Exploring Spiritual Direction: An Essay on Christian Friendship.* New York: Seabury Press, 1982. A literate and wise encouragement to seek spiritual friendship.

Kelsy, Morton. *Companions on the Inner Way: The Art of Spiritual Direction.* New York: Crossroads, 1983. Includes interesting aspects of psychology, contemplative practice, and Christian faith.

Leech, Kenneth. *Soul Friend: The Practice of Christian Spirituality.* San Francisco: Harper & Row, 1977. Excellent resource for anyone wishing to explore roots and practices of spiritual direction. More like a textbook. Very helpful.

May, Gerald G. *Care of Mind, Care of Spirit: Psychiatric Dimensions of Spiritual Direction.* San Francisco: Harper & Row, 1982. An excellent resource for individuals who are interested in both counseling and spiritual direction. Helps to clarify differences.

Nemeck, Francis Kelly, OMI, and Marie Theresa Coombs, Hermit. *The Way of Spiritual Direction.* Wilmington, Del.: Michael Glazier, 1989. Classic spiritual direction.

Neufelder, Jerome M., and Mary C. Coelho, eds. *Writings on Spiritual Direction by Great Christian Masters.* New York: Seabury Press, 1982. A fine collection of classic resources.

Peterson, Eugene. *The Contemplative Pastor: Returning to the Art of Spiritual Direction.* Dallas: Word, 1989. Recommends reshaping pastoral ministry from CEO models toward spiritual guidance models.

———. *The Wisdom of Each Other: A Conversation between Spiritual Friends*. Grand Rapids: Zondervan, 1998.

———. *Working the Angles: The Shape of Pastoral Integrity*. Grand Rapids: Eerdmans, 1987. Description of the role of prayer, Scripture, and spiritual direction in the life of ministers, but is equally applicable to any person seeking spiritual authenticity.

Rice, Howard. *The Pastor as Spiritual Guide*. Nashville: The Upper Room, 1998. Describing all pastoral ministries as flowing out of spiritual direction. A fine resource for shaping church life.

Ruffing, Janet. *Spiritual Direction: Beyond the Beginnings*. Mahwah, N.J.: Paulist Press, 2000.

———. *Uncovering Stories of Faith: Spiritual Direction and Narrative*. Mahwah, N.J.: Paulist Press, 1989. Listening to spiritual direction conversations from the inside and watching their development.

Sellner, Edward C. *Mentoring: The Ministry of Spiritual Kinship*. Notre Dame, Ind.: Ave Maria Press, 1990. Models of spiritual direction including the Irish soul friend. Excellent chapter on C. S. Lewis as spiritual mentor.

Thomas, Arthur D. "James M. Houston: Pioneering Spiritual Director to Evangelicals—Part 1." *Crux* 29 (September 1993). "James M. Houston: Pioneering Spiritual Director to Evangelicals—Part 2." *Crux* 29 (December 1993). Good for evangelicals who are considering spiritual direction.

Webster, Douglas D. *Finding Spiritual Direction: The Challenge and Joys of Christian Growth*. Downers Grove, Ill.: InterVarsity Press, 1991. Uses the Book of James to show spiritual direction in scriptural context.

Group Spiritual Direction, Group Spiritual Formation, and Small Groups

Benefiel, Margaret. "Spiritual Direction for Organizations towards Articulating a Model." *Presence* (an international journal for spiritual direction) 2, no. 3 (September 1996): 40–49.

Dougherty, Rose Mary SSND. *Group Spiritual Direction: Community for Discernment*. Mahwah, N.J.: Paulist Press, 1995. Group spiritual direction offers possibilities that are both similar and unique when compared with individual spiritual direction. This fine book could be used to understand, begin, and grow in spiritual direction groups.

Edwards, Tilden. *Spiritual Friend: Reclaiming the Gift of Spiritual Direction*. New York: Paulist Press, 1997.

Gorman, Julie A. *A Community That Is Christian: A Handbook for Small Groups*. Wheaton: Victor Books, 1993. A superior resource for Christian small groups.

Johnson, David W., and Frank P. Johnson. *Joining Together: Group Theory and Group Skills*. 6th ed. Boston: Allyn and Bacon, 1996. This book includes group development theory and practical exercises regarding every aspect of group life.

May, Gerald G. *Pilgrimage Home: The Conduct of Contemplative Practice in Groups*. New York: Paulist Press, 1979. Foundations and helpful methods for encouraging contemplative prayer and listening in groups.

Smith, Bryan James. *A Spiritual Formation Workbook: Small Group Resources for Nurturing Christian Growth*. San Francisco: Harper & Row, 1993. Describes five threads of Christian spirituality: holiness, contemplative, charismatic, evangelical, and social action. Illustrates them through the life of Christ and historical and contemporary practices. Excellent resource for use with small spiritual formation groups.

Scripture

Brueggemann, Walter. *Praying the Psalms*. Winona, Minn.: St. Mary's Press, 1983.

Hall, Thelma. *Too Deep for Words: Rediscovering Lectio Divina*. New York: Paulist Press, 1988. Helpful for people moving from vocal to meditative prayer through Scripture.

Mulholland, M. Robert, Jr. *Shaped by the Word: The Power of Scripture in Spiritual Formation.* Nashville: The Upper Room, 1985. Excellent suggestions for dwelling with the Word of God.

The Spiritual Formation Bible: Growing in Intimacy with God through Scripture. NRSV. Grand Rapids: Zondervan, 1999. A fine introduction to spiritual formation using Scripture. Includes spiritual formation articles and invitations to engage with Scripture through different methods on every page.

Vest, Norvene. *Gathered in the Word: Praying the Scripture for Small Groups* (Nashville: The Upper Room, 1996). Includes excellent helps that point toward spiritual direction. Helpful suggestions for groups.

Prayer

Brother Lawrence. *The Practice of the Presence of God.* Washington, D.C.: ICS Publications, 1994. This volume presents the reflections of a lay brother who endeavored to live consciously in the presence of God as he worked in the kitchen of a Paris monastery. (Author lived ca. 1605–1691.)

Brueggemann, Walter. *Praying the Psalms.* Winona, Minn.: St. Mary's Press, 1983. An excellent companion for prayer.

Callahan, William R. *Noisy Contemplation: Deep Prayer for Busy People.* Hyattsvillle, Md.: Quixote Center, 1994. Encouraging assistance in prayer.

Foster, Richard J. *Prayer: Finding the Heart's True Home.* San Francisco: Harper & Row, 1992. A comprehensive, contemporary, and in-depth review of prayer.

A Guide to the Stages of Prayer according to St. Teresa of Jesus and St. John of the Cross. Imprimatur Leo C. Byrne D.D. Coadjutor Archbishop of St. Paul-Minneapolis, 1971. Helpful for reading Teresa and John's wisdom, gathered into one resource.

Hallesby, O. *Prayer.* Minneapolis: Augsburg, 1975. This is a classic on prayer by a Norwegian theologian and evangelist and reflects the vital piety of the evangelical revivals in nineteenth-century Scandinavia. First published in English in 1931.

Herman, E. *Creative Prayer, A Devotional Classic.* Edited by Hal M. Helms. Orleans, Mass.: Paraclete Press, 1998. The realities of prayer in speaking, silence, meditation, and opening oneself to God are presented in ways that encourage and enable persons to pray.

Hulme, William E. *Celebrating God's Presence: A Guide to Christian Meditation.* Minneapolis: Augsburg, 1988. A balanced introductory treatment of Christian meditation.

Job, Rueben, and Norm Sawchuck. *A Guide to Prayer for All God's People.* Nashville: The Upper Room, 1990. A helpful one-volume resource for the spiritual life. Includes a daily suggested Scripture reading and a comprehensive anthology of spiritual readings.

Keating, Thomas. *Intimacy with God.* New York: Crossroads, 1995. Clearly describes the origins, theological basis, and practices of centering prayer.

Kelly, Thomas. *A Testament of Devotion.* San Francisco: Harper & Row, 1996. In addition to the Bible, this has been a strong shaping foundation for Christians who feel called to listening. In the introduction to this edition Gerald May writes, "A testament of devotion has been the single most helpful written resource for the most important endeavor of my life: practicing God's presence."

Loder, Ted. *Guerrillas of Grace: Prayers for the Battle.* Philadelphia: Innisfree Press, 1984. A fine collection of contemporary prayers.

Nesser, Joann. *Journey into Reality through Prayer and God-Centeredness.* Prior Lake, Minn.: Living Waters, 1998. Leads readers into an intimate relationship with God through prayer.

———. *Prayer: Journey from Self to God.* 1985. Available through Christos Center for Spiritual Formation, Lino Lakes, MN. Exploration of prayer as an inward journey from brokenness to wholeness.

Payne, Leanne. *The Healing Presence.* Grand Rapids: Baker, 1989. *Listening Prayer: Learning to Hear God's Voice and Keep a Prayer Journal.* Grand Rapids: Baker, 1994. *Restoring the Christian Soul through Healing Prayer.* Grand Rapids: Baker, 1991. These three

books are grounded in Scripture, theology, and experience and include concrete suggestions for listening to God.

Pennington, M. Basil. *Centered Living: The Way of Centering Prayer.* New York: Doubleday,
1988. A clear, pastoral approach to learning about and practicing centering prayer.

Peterson, Eugene. *Praying with the Psalms.* Grand Rapids: Zondervan, 1993. A clear, enjoy-
able text for prayer.

Prather, Charlotte C. *A Generous Openness: Praying the Spiritual Exercises of St. Ignatius.*
Petersham, Mass.: St. Bede's Publications, 1992. The author shares the impact of the
Ignatian Exercises on her own prayer and life, enabling readers to connect their help-
fulness with contemporary life and spirituality.

Steere, Douglas. *Dimensions of Prayer.* Nashville: The Upper Room, 1998. A depth of understanding of prayer that resonates. A foundational book that invites people to their own
prayer.

St. Teresa of Avila. *Interior Castle.* Translated and edited by E. Allison Peers. New York:
Image Books, 1961.

———. *The Life of Teresa of Jesus: The Autobiography of St. Teresa of Avila.* Translated and
edited by E. Allison Peers. New York: Image Books, 1960.

———. *The Way of Perfection.* Translated and edited by E. Allison Peers. New York: Image
Books, 1964. These three books containing the teaching of Teresa of Avila on prayer
are Christian classics.

Swanson, Kenneth. *Uncommon Prayer: Approaching Intimacy with God.* New York: Bal-
lantine/Epiphany, 1987. An autobiographical treatment of development in prayer.

Volkman, Bill. *Basking in His Presence: A Call to the Prayer of Silence.* Glen Ellyn, Ill.: Union
Life, 1996. Describes one Protestant's pilgrimage in faith leading to centering prayer
and contemplation. Autobiographical and practical.

Discernment

Barry, William. *Paying Attention to God.* Notre Dame, Ind.: Ave Maria Press, 1990. Includes
sections on individual and communal discernment.

Bouroughs, Philip C. "Using Ignatian Discernment." *Review for Religious* 51, no. 3
(May/June 1992): 373–87. A brief treatment of the three times of choice and five factors that influence the ability to discern as described by St. Ignatius of Loyola.

Chan, Simon. "The Discernment of Spirits." In *Spiritual Theology: A Systematic Study of
the Christian Life.* Downers Grove, Ill.: InterVarsity Press, 1998.

Farrow, Jo. "Discernment in the Quaker Tradition." *The Way Supplement* 64 (spring 1989):
51–62. Helpful for Protestants to consider.

Green, Thomas. *Weeds among the Wheat—Discernment: Where Prayer and Action Meet.*
Notre Dame, Ind.: Ave Maria Press, 1984. A fine overview and introduction to discernment through biblical materials, Jesus' discerning, and Ignatian ways of paying
attention.

Hardon, John. *Retreat with the Lord: A Popular Guide to the Spiritual Exercises of St. Ignatius
of Loyola.* Ann Arbor, Mich.: Servant Publications, 1993.

Hugget, Joyce. "Why Ignatian Spirituality Hooks Protestants." *The Way Supplement* 68
(summer 1990): 22–34. A splendid article about prayer and Scripture.

Hughes, Gerard. *God of Surprises.* Mahwah, N.J.: Paulist Press, 1985. Written by a Jesuit
priest, this book expresses the spiritual teachings contained in St. Ignatius of Loyola's
Spiritual Exercises, a classic of Western spirituality, in an easily accessible way for modern readers.

Job, Rueben P. *A Guide to Spiritual Discernment.* Nashville: The Upper Room, 1996. A collection of Scripture and other readings focusing on discernment. It is organized as a
forty-day guide to use in prayer.

Larkin, Ernest E. *Discernment as Process and Problem.* Denville, N.J.: Dimension Books,
1981. A small, clear book about discernment.

Lonsdale, David. *Listening to the Music of the Spirit: The Art of Discernment.* Notre Dame, Ind.: Ave Maria Press, 1992. A careful treatment of discernment with many details.

McDermott, Gerard R. *Seeing God: Twelve Reliable Signs of True Spirituality.* Downers Grove, Ill.: InterVarsity Press, 1995.

Morris, Danny E. *Yearning to Know God's Will: A Workbook for Discerning God's Guidance for Your Life.* Grand Rapids: Zondervan, 1991.

Morris, Danny E., and Charles M. Olson. *Discerning God's Will Together: A Spiritual Practice for the Church.* Bethesda, Md.: Alban Publications, 1997. Useful for group spiritual formation and churches.

Olsen, Charles M. *Transforming Church Boards into Communities of Spiritual Leaders.* Bethesda, Md.: Alban Publications, 1995.

Schemel, George, and Judith Roemer. "Communal Discernment." *Review for Religious* 40, no. 6 (November/December 1981): 825–36. Helpful article for considering how to pay attention to discernment in group settings.

Smith, Gordon T. *Listening to God: The Art of Discovering the Will of God.* Downers Grove, Ill.: InterVarsity Press, 1997. He distinguishes other views as "blueprint" models and "wisdom" models and says the heart of the matter is development of a very good relationship with God.

Wakefield, Jim. *Listening Prayer: A New Annotation and Introduction to the Spiritual Exercises of St. Ignatius.* Available from Our Saviour's Lutheran Church, 1040 C. Avenue, Lake Oswego, OR 97034; 503-635-4563. This version of the Ignatian Exercises was designed by a Protestant pastor with Protestants in mind. It includes excellent instructions for participating in the Exercises.

"Discerning the Spirits." *Weavings* 10, no. 6 (November/December 1995).

Willard, Dallas. *In Search of Guidance: Developing a Conversational Relationship with God.* San Francisco: Harper & Row, 1984. A book with clear thinking.

Wolff, Pierre. *The Art of Choosing Well.* Liguori, Mo.: Liguori Publications, 1993. Already a classic.

Spirituality

Ackerman, John. *Spiritual Awakening: A Guide to Spiritual Life in Congregations.* New York: Alban Institute, 1994. Practical, ministry-oriented with reflection sheets and clear directions to use with groups. Topics include telling your story, discernment, praying, practice, personality patterns, surrender and control. Excellent help for beginning spiritual formation groups.

Alexander, Don. *Christian Spirituality.* Downers Grove, Ill.: InterVarsity Press, 1998.

Au, Wilkie. *By Way of the Heart: Toward a Holistic Christian Spirituality.* New York: Paulist Press, 1989. Based on biblical and psychological research. Articulates a model of Christian spirituality flowing out of gospel love and aimed at integrating the human need for wholeness and holiness. Excellent resource.

———. *The Enduring Heart: Spirituality for the Long Haul.* New York: Paulist Press, 2000.

Au, Wilkie, and Noreen Cannon. *Urgings of the Heart: A Spirituality of Integration.* New York: Paulist Press, 1995. These are the topics people bring to spiritual direction.

Benson, Bob, and Michael W. Benson. *Disciplines for the Inner Life.* Nashville: Thomas Nelson, 1995. Includes a combination of Scripture, devotional readings from classic and contemporary works, hymns, and prayers. Includes an excellent bibliography.

Broyles, Ann. *Journaling: A Spirit Journey.* Nashville: The Upper Room, 1999. Journaling with Scripture, with guided meditations, in response to dreams, and journaling conversations. A nice resource.

Edwards, Tilden. *Living in the Presence: Spiritual Exercises to Open Our Lives to the Awareness of God.* San Francisco: Harper & Row, 1995. Contains many methods, processes, and experiences designed to facilitate deepening in prayer, openness to God, and possibilities for growth. An abundance of ideas that can be adapted to individual and group needs.

Foster, Richard J. *Celebration of Discipline: The Path to Spiritual Growth.* San Francisco: Harper & Row, 1978. A readable, welcoming introduction to Christian disciplines.

————. *Streams of Living Water: Celebrating the Great Traditions of Christian Faith.* San Francisco: Harper & Row, 1998. Identifies and describes six major traditions in Christian spirituality: contemplative, holiness, charismatic, social justice, evangelical, and sacramental. A fine sourcebook.

Foster, Richard J., and Kathryn A. Yanni. *A Journal Workbook to Accompany Celebration of Discipline.* San Francisco: Harper & Row, 1992.

Griffin, Emilie. *Wilderness Time: A Guide for Spiritual Retreat.* San Francisco: Harper & Row, 1997. This gentle guide reveals marvelous opportunities for spiritual renewal in contemporary Christian practice. This is a nice introduction to designing a personal or group retreat.

Hagberg, Janet A., and Robert Guelich. *The Critical Journey: Stages in the Life of Faith.* Salem, Wis.: Sheffield, 1989. The book helps people recognize their own spiritual journey and their part in attending to what God invites. Presents a helpful, constructive model that is useful to individuals and groups.

Huggett, Joyce. *The Joy of Listening to God.* Downers Grove, Ill.: InterVarsity Press, 1986. Description of evangelical, charismatic, and contemplative Christian spiritualities from the inside of one person's developmental journey. Potential hazards in spiritual development. Warm, personal, transparent, helpful.

Job, Rueben P., and Norman Sawchuck. *A Guide to Prayer for All God's People.* Nashville: The Upper Room, 1990.

————. *A Guide to Prayer for Ministers and Other Servants.* Nashville: The Upper Room, 1983.

Klug, Ronald. *How to Keep a Spiritual Journal.* Minneapolis: Augsburg, 1993. A clear, concrete resource for helping people consider and begin keeping a spiritual journal.

McGrath, Alister. *Christian Spirituality: An Introduction.* Malden, Mass.: Blackwell, 1999. A fine new treatment of Christian spirituality.

Mogabgab, John S., ed. *Communion, Community, Commonweal: Readings for Spiritual Leadership.* Nashville: The Upper Room, 1995. This is a fine collection of articles on spiritual disciplines that were originally published in *Weavings.*

Mulholland, M. Robert, Jr. *Invitation to a Journey: A Road Map for Spiritual Formation.* Downers Grove, Ill.: InterVarsity Press, 1993. Covers a broad range of spiritual formation topics including the nature of spiritual formation, creation, holistic spirituality, classic spiritual disciplines, and corporate and social spirituality.

Norris, Kathleen. *The Cloister Walk.* New York: Riverhead Books, 1996. One woman's journey and commitment to participate fully in Christian disciplines that shape life.

Nouwen, Henri J. M. *Life of the Beloved.* New York: Crossroads, 1996. Offers encouragement to see ourselves as God's beloved friends and what that implies.

————. *The Way of the Heart.* New York: Ballantine Books, 1981. Discusses solitude as preparation to be fully present with others; prayer of the mind, prayer of the heart, unceasing prayer, and where they lead. Excellent for considering the possible fruits of spiritual disciplines.

Oswald, Roy. *Personality Type and Leadership.* Bethesda, Md.: Alban Institute, 1988. A helpful guide related to the Myers-Briggs Type Inventory and how people of different types work together and serve others.

Pausell, William O. *Rules for Prayer.* New York: Paulist Press, 1993. Gives excellent examples of establishing a personal rule of life.

Seamands, David. *Healing Grace.* Wheaton: Victor, 1988. This book discusses how we break free from distorted images of God and the performance trap in discipleship.

Thompson, Marjorie J. *Soul Feast: An Invitation to the Christian Spiritual Life.* Louisville: Westminster/John Knox Press, 1995. A fine contemporary introduction and encouragement to participate in Christian disciplines with concrete suggestions.

Underhill, Evelyn. *The Spiritual Life.* Wilton, Conn.: Morehouse Barlow, 1955. One of the classics of the Christian spiritual life.

Willard, Dallas. *The Divine Conspiracy: Rediscovering Our Hidden Life in God.* San Francisco: Harper & Row, 1998. Fine theological treatises essential for reflecting on Christian faith in contemporary life.

———. *Hearing God.* Downers Grove, Ill.: InterVarsity Press, 1999. Articulate, clear, and helpful.

———. *The Spirit of the Disciplines: Understanding How God Changes Lives.* San Francisco: Harper & Row, 1988.

Periodicals

Presence: The Journal of Spiritual Directors International. Published three times a year. Provides a forum for spiritual directors. Includes articles related to the training of spiritual directors and the practice of spiritual direction. 1329 Seventh Avenue, San Francisco, CA 94122-2507.

Weavings: A Journal of the Christian Spiritual Life. Nashville: The Upper Room. This is a bimonthly journal that presents topics in spiritual formation.

Web Sites

The Center for Spiritual Formation; http://www.cpcumc.org/spiritual/spirdir.htm

Shalem Institute for Spiritual Formation, 5430 Grosvenor Lane, Bethesda, MD 20814; http://www.shalem.org

The Spiritual Director: Helping People Hear God's Direction and Guidance; http://thespiritualdirector.org

Spiritual Directors International, 1329 Seventh Avenue, San Francisco, CA 94122-2507; http://www.sdiworld.org

The Upper Room, 1908 Grand Avenue, Nashville, TN 37202, has a fine web site dedicated to spiritual formation. It includes information about electronic and printed resources; http://www.upperroom.org

You can also do a general Internet search using keywords spiritual + direction.

Jeannette Bakke (Ph.D., University of Minnesota) was a professor of Christian education at Bethel Theological Seminary from 1978 to 1994 and continues to teach there as a faculty associate. Besides her Ph.D., she has a certificate in Spiritual Direction from Shalem Institute for Spiritual Formation and a D.Min. in Spiritual Direction. A spiritual director herself, she regularly teaches on the subject for church and para-church groups. Most recently she was part of an ecumenical team that provided continuing education courses in spiritual formation and spiritual direction for U.S. Navy, Marine, and Coast Guard chaplains. This book is a product of more than fifteen years of study, receiving and giving spiritual direction, reflection, and teaching.